Family Finance

An easy to read guide
to your money problems

Colm Rapple

Not forgetting the able subs Nuala and Simone

While every attempt is made to ensure accuracy, no legal or other liability can be accepted for the information and advice given.

The moral rights of the author have been asserted.

ISBN 0 9530042 1 X
ISSN 0790-9683

ILLUSTRATIONS BY JOHN BRENNAN

COVER DESIGN BY KAREN DOYLE

PUBLISHED BY SQUIRREL PRESS

Printed and bound in Ireland by
MOUNT SALUS PRESS LIMITED

By The Same Author
Your Guide to Pensions, Squirrel Press
Start Your Own Business, Ward River Press
Living with the Recession, Ward River Press

Contents

Checklists

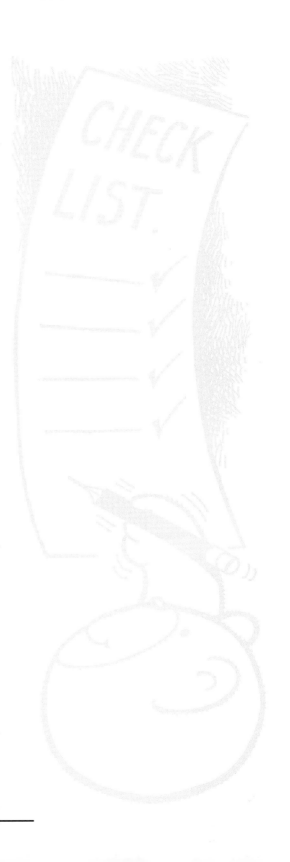

Your 1998 checklists

1.

Income tax will be taking a smaller proportion of everybody's income in 1998. Tax allowances are being increased and tax rates are coming down. The prospects look good on the interest rate front too. Rates are already low and are expected to fall further during 1998 unless there is an upset in the progress towards the single European currency. But while most people will be better off in 1998, the extent to which you personally benefit depends on making the right decisions. It is up to you to reduce your tax bill and get better value in financial products such as insurance, savings, investments, pension plans etc..

You can save tax by making the best possible use of allowances and reliefs. All it requires is a bit of knowledge and some planning. The end result can be very worthwhile. There is plenty of scope to save money in other areas too. Increased price competition in the financial services sector is making it more important than ever to shop around for the best deal. Competition in both the general and life insurance markets is bringing down premium rates and producing better products for the consumer. Increased competition has also prompted major changes in the general banking area with the main banking groups no longer having anywhere near a monopoly for low cost loans and current accounts.

All of these changes in the financial environment and in the budget have implications for personal finance decisions. Past decisions need to be reviewed and altered, if necessary, in the light of the new circumstances. Such a review should be made at least once a year. The following checklists may be used as a guide which will refer you to the more detailed information contained elsewhere in the book.

Savings and Investments

Low interest rates are a mixed blessing — good for the borrower but not good for the saver. Higher returns can be obtained, for instance, by putting money into a longer term account, or one of the Post Office savings schemes. Special Savings Accounts have lost a lot of their appeal with the DIRT tax rate raised to 20% in the December 1997 budget — not much below the 24% normally stopped on deposit interest. There are lots of alternatives for those willing to take some risk. There can be a significant difference in the potential returns so it pays to take a little time to consider the options.

Details can be found as follows:

Saving for children — page 51.

Saving for retirement — page 52 and 169.

Lump sum investment to provide income — page 53.

Lump sum investment for capital growth — page 55.

Invest in paying off a loan — page 50

Getting the best from financial advisers — page 48.

Managing your budget

Simply managing your money between paydays has tended to become more complicated and more expensive. Bank charges are tending upwards and an increasingly diverse range of money transfer services for paying bills are becoming available. The banks no longer have a monopoly in this area. Building societies offer alternatives.

Details of the options are given in **chapter two:**

The options outlined — page 14.

Bank charges compared — page 18.

Interest bearing current accounts — the banks page 23, Irish Permanent page 19, TSB page 25, ACCBank page 25.

Plastic money — page 29.

Tax

I t is surprising how many people do not even bother to check their certificate of tax free allowances, let alone look for legitimate ways of reducing their tax bill. The taxman can make mistakes on the certificate of tax free allowances but most errors are the fault of the tax payer himself. People often fail to claim all the allowances to which they are entitled. For the PAYE payer whose allowances are increasing — higher medical insurance premiums, medical expenses, rent in some circumstances or higher mortgage interest as a result of moving house — any delay in claiming the additional allowances is simply money lost. Tax reliefs can be backdated when you claim them but in the meanwhile you will have been out of pocket.

Each successive budget brings changes in the tax code which may warrant some action. New taxes are imposed, old concessions closed off and new concessions introduced. There are plenty of old concessions still around, of course. Even PAYE taxpayers can take part of their income out of the income tax net by putting money into a pension fund, making use of profit sharing schemes, or by investment in a company under the Business Expansion Scheme. For more information see:

Summary of tax rates — page 302.

Getting a tax rebate — page 241.

Saving tax by employing your child— page 268.

Saving tax by investing in your pension scheme — page 169.

Getting tax-free income through a profit sharing scheme — page 280.

Mortgage tax relief — page 136.

Your PAYE tax guide — page 224.

Tax and the company car — pages 234 and 248.

Planning to reduce inheritance taxes — page 261 and 270.

Capital gains tax — page 256 and 310.

Tax and marriage— page 273

Low income exemptions — page 229.

Life Assurance

It's important to review your life assurance from time to time making sure that you have adequate cover. Pure life cover, the type which only pays out if the insured person dies within a fixed term of years, is relatively cheap. But the dearest company may charge you over twice the premium you'd pay to the cheapest company for exactly the same cover. So you do need to shop around or get someone to shop around for you. You may also want to consider insurance-linked saving plans as a vehicle for long term saving. Do not, however, get the two roles mixed up. And don't forget that there are two parents in most families whose lives may need to be covered by assurance.

Life assurance as family protection is examined in **chapter four.** The topics covered include:

House Insurance

The house insurance market has become more expensive but also more competitive over the past few years. So it pays to shop around. You could, just possibly, halve your insurance costs by changing companies. And check just what cover your policy provides: Does it cover the present day values of your house and contents; just what does the fine print exclude. Policies differ greatly in both cover and price. It makes sense to shop around well before the premium is due and also to update your cover with regard to the current value of the house and contents.

See **chapter nine** for an outline of what the basic policy normally covers:

Borrowing

Interest rates are at a low level and likely to fall further during 1998. There is a danger, decreasing with time, of sharp movements in rates if uncertainties arise over the European Monetary Union. Also, relative to inflation, borrowing is still expensive and the tax relief on mortgage interest relief has been curtailed for top rate tax payers. It's a time for reviewing your borrowings. Apart from shopping around to get the cheapest rate on fresh loans, there may be some advantage in switching your existing borrowings.
Remember that the lenders want your custom. They are not doing you a favour. It is the other way around. Without your custom, they wouldn't make any profits.

The options are looked at in **chapter five.**

Shopping around, where to go — page 102.

Banks — page 103.

Credit Unions — page 111.

Loan repayment tables — page 105.

Mortgages, the alternatives — page 121.

Six point plan for tackling debt problems — page 113.

Wills

If you are over eighteen and have not made a will, it is time to do so. It is downright irresponsible for a married man or woman with children not to have a will drawn up. Indeed, both spouses should have wills drawn up. If you have made a will, check it to see that it still reflects your wishes. Circumstances change. Is the executor you named still willing and able to act? Have you thought of the possible tax implications? There are ways of reducing future liability to inheritance taxes.
Wills are covered in **chapter seven.**

Why make a will — page 141.

Duties of executors — page 145.

Reducing the impact of the inheritance taxes — page 261 and 270.

Pension rights

It is never too early to start planning for your retirement. If you are self-employed you need to make your own provisions. If you are in a company scheme you are not precluded from looking for improvements or, at least, making extra voluntary contributions yourself in order to secure higher benefits.

But you need to take stock of where you are and where you want to be. Within generous limits, contributions to pension schemes are allowable in full for tax relief.

Social Welfare

The social welfare code is constantly changing. You could be entitled to some assistance. Unless you claim your entitlements you are unlikely to get them:

Self-Employed

A growing number of people are now self-employed either by choice or necessity. They face the same range of personal finance problems as anyone else except they can be even more complicated and more time consuming. Most of the items covered in later chapters relate as much to the self-employed as anyone else but there are sections dealing specifically with their particular concerns. The following signposts some of them:

Tax on self-employed income — page 243.

PRSI — page 184.

Motoring expenses — page 248.

Civil service motoring expenses — page 312.

Rental income — page 247.

Pensions — page 179.

Save tax by employing your child — page 268.

Reducing inheritance tax liabilities — page 261 and 270.

Banking

Routine cash management

2.1

Most of the money which comes in each payday is spent before the next payday. Less and less of it is spent as cash. Increasingly money is being transferred either on paper or in computers from one account to another. This is true not only for the well-off. Many social welfare recipients can now have some of their bills paid directly by the Post Office from their benefit. The Post Office does not charge for that service but most financial institutions do charge for handling your money and the charges have been rising.

But there is increased competition. The old traditional demarcation between banks, building societies and other financial institutions has broken down. Personal banking services are now provided by more than the high street banks. Some building societies provide fully fledged cheque book accounts while others offer banking facilities in a different way. They provide cash withdrawal services through ATMs and payment services by way of Laser Cards.

Introduced in 1996 the Laser card provides an electronic alternative to a cheque book. In all cases it is cheaper to use than a cheque. It is issued by a wide number of banks and building societies and some don't charge for its use. There is more about the Laser card in chapter 2.2 which deals with plastic money.

Bank charges have become a bone of contention with many consumers but they are not the only factor to take into account when choosing a banking service. Cost is important but convenience is equally important. A few pennies saved in direct charges can easily be offset by inconvenience costs if, for instance, your bank or building society doesn't happen to have an ATM where you most need it.

Avoid those unapproved overdrafts

Overdrawing your cheque-book account without permission can be a very costly business, more so with some banks than with others. In all cases you will be charged a penal rate of interest on the overdrawn amount — perhaps six percentage points above the normal. On top of that you can be charged up to £3.50 per item. The cost can quickly mount up. Suppose you write one cheque which pushes you over the limit and then another three cheques, standing orders or direct debits are presented which push you further into the unapproved red you are charged an additional £3.50 per item — a total of £14.

The charges mentioned above are imposed when the bank actually honours the cheque, standing order or direct debit. But the bank may simply refuse to pay. In that case the person presenting the cheque for payment and the person who wrote it can end up paying other charges. The person who wrote the cheque — the drawer — loses some credibility, and maybe credit worthiness, too. The charges imposed are as follows:

Bank	Presenter	Drawer
AIB	£3.50	£5.00
Bank of Ireland	£2.60	£8.00
First National Building Society	£2.60	£5.00
Irish Permanent	£5.00	£5.00
Ulster Bank	£3.50	£8.00
National Irish Bank	£3.50	£7.00
TSB Bank	£3.50	£5.00

So what can you do to avoid paying these charges? The best advice, of course, is not to overdraw your account at all. In that way you risk no charges and can qualify for free banking. But one of the advantages of a current account is that you can overdraw in times of need. To ensure that you have that flexibility make sure to negotiate an adequate overdraft permission. Check every now and then that it is still in place and have it increased from time to time if you think it necessary. If you think that you are going to exceed your permission, let the bank know in advance. Banks will normally be only too pleased to increase your overdraft permission. AIB and Bank of Ireland charge £20 to approve an overdraft. The other banks make no charge.

So what is the best way to manage your money in the short term? There is no single choice suitable for all individuals. It depends on circumstances but most people need access to some method or methods of paying bills other than by cash. There are benefits in having wages paid directly into a financial institution provided there is ready access to your money through a good branch network, long opening hours, and/or cash dispensing machines. Access to short-term loans is also useful in meeting occasional heavy demands for money. Developing a track record with a financial institution which can provide longer term loans at competitive rates can also be a benefit. And you obviously want to do all that at the lowest possible cost. There are pluses and minuses for all the financial institutions. You need to weigh up the benefits and costs yourself. First you have to decide what you actually need. Let's consider some of the options and examine what's available.

Do you need a cheque-book, for instance? Don't be too quick to answer yes! There are a growing number of alternative and cheaper ways of paying bills. And what else do you want the cheque-book for? It used to be the case that only those with cheque-books had access to overdrafts and overdrafts are the most flexible form of loan and can be the cheapest. The interest rate is low and the flexibility keeps interest costs to the minimum in that you only borrow what you need as you need it. But there are now current accounts which provide access to overdrafts without a cheque-book. A number of building societies, EBS, First National and Irish Nationwide operate such accounts. Customers use ATM/Laser cards to withdraw funds and make payments.

So if you need access to an overdraft — and more about overdrafts below — you have a wide range of alternatives. You have to ask yourself which is best and one of the considerations has to be cost. Interest rates can vary and some lenders charge an arrangement fee. Both Allied Irish Bank and Bank of Ireland, for instance, charge £20 for approving an overdraft permission. Another cost factor is that once you get an overdraft on your account you generally lose any entitlement you might have to free banking.

Those extra costs may be small enough if you make good use of an overdraft permission.

Another factor to consider in choosing your banking service is your possible future needs. If you think you might need a business loan in the future then it may be worthwhile building up a record with one of the larger banks and establishing a relationship with a bank manager.

The average personal bank customer needs a relatively small range of services. He may like to have his wages paid directly into some safe depository from which he can draw cash readily

There are cheaper ways of paying bills than through a bank account. There is a growing number of alternatives.

Cheque book account charges — a comparison

Transaction	AIB	B of I	NIB	Ulster	TSB	Irish Per.[1]	First National
Paper	24p	26p	24p	25p	23p	25p[2]	nil
Automated	17p	19p	15p	18p	10p[3]	nil	nil
Standing order setup	£3.00	£2.70	nil	£3.00	£2.50	nil	£2.70
Standing order fee	29p	31p	27p	30p	30p	nil	nil
Cheque card (annual)	£3.00	£3.15[4]	£5.00[4]	£3.00[5]	£2.50	nil	nil
Overdraft permission	£20	£20	nil	nil	nil	nil	£20
Quarterly fee	£3.75	£4.15	£3.75	£3.90	£3.00	£10/£15	£10[6]

1. Interest paid on credit balances (0.75% up to £1,000 and 1.25% on £1,000+). 2. First 25 transactions free each quarter. 3. Only on TSB's own ATMs — 20p if cash withdrawal from AIB machine. 4. ATM card included. 5. Charged only every two years. 6. £5 if the account is kept in credit.

Qualifications for free banking

No transaction charges are applied where customers meet the following conditions:

AIB: A minimum credit balance of £100 is maintained in the account during the accounting period; retired, widowed and customers over 60 years of age; members of institutions for the blind; full time students who stay in credit.

B of I: A minimum of £100 credit balance is maintained in the account during the accounting period; all customers over 60 years of age; full time students with Ascent accounts.

National Irish: The account is kept in credit for the full charging period.

Ulster: The account is kept in credit for the full charging period.

TSB: Customers over 60 years of age; accounts which never go under £100 credit or have maintained an average balance of at least £300. Students may also qualify.

Where free banking does not apply, some banks give an offsetting credit against charges for balances kept in the account.

Bank of Ireland: An allowance calculated at the lowest deposit interest rate on average credit balances of £200 or over. If the allowance exceeds the bank charge, the excess is ignored.

National Irish Bank: An allowance calculated at the normal minimum deposit rate on the average credit balance is offset against charges.

when needed, arrange to pay regular and irregular bills, and maybe get interest on any surplus. All of those services can be obtained free outside the banking system. Indeed most building societies already provide them to holders of saving accounts.

The larger building societies have a growing network of ATM machines. You can make direct debits or standing orders from the account — all at no charge. And if you want to send a once-off payment you can get a third party cheque from the building society office — again at no cost. Some, such as the EBS, also offer an alternative way of paying bills by phone. Once you arrange in advance for particular payments — the ESB, telephone or gas bills, for instance — you can arrange for the payment to be made from your account simply by dialing a freephone number. The Irish Permanent which is now a bank rather than a building society, offers four different types of cheque book accounts with access to overdrafts and interest paid on credit balances.

There are ways of paying bills at no cost. Sending a cheque off by post is a very expensive way of paying a bill, indeed. It can cost as much as 62p. That is made up of 25p to the bank, 7p to the government for the stamp duty on the cheque, and 30p for the stamp. And that's not including the cost of the envelope.

Paying the same bill by credit card costs nothing for the actual transaction. That's assuming you have a credit card. There is an annual stamp duty of £15 while Bank of Ireland and AIB also impose flat annual charges of their own — £8 with Bank of Ireland and £10 with AIB. But if you have a credit card you have already incurred those costs and hopefully you get that money back by making use of as much free credit as possible. If you always pay your bill in full and on time you'll pay no interest.

You can pay your telephone or gas bill in any post office. So there are plenty of alternatives. But a current account has its advantages and it doesn't cost the earth. You can reduce the cost by careful management. By meeting certain criteria you can qualify for free banking. The banks claim that most customers do. But you won't qualify if you run up an overdraft. So don't get overdrawn except for a reasonable amount. Use as few direct debits and standing orders as possible. That gives you the flexibility to delay payments when the finances are tight. A bit of careful management can work wonders.

But let's have a look at the alternatives in detail.

The Associated Banks

The Bank of Ireland, Allied Irish Bank, National Irish and the Ulster Bank are known as the Associated Banks. Apart from their role as holders of savings, they provide a wide range of services in lending money and in transferring it from one person to another. They also, indeed, create money under the control of the Central Bank — the Government's bank. As far as many consumers are concerned, however, there is now little to distinguish between them and other banks and building societies but they do provide the widest range of services.

There are a large number of options. The traditional division was between a simple deposit account and the current (or cheque-book) account. But bank services are changing rapidly with increasing emphasis on the expanding network of 24 hour automatic teller machines (ATMs) and in the case on AIB and Bank of Ireland, on 24 hour telephone services.

Plastic money in the form of credit cards and ATM cards is growing in importance and there is an expanding range of account types combining various elements of the old deposit and current accounts. A bank account gives you access to all of these services and it also offers loan facilities. But let us first look at the different types of accounts available. They all have their different uses, advantages and disadvantages.

Current Accounts

The operative word is "current". It is the ideal place to keep money which will be spent in the short-term. The holder of such an account is given a cheque book and can write cheques which are, in effect, money. They also automatically receive a Laser Card. The bank may also issue a Bankers' Card which guarantees that any cheque written by the holder, up to one hundred pounds in value, will be honoured even in certain countries abroad.

Normally, of course, the cheque is covered by funds which the current account holder has in the bank, but he may be given an overdraft permission, which allows him to borrow money over and above what he has in the bank by simply writing cheques as he needs the money. Overdrafts are one of the cheapest forms of loan in interest rate terms and they are also the most flexible available so it is worth having access to them. The interest is only charged on the amounts actually withdrawn and at the

Joint accounts and inheritance

There are many reasons for opening a joint bank, building society or Post Office account. People sharing living expenses may find it the easiest way to operate. Elderly people sometimes open joint accounts with a relative or friend to ease access to their money. They may give the other person the right to withdraw money but they can also maintain that right to themselves. In this type of situation the intention may be that the money will automatically pass to the survivor. But that is not always the case.

Indeed up to fairly recently the opposite was more often the case. Where there was a joint account into which one of the joint owners had contributed the money, the other account holder did not automatically acquire sole ownership of the funds after the death of the other person.

This had been decided in a court case back in 1932 where it was decreed that the money in such an account should pass into the estate of the deceased person to be divided up in accordance with the terms of any will or, where there was no will, the division laid down by the courts or the Succession Act. It was considered that this was necessary to curtail fraud and that it was, in any case, an attempt to avoid inheritance taxes.

Last year this earlier judgment was effectively overturned by the Supreme Court in a ruling on a new case. It concerned an elderly woman who opened a joint account with a niece. She clearly wanted her niece to inherit the money after her death but also wished to retain sole access to the account during her own lifetime. Both aunt and niece were in the bank when the account was opened. Both signed the documentation. The account was made payable to the aunt or to the survivor. In other words only the aunt could withdraw money during her life time but it was her clear intention that after her death her niece should have access to the money.

After her death other claimants on her estate took a case against the niece and the bank and a lower court found in their favour citing the 1932 case. It was appealed to the Supreme Court which found in favour of the niece. But the judgment does not give an automatic right of ownership to the survivor. There should be no problem, of course, where account holders have each contributed to the account but where only one has contributed, the other or others will gain ownership where there was a clear indication that this was the deceased person's intention.

So the advice is in a case like this to make the intention clear in writing. Money in a joint account escapes the two per cent Probate Tax in the event of death but it may still be liable to Capital Acquisitions Tax in the hands of the survivor — see chapter 13.6 for more details of inheritance tax and the transfer of assets on death.

same rate as on term loans. Borrowing options are dealt with in detail in chapter 5.

Current accounts can be expensive to operate but they do give access to the cheapest possible loans.

A cheque-book and an overdraft permission does provide a valuable degree of financial flexibility. With an overdraft you only pay interest on the amount you actually overdraw but running a current account can cost you money over and above any interest you pay. Both AIB and Bank of Ireland, for instance, charge a £20 'facility fee' for providing an overdraft permission. None of the other banks do but they all impose transaction charges although if you meet certain conditions — such as keeping a minimum amount in the account — these charges are waived.

If you do not qualify for free banking then you become liable for fixed quarterly maintenance charges and additional charges for every transaction made. Each paper transaction i.e. lodgment, cheque, withdrawal etc., costs at least twenty to twenty-six pence, depending on the bank. Writing a cheque costs more because of the additional Government stamp duty of 7p charged on each cheque. Even if you are eligible for free banking you still pay that stamp duty. You can avoid the stamp duty by using a Laser Card. The facility is included on your cheque or ATM card. For more on Laser Cards see chapter 2.2. They are an alternative to a cheque book but in most cases you are liable for a charge on each transaction. If you are doing a lot of shopping it would be cheaper to use your ATM to withdraw cash and use it for the transactions. That way you only incur one transaction charge.

The table on page 18 gives details of current account charges. They are the charges which apply on cheque book accounts held by personal customers. Higher charges generally apply to business accounts.

Deposit accounts

Most banks also offer traditional deposit accounts. The holder may be given a book or record sheet into which his deposits and withdrawals are written and/or he may get regular computerised statements. He can withdraw his money on demand, and is paid interest. The big four banks all provide plastic cash cards with deposit accounts so that there is access to your money from the automatic dispensers 24 hours a day. There may be transaction charges and, of course, the interest paid is not as good as on accounts with a longer notice of withdrawal. It is not possible to get an overdraft but, as a bank customer, you are more likely to get a term loan when you need one.

Other accounts

A number of banks offer interest-bearing cheque book accounts. They include the big four and TSB Bank, Irish Permanent and ACCBank. They pay fairly low rates of interest and are all less flexible than basic current accounts but all in different ways. If you can live with the restrictions, they obviously have some advantages. But they can be costly. So be careful. Let's look at what each of the banks has to offer.

Allied Irish Bank: In order to earn interest on an AIB "Credit Interest" account you have to keep a minimum of £300 in the account. You are not allowed to get overdrawn and no ATM card is given. It is possible to make standing orders or direct debits from the account and normal bank charges apply with no 'free banking' for being in credit.

Bank of Ireland: Known as an "Ascent" account it is only available to people under 25 years of age. All of the normal current account facilities are provided including an ATM card. Normal charges apply if the account goes into the red.

National Irish: Its "Cheque Plus" account allows overdrafts but at an abnormally high rate of interest — five percentage points above the normal overdraft rate. There are no transaction charges but there is a quarterly maintenance charge of £5 when an account is overdrawn. An ATM card is provided.

Ulster Bank: Its "Premium" account is aimed at a relatively small market of people who hold fairly large amounts in an account and want the facility to be able to write cheques from it. The interest rate paid is higher than the other banks but it is necessary to deposit an initial £2,500.

The larger building societies have greatly enlarged their branch network in recent years and now have outlets in most large cities and towns. They also have their own ATM network. So for the bulk of the population there is little problem about making deposits or arranging withdrawals.

Both the EBS and the First National provide account holders with Laser Cards while the Irish Nationwide will be launching it's Laser Card account early in 1998. First National account

All the big banks offer some form of interest-bearing cheque book accounts.

Building Societies

holders can also get a cheque-book. Its current account details are included in the table of page 18. All three accounts offer access to overdrafts at competitive interest rates and also provide other current account facilities such as standing orders and direct debits.

But there is usually a hidden cost in opting for an account which provides ready access to your money. You have to accept a lower interest rate than you would get on longer term deposits. But on ordinary demand accounts the interest rate is usually competitive with the big banks. Often it is a little higher. There is no difference in terms of tax.

When mortgage funds were scarce, it made a lot of sense for people planning an eventual house purchase to save with the building societies since a record of saving was necessary to get loan approval.

Building societies now offer almost as wide a range of services as the bigger banks.

At present that's not a major consideration since mortgage finance is easily obtained. But some societies do charge lower interest rates to borrowers who meet certain savings requirements i.e. having a minimum level of savings on deposit for a minimum period. It is something to ask about before you open an account if your intention is to eventually borrow. And, of course, mortgages could get scarce again in the future although there is no sign of any potential mortgage famine at present.

Post Office Savings Bank

An Post schemes are, of course, government guaranteed so, in terms of security, they are second to none. It offers a number of different savings schemes, but in this chapter we will only consider the normal Post Office savings bank account. This is the one most suited to the short-term saver who may want to withdraw all his money quickly. There are other schemes aimed at regular savers or those with lump sums to invest either for growth or income. These are considered in the next chapter. As we mentioned, security is no problem and neither, indeed, is ease of access. The Post Office has about 1,400 branches throughout the country and they stay open for longer hours than banks. With a post office savings book the depositor can withdraw up to fifty pounds daily on demand. Larger amounts can be withdrawn at a few days notice. Withdrawals can be made at any post office.

Interest on an ordinary post office savings account is credited on a daily basis. The interest rate is normally as good — and is currently a good deal better — than that given by the associated banks on small deposits. There are Special Savings Accounts liable only to the special low rate of DIRT tax but money can only be withdrawn at a month's notice so they are to be considered more for saving than as a means of managing your short term money.

As an adjunct to the normal Post Office Savings Bank book, there are schemes aimed at encouraging you to save. Group schemes are organised in work places and schools, and there is a savings stamp scheme specially for children. There is also the Installment Savings Scheme which is dealt with in chapter 3. Here we are only concerned with short term savings and in a number of areas the Post Office must be considered better than the banks. But there are no other benefits.

The Post Office does not lend money, so no matter how good your record of saving, you won't be able to get a loan if you need it. It does act as an agent for a finance company offering fairly expensive loans but you can get that type of loan just as easily by going to a finance company directly. Regular savers with the banks on the other hand have access to much cheaper overdrafts and term loans unless credit is very tight.

TSB Bank

TSB Bank is a nationwide bank providing the full range of banking services to individuals and small businesses. It offers normal cheque book accounts and cheque cards, and has its own cash dispenser network providing access round the clock. It operates a Visa card and prides itself on longer opening hours than the big four commercial banks. It also provides a Laser Card.

Their 'High Interest Cheque Account' pays interest on sums in excess of £4,000 while providing the depositor with a cheque book. Monthly income accounts are available for those with more than £3,000 to invest. Otherwise the TSB Bank offers the same range of services as other commercial banks and its ATM card can be used in AIB machines. So, although it still has a limited number of branches nationwide there is good access to cash through both the AIB and its own ATM networks.

State banks

There are two state owned banks providing financial services to the public — ACCBank and ICCBank. Both are Government owned and offer relatively high rates of return. While their branch networks are growing they are still not as extensive as the major banks or post offices.

ACCBank has grown far beyond its traditional role as a farming bank. It has greatly broadened its branch network in urban areas and offers a full range of services including a special cheque book account which pays interest on credit balances and a Visa card which doubles as an ATM card with the Visa account linked to the customer's normal account. The Visa debits are automatically paid out of the cheque book account at the end of the free credit period. There is no charge for the card and the interest rate is the lowest around — see the next section on plastic money. Interest is paid on money in the cheque book account. The only draw back is that transaction charges are high, but for someone making relatively few transactions that is not a major worry. ACCBank provides a full range of loan types: overdrafts, term loans, and mortgages.

Other banks

There are also a wide range of smaller banks which take deposits from the public. A comprehensive list of these and the rates they offer are published regularly in the newspapers. Most are not suitable for the type of short-term saver we are considering here — they have relatively few branches and many have a minimum deposit (usually at least £1,000). For the most part they prefer not to have to deal with too many transactions in or out of an account. The main exception has to be the Irish Permanent Bank. It is no longer a building society and, of course, offers a full range of services aimed at the individual customer. Its ATM card can be used on Bank of Ireland machines for cash withdrawals and it also, of course, has a cheque book account.

Credit Unions

Credit unions are cooperative nonprofit making ventures established within a community covering perhaps a locality or a work place. Through that community all the members enjoy what is known as a "common bond". Their basic role is to encourage saving and provide loans but they are in the process of greatly expanding the range of financial services they provide. New laws which came into force on October 1, 1997 pro-

There are over 400 credit unions in the State with about 1.4 million members and £2,000 million in savings. Before the new legislation members could hold no more than £6,000 in a share account. Additional savings were kept in deposit accounts. The limits on share accounts, deposits and the size of loans have been significantly increased. Members can now have savings of up to £50,000 subject to the amount being no more than 1% of the Credit Union's total assets. Individual loans may not exceed 1.5 per cent of a credit union's assets although loans up to £30,000 are allowed even if they breach that 1.5% rule.

In addition to being a home for savings and a source of loans many credit unions operate budget accounts which provide for the payment of regular bills. Members may also have access to group rate VHI premiums which offer a 10% discount on individual rates and increasingly credit unions are providing a wider range of financial services. Most are members of the Irish League of Credit Unions which provides insurance services and is currently planning a nationwide credit union network of ATMs and the introduction of cheque book accounts, credit cards, and facilities for direct payment of wages and social welfare benefits into credit union accounts.

> Credit unions will be increasingly offering a wider range of services — sufficient to cover many people's money management needs.

A growing number of credit unions are issuing ATM cards to their members. A few have their own ATMs but in all cases the cards can be used at AIB and Bank of Ireland machines.

The interest paid on deposits and the dividends paid on share accounts vary from credit union to credit union. But the rates are likely to be higher than bank rates during times of relatively low market interest rates as at present. No DIRT tax is stopped on the interest although it is considered to be taxable income and some have devised ways of paying tax free dividends in the form of bonuses. So members can be sure of getting a good deal in the knowledge that all 'profits' are either paid out in dividends or ploughed back into the credit union.

A major benefit, of course, is the access to loans at very reasonable rates of interest compared particularly to the more expensive finance houses — see chapter five. Most credit unions charge the maximum rate of 12.6% APR but some give subsequent discounts out of whatever surplus is generated. Loan protection insurance providing for the repayment of the loan in the event of death or permanent disablement is included. Limits may apply to the size of the loan and the cover is curtailed for the over 60s and not available for the over 70s.

Another built-in insurance provides for the payment of a benefit to a member's estate in the event of death. In the case of a member aged under 55 the benefit is equal to the amount on deposit or in shares at the time of death. The benefit is lower for those over 55 and not applicable in the case of the over 70s.

Credit unions will be increasingly offering a wider range of services — sufficient to cover many people's money management needs. If the offices are close to your home or in your work place it is obviously easy to deposit or withdraw money, although normally a week's notice is required for withdrawals. It depends on the credit union although the law requires a minimum notice of 60 days in the case of shares and 21 days in the case of deposits. Individual credit unions may, by rule, impose longer periods of notice, so it can vary from union to union.

The security aspect also varies from one credit union to another. Depositors are insured against loss resulting from fraud on the part of officials, and there is a savings protection scheme which covers loans up to £10,000. The Irish League of Credit Unions also provides back-up funds and assistance to member credit unions should they run into difficulties. Credit union members also have the benefit of knowing that theirs is a self-help nonprofit making organisation.

Plastic money — use sensibly

THERE is increased competition in the credit card market. Mastercard and Visa cards are being offered by a wider range of banks and building societies and even by one specialised credit card company. They are all basically the same in the services they provide but there are some very important differences between them — not least in interest rates and other costs. There is money to be saved by shopping around. Mastercard and Visa, of course, are not the only forms of plastic money. Cash is being rapidly replaced by plastic — so many different types as to be downright confusing by times. They can all be used to advantage but, without care, they can all prove costly in one way or another. The first step towards avoiding the pitfalls is to understand how the types of card differ.

The most common plastic is the 'credit card' — Mastercard and Visa — which are issued by banks, building societies and specialised credit card companies. Credit unions may now issue credit cards and will possibly do so in the not too distant future. So there is plenty of choice. The one thing all the cards have in common is that the operators want to lend you money. You do not have to pay the outstanding balance in full each month. In that they are different from 'charge cards', like American Express and Diners Club which do expect you to pay your monthly bill in full. Some of the charge card companies provide "Gold Cards" for people who are genuinely high spenders or for those who just want to pretend that they are.

Plastic money

A third category of plastic money are the store cards issued by individual retail outlets or chains. They can either be credit cards allowing the purchaser to spread the cost of goods over a period, or else charge cards, the accounts of which have to be settled at the end of the month. And that does not exhaust the possibilities. There is also the Esso Charge card for use in Esso garages and, doubtless, other similar cards to come. The Ryan Hotel Group also has its own charge card. Both the Esso and Ryan cards are similar to store charge cards.

A fourth category first issued in Ireland in 1996 is the debit card. Only one has so far been issued, the Laser Card, but it's available from a wide range of banks and building societies. It operates like an electronic chequebook. It can be used to make purchases and limited cash withdrawals. The amounts involved are debited directly to the holder's current account.

There are, of course, other forms of plastic money like the cheque guarantee card and the cash dispenser card. They are not credit cards as such since there is no automatic entitlement to credit with them. Holders may, of course, be allowed to overdraw their account with the permission of the bank. The cash dispenser card is usually the cheapest way of getting cash — far cheaper than using a credit card. But more about that later. Let us look at each type of card in some detail — listing their pros and cons.

Mastercard and Visa

Mastercard, previously Access, is issued by the Bank of Ireland, Ulster and National Irish Bank while Visa is issued by Allied Irish Banks, Bank of Ireland, National Irish, TSB Bank, Irish Permanent Bank, ACCBank, EBS Building Society, the First National Building Society, and MBNA.

There are also so-called 'affinity' cards in the names of various organisations, universities and charities. The interest rates on such cards is usually lower and the credit card companies makes payments to the organisation involved on the basis of a small percentage of the amount transacted on the card.

Eircell, the mobile phone company, also issues its own Visa card.

You do not have to be a customer of the issuing bank to get one and, indeed, it is possible to have both, either from the same bank — where they issue both — or from different banks. They are true credit cards which enable the holder to spread the cost of purchases, or cash withdrawals, over a period of months. And, of course, both provide some free credit.

Mastercard and Visa cost very little to obtain. Some issuers make no charge other than the annual Government stamp duty of £15. Bank of Ireland and Irish Permanent Bank charge £8 a year while Allied Irish Banks impose a supplementary charge of £10 on some holders. The charge is waived in the first year and is also waived in subsequent years provided the card is used

Credit Cards — the costs

Issuer	Card	Interest rate	Annual Charge	Foreign exchange	Interest charged from
ACCBank	Visa	21.0%	None	£2 plus 1.75%	Statement
AIB	Visa	26.5%	None[1]	1.5%[2]	Purchase[3]
	Visa	24.7%	£10[4]	1.5%[2]	Purchase[3]
Bank of Ireland	Mastercard and Visa	25.5%	£8	1.75%	Purchase[3]
EBS	Visa	27.7%	None	None	Purchase[3]
First National	Visa	25.5%	£8	None	Purchase[3]
Irish Permanent	Visa	25.3%	None	1.5%[5]	Purchase[3]
MBNA	Visa	18.9%	None	2.65%	Purchase[3]
National Irish	Mastercard and Visa	22.4%	None	1.75%	Purchase[3]
TSB Bank	Visa	23.1%	None	1.75%	Statement
Ulster Bank	Mastercard and Visa	24.6%	None	2%	Purchase[3]

Notes: 1. Bill must be paid within ten days of statement. 2. Minimum £1.50. 3. Date of processing purchase. 4. Waived in first year and if there have been 50 transactions with the card during the preceding year. 5. Subject to a maximum of £2.

more than fifty times during the preceding year. So the minimum cost of a card is £15 a year — the stamp duty — but it can be as high as £25. If used wisely, however, that is the total annual cost and it can be more than repaid in free credit or just plain convenience.

With both cards the customer is billed for his purchases once a month and then usually has about 25 days to pay. If the account is paid in full during that period, no interest charges are incurred. But if the full amount is not paid by the due date, interest is charged at the rather high rate — it can be over 25%. And the interest is charged from the date of the statement or, in some

Credit cards are a boon if used wisely. That means paying up in full and on time each month.

cases from the date at which the transaction was presented for payment by the seller — not from the date on which payment was due. So it makes sense to pay on time, allowing a few days for your payment to get through the system. Interest is charged on cash withdrawals immediately from the date of the withdrawal so it is an expensive way of getting cash.

Competition started between the card issuers a few years ago when National Irish Bank cut its rate significantly. That competitive edge was subsequently narrowed and more recently the new entrant MBNA, a US bank which is only offering credit card services in Ireland, has entered the market with a lower rate than any of the other card issuers.

It is well worth having at least one credit card. It can be worthwhile getting both a Mastercard and Visa card alternating their use to get the longest possible period of free credit. This simply means using the card whose bill you last received. Remember the interest rates are no longer all the same.

The gap between the cheapest and dearest is significant ranging in late 1997 from a low of just under 19% to a high of almost 28%. These are annual percentage rates (APRs). But even 19% is a very high interest rate and it is best not to borrow on a credit card at all. A significant proportion of credit card users do manage to do just that. You should try to be one of them. But it is all too easy to incur charges even by simply making a late payment so it obviously makes sense to get the cheapest card in terms of interest. There are other considerations. Only AIB, Bank of Ireland, and Irish Permanent charge for their cards. You can save that £8 or £10 a year by getting your card somewhere else and remember you do not have to have an account with a bank or building society to get one of their credit cards.

AIB does offer a Visa card without any annual charge but the interest rate is higher and you are required to pay within ten days of the statement date if you are not to incur interest.

Interest is not the only cost and it can, of course, be avoided. Some companies also make a flat charge for late payments. If the minimum payment is not made on time MBNA makes a flat charge of £12. The commission charges on foreign transactions also vary from company to company.

Another factor to bear in mind is the date at which interest starts clocking up. As mentioned above, interest is charged on most cards from the date on which the bill is presented for payment by the retailer or trader. That can be a good deal earlier than the actual statement date. But with ACCBank, National Irish Bank and TSB Bank the interest is back dated only to the date of the statement. That can also save you a little.

Both Mastercard and Visa offer up to £30,000 in free travel insurance if you buy your ticket with the card; and there are special discounts. These are perks which are often forgotten — keep the leaflets sent with the card. Both are accepted worldwide — Mastercard being interchangeable with Access and Eurocard. It is also possible to use them to withdraw cash abroad. With Mastercard there is no charge if you put money into your account so that it is in credit and then draw it out as needed during a holiday.

This free withdrawal through Mastercard where an account is in credit could be usefully employed by emigrant workers wanting to send regular amounts home to their families. A man working in England, for instance, need only open a Mastercard account and get two cards — one for himself and one for his wife. He can then lodge money into the account in Britain and she can draw it out through a bank automatic teller machine in Ireland. It is completely secure and there is no cost involved.

Do not be tempted to make a habit of postponing payment of the accounts beyond the due date. If you find yourself permanently in debt to the credit card company you could save money by getting a bank loan at a lower rate of interest and paying off the credit card. If you have built up a credit card debt already, or intend making a big purchase get a term loan from one of the big four banks, or from a credit union. Any of those options would be far cheaper than borrowing on the credit card.

Charge cards

For those who travel a lot, the extra cost of getting one or both charge cards is possibly small when set against the extra flexibility and security provided. But for most individuals, the cheaper Mastercard and Visa cards should be sufficient.

The front runners in this area are American Express and Diners Card. Both have attractions for individuals who are high spenders or who do a fair amount of travel. But both Mastercard and Visa can be used at a far greater number of outlets world wide. But, if the quantity of outlets is smaller, the quality may be slightly better and the big spender will possibly find his charge card accepted in most of the outlets he will want to frequent.

The charge cards have another advantage. It is possible to use them as super cheque guarantee cards to get cash from one's own account. As mentioned above, if you borrow cash on your Visa or Mastercard card you are immediately liable for interest at about 25%. With the charge card the cash can come from your own bank account incurring no interest if there is a credit balance in your account and only the relevant bank rate if there is not. With American Express, for instance, the ordinary card holder can cash personal cheques for up to £500 at any office of American Express worldwide. Within Ireland seven days must elapse between every such transaction — abroad the period is 21 days.

Like Mastercard and Visa, the charge cards offer some free insurance cover when you buy your travel tickets with the card — a point sometimes forgotten by the holders. Indeed the charge cards are more generous in this regard. For instance, if you have charged the cost of a scheduled flight to your American Express card and it is delayed for four hours or more, you can claim up to £50 for meals, refreshments and hotel accommodation. There is also insurance for lost or delayed luggage. Charge cards are, however, not free. In addition to the £15 stamp duty there is an annual subscription — £37.50 a year.

Both American Express and Diners Club provide cash withdrawal facilities too. In addition to its cheque guarantee facility American Express can be used at cash dispensers worldwide. Diners Club lets you draw up to the equivalent of $1,000 in local currency each week from its dispensers.

Charge cards can provide an increased spread of outlets which may be important to the international traveller but most individuals will get by with Mastercard and Visa. The charge cards do provide emergency access to cash which may be important to some and worth the extra expense.

Gold cards

These are just super charge cards for high fliers. The American Express Gold Card, for instance, provides access to an unsecured borrowing facility of at least £7,500 from the Bank of Ireland; cheque encashment of up to £300 a day from Bank of Ireland branches and up to £1,000 from any American Express office during any 21 day period. It costs £70 a year plus the standard £15 annual stamp duty.

If you are the type of person who might make use of the facilities offered, the cost is possibly insignificant. Alternatively, you may be willing to pay for the impression a Gold Card can create. But that's hardly worth the extra cost for most people.

Laser cards

The Laser card is the first of a new generation of plastic money known as debit cards. In essence it is an electronic cheque. It is issued by ten banks and building societies linked to their current accounts. In most cases that means a cheque-book account but some of the building societies which issue Laser Cards don't have cheque-books. There are some 200,000 cards issued in Ireland and they are accepted in more than 4,000 retail outlets.

You use a Laser card as you would a cheque-book. Payments made with a Laser Card are debited to the holder's account in exactly the same way as a payment made by cheque or a withdrawal from an ATM.

Laser Cards — who charges what?

Issuer	Type of card	Transaction Charge
ACCBank	3 in 1 (ATM, cheque guarantee and Laser)	20p
AIB	2 in 1 (cheque guarantee and Laser)	17p
Bank of Ireland	3 in 1 (ATM, cheque guarantee and Laser)	19p
EBS Building Society	2 in 1 (ATM and Laser)	nil
First National	2 in 1 (ATM and Laser)	nil
Irish Nationwide	2 in 1 (ATM and Laser)	nil
Irish Permanent	3 in 1 (ATM, cheque guarantee and Laser)	15p
National Irish Bank	3 in 1 (ATM, cheque guarantee and Laser)	17p
TSB	3 in 1 (ATM, cheque guarantee and Laser)	18p
Ulster Bank	3 in 1 (ATM, cheque guarantee and Laser)	20p

The money may come out of your account a bit quicker but transaction charges are lower — there's no 7p stamp duty for one thing — and the upper limit for single payments is £1,000. Cheque payments are often limited to a maximum of £100 because that's the limit of the cheque guarantee card.

Apart from that limit the same sort of rules apply to the use of Laser as apply to the use of a cheque-book. You should have the money in your account or an overdraft permission. If you run up an unapproved overdraft you'll be liable for penal charges. They were outlined in the previous section.

The shops accepting the card are charged about 15p per transaction by the operators of the system and, in most cases the customer is charged for the transaction too. With most of the banks the charge is similar to that imposed on a transaction at an ATM. Some of the building societies charge nothing, however — see the table on the previous page. Where charges are applicable they are added to the customer's current account in the normal way. But they are also waived in the normal way if the customer qualifies for 'free banking'.

There is no cost in actually getting the card. The facility has been bundled with existing ATM and/or cheque guarantee cards. The building societies are linking it with their ATM cards and all of the banks except AIB are issuing three-in-one cards combining Laser with their cheque guarantee and ATM withdrawal cards.

The main advantage of having a Laser card is that you don't have to carry cash around. For those liable for bank charges Laser is cheaper than writing a cheque for single transactions. But someone out on a mini spending spree could save money by withdrawing cash from an ATM and using it for his or her various purchases. An ATM withdrawal only attracts a single charge while there would be a separate charge for each Laser transaction. In some outlets shoppers are able to draw out up to £75 in cash in addition to paying for their purchases.

The mechanics of using a Laser Card are similar to using a credit card. You present your card to the sales assistant who 'swipes' it through the till and gives you a receipt to sign. The money doesn't come out of your account immediately although that will eventually be the case, no doubt. At present, however, the process takes a couple of days so that there is time to make a deposit to keep yourself in credit. But you'd have to act quickly and make the lodgement at your own branch.

Some of these are operated by the stores themselves but most are now operated for them by finance houses. There are a number of different types of account. There are monthly accounts which are like charge cards. The amount due has to be paid each month and no interest is charged. It is obviously a worthwhile facility to have if you do a lot of shopping in one store or with the one group.

Then there are budget accounts. The store generally sets a credit limit calculated on the basis of a set number of times the

Plastic Money — Some Rules

Do not draw money on your Visa or Mastercard Card except in an emergency or unless you have already put the money in. Interest at up to almost 30% is payable from the date of withdrawal.

The accounts of charge cards like American Express and Diners Club must be paid in full each month. Otherwise penal charges are imposed.

Store cards are best avoided since they discourage shopping around, encourage overspending, and some charge hefty rates of interest.

Do not keep constantly in debt to the credit card company. The interest rates are too high. There are much cheaper ways of borrowing.

Keep a couple of separate notes of your credit card numbers and the phone numbers of the relevant companies so that you can act quickly if they are lost or stolen.

Make sure to check the accounts. Did you hear about the petrol pump attendant who regularly ran two slips off some cards? The spare one was put through for a fictitious fill of petrol a few days later. Slips can also be altered. Be careful how you dispose of your copy of the slips. Remember they have your signature and credit card number on them.

Do not forget that there are other benefits going with most cards, like travel insurance. Read the leaflets fully and know what you are entitled to.

If you are making a large purchase and have the cash, see what sort of a discount you can get by offering it as an alternative to the credit card. Remember that the shop has to pay the card company a commission of up to 6 %.

minimum monthly payment. It may be twenty times so that if you are prepared to pay £50 a month, the limit is set at £1,000. The interest rate is usually quite high — about the same as on a credit card. The credit limit remains set so that the customer can continue to buy more goods as the amount due goes down.

There are other accounts which are like a Mastercard or Visa account. They are known as option accounts and allow the customer to pay off in full at the end of each month — incurring no interest — or else make a minimum repayment and incur the interest. There is usually no charge for getting a card — other than the interest.

Store cards encourage you to shop in that particular store or group and not to shop around for the best price. A budget account may be worthwhile to cover the cost of a major purchase but not if the money could be borrowed from one of the larger banks instead. An overdraft or term loan would cost far less in interest charged.

So the advice must be to generally steer clear of store cards. Mastercard or Visa would provide similar benefits in most cases without the drawback of confining you to shopping in one store.

There may be some exceptions. Monthly cards involve you in no cost and you can benefit from promotions which stores sometimes put on for card holders — special sales and pre-Christmas openings for instance. The Brown Thomas Group issues a card which is a true credit card which does not have to be used only in Brown Thomas outlets.

The Esso charge card is another exception in so far as it provides a company with a better control of spending on motor fuel. Companies with a number of people on the road can benefit from getting an itemised monthly account with the VAT shown separately. A lot of reclaimable VAT can be lost if the accountant has to rely on drivers keeping "invoices".

Cheque guarantee cards

To make full use of a cheque-book account you need a cheque guarantee card. It will cost you about £2.50 and guarantees your cheques up to a value of £100 each. Without the card you may find it very hard to cash cheques except where you are very well known. But remember that cheques are an expensive way of paying bills. It is far cheaper to pay by credit card provided you don't run up interest charges. If you need cash it is cheaper to draw money out of a bank machine. The charges for automated transactions are generally much lower and there is no stamp duty.

Automatic teller cards

All the major banks and the building societies have their own ATM cards and they all use different names. With AIB it is Banklink while Bank of Ireland has PASS; Ulster Bank has Service Till and the National Irish card is known as Autobank. The building societies operate the Cashere network.

All of the bank systems are interlinked so it is possible to use your bank card on any of the other banks' machines. On the basis of the queues it seems that many people don't realise this. The ICS Building Society machines and cards are also linked with those of the Bank of Ireland. The TSB Bank has its own separate network but its cards can be used in AIB machines too. The Irish Permanent has linked up with the Bank of Ireland network.

It is, of course, necessary to have an account with one of the institutions concerned and to either have some money in it or else have permission to overdraw. The machine is simply an automated teller and the transactions are just computerised versions of what was, and still is, done at the bank counter. Most of the machines operate on a round-the-clock basis providing the most flexible way of getting ready access to cash.

2.3 Managing the holiday finances

GETTING the necessary funds to pay for a holiday is not the only problem which has to be faced in this area. If you are going abroad there is also the question of getting the best exchange rate for your Irish pounds and also the matter of how best to carry your spending money. Like most money problems there is no single correct answer. There are four basic options — the best solution contains elements of each. The mix depends on individual choice and also on the holiday maker's destination. A Visa card is great in Paris but it is not likely to be much use in an out of the way Greek island. But let us first have a look at the broad options:

Cash

Cash is the most readily acceptable form of money — not Irish cash, of course, but rather the local currency. Some other currencies, such as the US Dollar, the D-Mark or Sterling are also widely accepted in many popular holiday resorts. And in Eastern Europe, of course, there may be advantages in having Dollars or D-Marks. But apart from that, there is not much sense in changing Irish money into anything but the local currency.

The simplest thing, of course, is to change all your holiday money into local cash before you leave Ireland. You can shop around for the best exchange rate and incur only one set of commission charges. The only drawback is the risk — and it is a major one. Cash is too easily lost. But it is advisable to have some local cash to take with you — if only for incidental expenses when you arrive.

Travellers' cheques

Travellers' cheques can now be bought in a number of currencies and there is some advantage in buying cheques denominated in the local currency of wherever you are going. But it can be harder to get refunds on some of the more obscure local currency travellers' cheques. Usually a commission of 1% is charged when the cheques are bought and a further commission may be charged when they are cashed. That cashing commission varies from place to place. If your cheques are not in the local currency it is best to cash them in a bank — shops and hotels often give bad exchange rates. There should be no commission

What to bring with you abroad

FRANCE:
Franc travellers' cheques are the best value, since you should not have to pay a commission when cashing them although there may be a charge per transaction. It is better to change them in banks. Cash is a must for smaller shops. There can be a very wide variation in exchange rates so it can pay to shop around. Mastercard is not all that well known. Visa is more readily accepted but it is not as widely used as in Ireland.

SPAIN:
Peseta travellers' cheques are as good as any. If you have sterling or other currency cheques, the usual commission is between 1% and 2% cent in banks and travel agencies. They may also charge for changing Peseta cheques. Exchange rates among bank and travel agencies do not vary very much but shops and hotels may provide poorer rates. Credit and charge cards are widely accepted in the holiday resorts but not in many garages.

UNITED STATES:
Dollar travellers' cheques are best. They are readily accepted in shops, hotels, etc. Credit cards — Mastercharge (Access) and Visa are also widely accepted. If you are going to make heavy use of a credit card it is a good idea to actually lodge money in it before you travel so that you won't exceed your credit limit and can withdraw cash without incurring heavy interest charges.

GREECE:
Drachma travellers' cheques are not readily available, so sterling or dollar cheques are the thing to take. Like most places, the banks give the best exchange rates and, in general, charge relatively low commission. Depending on the area, credit and charge cards can be useful or useless — readily accepted in the tourist areas but unknown in the more remote areas.

PORTUGAL:
It is possible to get escudo travellers' cheques, and avoid double exchange costs but you may still be charged a commission on cashing them, even in banks. Sterling or dollar cheques are an alternative. The banks and tourist offices offer the best exchange deals, so only use shops, hotels, etc.when there is no alternative. Like Spain, credit and charge cards are widely accepted in the tourist areas.

on cashing local currency cheques, at least in banks but there is a commission of 1 to $1\frac{1}{4}$% charged when you buy them. Sometimes those cashing travellers' cheques abroad charge a fixed commission on each transaction, so using them for small purchases can be very expensive. It is best to change them in bulk every now and then in a bank — weighing the risk of holding the extra cash against the cost of a multitude of transactions.

Credit cards

The credit cards, Mastercard (Access) and Visa, together with the charge cards, American Express and Diners, can all be used abroad. Not all outlets accept them, of course. So in many continental countries — and particularly in the more remote areas — they are not to be relied on. But they are, at the very least, a very useful standby and in the more popular holiday resorts they may cover most requirements — although they would always need to be supplemented with some local cash.

The cost of purchases abroad are translated into Irish pounds at the exchange rate on the day the item is debited to the credit card account. A commission is also usually charged. Most banks charge 1.75%. The Ulster Bank charges 2%. The EBS Visa card is an exception with no commission charge.

They can, of course, be used to draw cash as well as simply paying bills. The charge for this is usually 2% although again the EBS Visa is an exception in not making any charge while the Ulster Bank charge is 2%.

But in addition to those charges interest is normally applied on any cash withdrawal from the day it is made. You can get around this in some cases by lodging money to your account in advance. The amount you can withdraw abroad varies but it can be as low as the equivalent of $200 a day. So it's best to see the cash withdrawal facility as a useful standby for use only in an emergency.

Eurocheques

This is a facility available to bank customers allowing them to issue foreign currency cheques on their existing bank account. You have to buy a special cheque card — for about £4 to £6 depending on the bank — and get a book of special cheques from your bank. The cheques are written in the local currency up to a limit of about £140 for each cheque. The cheques are debited to your bank account at home — in Irish pounds, of course. There is a commission charge of 1.6% on the amount of each cheque — subject to a minimum charge of about £1 — plus the usual handling charges at your own bank.

Holiday checklist

A bit of advance planning can help you avoid some unpleasant financial surprises while on holiday. The following are some pointers:

Credit cards:

- Increase your credit limit just in case you need it — unless, of course, that might prove too much of a temptation to overspend.

- Check that the magnetic strip is in good order.

- Get additional cards for your partner.

- Get the PIN number to use for withdrawing cash. It's an expensive way of getting cash but useful in an emergency.

- Make a note of all your card numbers and details of where you have to ring to report their loss. Keep a couple of copies so that you can report any loss quickly.

Eurocheques: Order them a few weeks in advance. You need to get a special Euro chequecard.

Form E 111: If you're going to a country within the European Community make sure to get a Form E111 from your local Health Board. It will ensure that you get the same sort of free medical insurance as the locals in whatever country you go to. You can pick up a blank form at your local health centre or dispensary. You need to fill it in and get it stamped. That can take a few weeks.

BUPA/VHI: If you have medical insurance check what cover it provides when abroad and make a note of any special contact telephone numbers to be used. It's not an alternative to travel insurance but it is a very useful addition.

Travel insurance: Don't forget to take out some form of travel insurance. Read the section on page 44.

Eurocheque cards can also be used to withdraw cash from some 6,000 automated teller machines throughout Andorra, Britain, Denmark, France, Germany, Italy, Portugal, Spain and increasingly in Eastern Europe. The fee is 0.25% of the amount withdrawn plus a flat charge of about £1.25. Eurocheques are not accepted everywhere, however. They are more generally accepted in northern Europe than in the southern areas.

Eurocheques provide great flexibility but must be ordered some weeks in advance.

A point to remember about Eurocheques is that it can take a couple of weeks to organise your cheque book and card. So do not leave it until the last moment to organise yours. Order them from the bank in plenty of time.

Travel Insurance

Travel insurance can provide a real benefit in the form of peace of mind even if you never have to make a claim. But be sure to read the fine print and know exactly what you are covered for and what you have to do to make a claim. It's usually necessary to report any loss to the local police, for instance, and to make the claim within a fixed time period.

There are a wide range of policies available and the cover varies greatly: as does the cost. Travel agents normally offer insurance with their holidays and may charge an extra fee — perhaps £5 — if it is not taken out. But it can still be worthwhile shopping around. It is not too difficult to save £5 on a holiday insurance premium and still get wider cover. Don't forget that you may already have insurance cover for some risks. You may have items like jewellery, cameras etc. covered for "all risks" on your household policy.

People who travel a lot should consider taking out an annual policy rather than one for each trip. There's certainly a saving to be made if you make three or more trips a year.

You may want cover for the potential loss of having to cancel a holiday in the event of the death of a close relative. This cover is usually fairly restrictive. You also need cover for medical expenses. BUPA and VHI provide some cover but not enough. Most policies also provide cover for delays and the loss of baggage and personal belongings.

The Irish League of Credit Unions offer travel insurance through member credit unions. A summary of the cover it provides can be used as a guide to what's available. At a cost of £7.50 for up to 18 days holiday in Ireland, £10 for holidays in Britain; £16 elsewhere in Europe and £36 worldwide, the policy will pay out up to £2 million for medical expenses, £3,000 if you have to cancel because of the death of a spouse or close relative, jury service or the burglary of your home or business, £2 million for personal liability, up to £1,500 for loss of baggage and up to £500 for loss of cash.

There is a 10% discount for people taking out holiday loans through the credit union. Holidays involving winter sports attract twice the premiums listed above. The basic rates apply up to age 75 — many insurance policies charge an extra premium for anyone over 70.

Savings

Saving — the best options

3.1

Everyone is a saver to some extent even if it only a matter of spreading money from one payday to the next. That short-term management of money was the subject of the last chapter. Saving, in the normal sense of the word, involves putting money away for a longer period. At the basic level money is put away simply to meet the occasional bill which comes in less regularly than paydays — a holiday, the car or house insurance, even the ESB or gas bills.

But there are other times for saving with an eye to a more distant future. The time scale is longer and the sums involved are likely to be bigger so the rate of return becomes more important. The short-term saver is more concerned with having ready access to his or her funds. The longer-term saver or investor places a higher priority on interest rates. There is, of course, no clear-cut division between the short-term saver and the investor. Some of the options listed in the last chapter may be used — and are used — by those with no immediate use for their money. And some of them have attractions in this regard. The building societies, smaller banks and the State institutions such as ICCBank and ACCBank all offer higher rates for those willing to leave their money untouched for longer periods. And they all offer higher rates for those with larger sums to invest. So they would be equally relevant in the present chapter. The division between the two is therefore somewhat arbitrary.

For most savers, the progression is from short-term to medium term and finally to long-term saving. In other words it is a matter of saving up small amounts regularly over a period to eventually build up a lump sum which can be put aside for some years.

Getting the best from financial advisors

The old legal adage of caveat empore or let the buyer beware has not been supplanted by the range of consumer protection legislation enacted in recent years. There is still little enough protection in the financial services area and wrong decisions can be very costly for consumers. Taking out the wrong insurance policy or making the wrong investment can be very expensive and it is not necessary to take out a "bad" policy or make a "bad" investment to lose out. Just as there are horses for courses, there are policies and investments which, while excellent in some circumstances, may be disastrous in others. And the salesman or advisor may err simply by not knowing enough or not having access to a wide range of products. There is no shortage of one-product salesmen in the financial area who are simply geared to sell that product irrespective of the client's needs.

The first bit of advice is to be wary of the advisor who does not ask you a lot of questions to start with. To give adequate advice, a financial advisor needs to know something of his client's circumstances: a broad idea of income and responsibilities; tax situation; attitude to risk etc. It is also up to the client to ask some questions of his own. Make sure that you understand the answers.

1. **WHAT — What do I need?**

2. **HOW — How is the product going to supply that need?**

3. **WHY — Why that product rather than something else?**

4. **WHEN — Don't be rushed?**

The "What?" question is one that you have to ask yourself. Supermarkets and shops are very much into encouraging impulse buying. That can be discouraged by making a shopping list and sticking to it. The same is true in the financial area. It's up to you to decide what you want. Don't let the salesman decide what you want. He or she may make suggestions but make sure that you make the decisions. Before you take any advice decide what you want yourself — if only in very broad terms, such as "I need to save for the children's education" or "I need insurance cover".

Then try to go a bit further than that. If the product is insurance what cover do you need? Do you need it on yourself or your spouse or both? Try to put broad figures on your needs. For instance, if you are considering saving for the children's education how much are you likely to need? And when? Do you think you'll need it to pay for secondary school or third level. Fees may have been abolished but other costs remain. Why do you need it — will your income not be sufficient at the time to cover the expense? Are you willing to take a risk with your savings? How much can you afford to save? Scribble down your answers. Use it as a check list to see if the salesman or advisor has got you to deviate from your original objectives. If so, did he give adequate reasons why you should?

The other three questions in your check list are asked of the salesman or the advisor. It is a matter of "how and why". How is that particular product going to satisfy your particular need and most important, why that product rather than something else? And that includes the most important question of why one company's products rather than another's.

Make sure you get adequate answers. Do not be afraid to keep asking why or how and make sure you understand the answer. Ask about alternatives. You can be sure that there are alternatives even if you don't know what they are. The salesman or advisor should know what they are and be able to justify the alternative he has chosen for you.

And remember that if you don't understand it, it is not your fault. There is nothing so complicated in financial products that it can't be explained in simple, easily understood, language. If your salesman or advisor can't do that, maybe he doesn't understand it himself. If he or she is calling to your home it can be no harm taking out a tape-recorder explaining that you are a bit muddle headed and may forget what he has to say. Explain that you would like to be able to go over it after he has left. That should stop him making excessive claims.

The final question is "When?". That is really a reminder not to be rushed. In the financial area you can be making very expensive decisions. A premium of £5 a week seems small but it is £260 a year and £2,600 over ten years. Take your time. Sleep on it.

It is, of course, always better to get advice from more than one advisor if possible. It is usually free. Then you can compare one with the other. And, do not forget, that although the advisor or salesman is not charging you anything, he is getting some commission. In some cases it can be considerable. In the case of many savings-type insurance policies it can eat up more than half of the first year's premiums. It is similar with pension schemes. The point is not that you are paying too much — a good advisor is worth his commission. Just remember that you are actually paying — and paying adequately, even generously — for the adviser's time and knowledge. So there is no need to feel guilty about asking questions and getting answers before you make your final decision.

Invest in paying off a loan

Paying off a loan can sometimes be the best use for some spare savings. It can yield a far higher return than any alternative safe investment. Let's use Post Office Savings Bonds as a benchmark investment. It's safe and tax free and yields an average of 4.5 per cent over three years.

Invest a £1,000 in Savings Bonds and you effectively earn £45 a year in interest. Invest the same money in paying off a bank term loan - currently costing 11 per cent — and your gain is £110 a year. It makes sense to pay off the loan. Paying off the loan does reduce your flexibility but loans are readily available at present and seem set to remain so for the foreseeable future. So if you do need the money later, you can always borrow again. Mortgages are the exception. The interest rate is low and the interest may be eligible for tax relief. The true cost of a mortgage at 7 per cent is only 5.6 per cent after tax relief.

Taking the example above the gain from paying £1,000 off such a mortgage is £56 a year which is more than the £45 to be gained from an investment in Savings Bonds. But it still may not be worth using the money to pay off the mortgage. There are longer term considerations to take into account.

If you once pay off the mortgage, it's not so easy to borrow again at such a favourable rate. It would, of course, be possible to get a top up mortgage but it would not be eligible for tax relief. And there'll be set up costs. It would be rather foolish to pay off a loan on which the effective interest rate is only 5.6 per cent and then, perhaps, have to borrow in a year or two at 11 per cent to buy a car.

So as a rule of thumb it does make sense to use surplus cash to pay off most loans provided there are no early repayment penalties involved. The exception is a mortgage on which you are getting tax relief. It may not even be worthwhile paying off a mortgage on which you are not getting tax relief if you leave yourself in a position where you'll have to borrow again at a higher rate in the future. Assuming a mortgage rate of 7 per cent a married couple get tax relief on mortgages up to about £71,400 while a single borrower gets relief on a loan up to £35,700. There is no tax relief on the portions of the loans above those levels.

For this type of regular saver the normal short-term outlets, dealt with in the last chapter, offer many alternatives. There are other schemes such as the Post Office Instalment Savings Scheme, and endowment assurance linked plans, which are particularly attractive to those able to save regularly. These schemes, however, are not really suitable for short-term savers since there are penalties involved in taking your money out too soon.

There are other people who may already have a lump sum to put aside. These could also use the short-term outlets. As outlined above, many of the banks and financial institutions mentioned in the last chapter give higher interest rates for money left in for longer periods. So do not rule those out. But there are other options which can yield higher returns. Some of these are considered later in the chapter.

The final decision rests with the saver and a lot of personal idiosyncrasies can influence that decision. These include the amount of risk desired to be taken; the weight given to the possibility that medium-term savings may be needed more urgently than first anticipated and, of course, the individual's tax situation. Tax, indeed, is a very important element in the rate of return a person gets on his savings. Some schemes are particularly attractive to people on high rates of income tax yet may have no attractions for people not liable to tax, or simply liable for tax at the standard rate. While a general consideration of tax liability is left to a later chapter, the tax implications of the following saving options are dealt with as they come.

As mentioned above there is no single best option. It all depends on individual circumstances and objectives. And, of course, the relative attractiveness of different options can change with time. So the following should only be taken as pointers. A more detailed look at the various options mentioned is contained in the following sections.

Saving for the children

Even with fees abolished, putting children through third-level education can be a costly business and it makes sense to make some provision for that expense in advance. It is never too early to start saving whatever you can afford on a regular basis. There are a number of different alternatives:

Deposit Account: The easiest way of saving is in a bank, building society, post office, or credit union account. You can put aside as much as you like and as you build up larger sums you can switch them into longer term accounts which pay higher rates of interest. Some people, however, like to have a more formalised plan which will put some pressure on them to fulfill their good intentions.

Post Office Instalment Saving: The idea is that you agree to save a regular amount — up to £300 a month — for a year and then leave it on deposit where it earns about 4.9% a year tax-free. At the end of the year you can start off again. It is risk free and is currently yielding a good safe return. You might decide, for instance, to put in the child benefit money each month. While it is obviously a longer term savings plan it is possible to get your money out at any time if you need it.

Assurance Policy: Life assurance companies and other fund managers also offer savings plans with or without life insurance cover included. The life cover is usually very small but re-member that it's not free. Part of your savings will be going to pay for it. There is a wide range of options available. Your savings go into an investment fund of some kind. In most cases the value of those investments can move down as well as up so that there is no certainty about the return you can expect. Among insurance linked plans, endowment policies carry the least risk.

There are relatively high setup costs so it is important to be sure that you are going to stick with it. New products are being introduced which spread the cost over a longer period but as a rough rule of thumb you are unlikely to get much, if any, return if you cash in within the first five years.

It can be a good idea if you are taking out such a policy with a view to saving for a child's education to take it out on the life of the non-wage earning spouse — usually the mother. It is very common to find that there is ample life assurance on the life of the husband but little or none on the life of the wife. Yet her death can involve severe financial strain if the family is to be kept together. Replacing a non-wage earning wife with a housekeeper is a very costly business — a fact that is very often forgotten but be clear that you are making two decisions, one is to save for the future and the other is to take out some life insurance cover. Be sure that you know how much the life insurance cover is costing. Most of the "special" education plans offered by the insurance companies are based on such unit-linked policies. In fact, the same investment could be used equally well for saving for retirement or any other purpose.

Saving for retirement

This is just a variation on the objective mentioned in the last section and all the options mentioned are just as relevant. There is one other possibility: contributing to a pension scheme. If you are already in a company scheme it may be possible to make extra contributions to improve your benefits. If you are self-employed, it is possible to organise your own scheme. The great benefit is that up to generous limits, there is full tax relief on the contributions paid into the fund and the money grows tax-free within the fund. For more details see chapter ten on planning for retirement (page 161).

Income from a lump sum

With retirement or redundancy lump sums the usual objective is to provide the best net income with an acceptable degree of risk. In many cases no risk will be acceptable. Some people may be willing to take a risk with at least some of their lump sum. It all depends on the individual. Tax may have to be taken into account. For instance, unless the recipient is over 65 or incapacitated, there is no way of claiming back the DIRT tax stopped on deposit interest even if the recipient is not liable for income tax.

Interest rates are at a low level going into 1998 and they are expected to fall further, so it is all the more important to shop around for the best possible return. And that means continually shopping around, keeping an eye on what is available. That does not mean always keeping your money on short notices of withdrawal, but simply examining the options afresh each time you have the flexibility to switch. Let us have a brief look at some of the options. They are all dealt with in detail later in the chapter.

Pay off loans: It can sometimes make more sense to use part of a lump sum to pay off loans than to invest it. In general if you are paying a higher rate of interest on the loan than it is possible to get from an investment, then it makes sense to pay off the loan. Be careful, however, about penalties for early repayment on some loans and don't pay off a relatively cheap loan if that will leave you in a position where you may have to borrow later at a higher rate. For instance, don't pay off a mortgage on which you are getting, or may again get tax relief. You lose flexibility and you could be forced to borrow at much higher rates in the future — and without tax relief — if you need to replace your car, say, or need money urgently for something else.

Post Office Schemes: Saving Certificates and Savings Bonds offer tax-free returns with complete security. The returns are not liable to income tax. With Saving Certificates it is possible to get a six monthly income by cashing in some of the certificates. It is more difficult to get a regular income from Savings

Bonds. No interest is payable if you withdraw bonds during the first year, for instance. With both schemes it is always possible to withdraw some or all of your money on short notice but you can lose up to six months interest with Savings Certificates and up to a year's interest with Bonds. But depending on the timing of the withdrawal you may lose nothing. A bit of care is needed.

Government stocks: These can be attractive for investors not liable for income tax but because they are under 65, are not entitled to reclaim the DIRT tax which would be stopped on most deposit interest. Dividends are paid out every six months without any tax being stopped. There need not be any great mystery about them. All is explained later in the chapter.

Annuities provide a secure way of spreading a lump sum out over the rest of one's life.

Annuities: These are another alternative — particularly for elderly investors with limited means. On offer from insurance companies they provide a method of spreading a lump sum out over the rest of one's life. The company promises to pay an agreed income until death. The longer you live the better the overall return. The advantage is that you know the income will continue until death no matter how long you live. The disadvantage is that there is nothing left of the investment when you die.

Investment funds: These funds, run by assurance companies and other professional managers, allow investors to get involved in shares, property and other investments on a cooperative basis with other investors. For a fee you get the benefit of professional management of your investments. Most units can move down as well as up in value but there are some funds which guarantee to at least return the bulk of your money at the end of a set period. You can reduce the risk with your choice of fund. Managed funds, for instance, which have a spread of investments usually carry less risk of a downturn than funds which are only invested in the one type of outlet — say property or equities. And there are 'money' and 'guaranteed' funds where the risk is insignificant. But they should be viewed as medium to long term investment options. They are hardly the place to put all of a redundancy or retirement lump sum although they might be considered as a long-term investment for a small portion of it. It is possible to get a regular income by cashing in some of the units but if unit values are falling, or not rising fast enough, some or all of that income has to come out of capital. See also below.

Shares: Shares can provide some income in the form of dividends but a good part of the hoped-for return generally comes from increases in the share price — if you are lucky. But, of course, share prices can move down as well as up — sometimes quite dramatically as they did during the 1987 crash or most recently, although not quite as dramatically, in October 1997. Over the long term share values tend to go up faster than inflation. But you do need to pick the right shares at the right time. If your income needs are limited and you can take a long term view, shares might be a consideration. You do need to know what you are doing. Share values on many markets were believed to be near a peak late in 1997 even though they recovered from the threatened crash so it may not be the best time to invest.

At the same time, however, interest rates are low and are expected to fall even further during 1998 in the run up to European Monetary Union. Final decisions on the countries which are to join the single currency bloc are to be taken by April 1998 and the euro is to come into being on January 1, 1999.

If all goes according to plan interest rates in Ireland are expected to move down to the lower levels obtaining in Germany. That is, of course, assuming all goes according to plan.

Investment funds: Again taking a long term view unit-linked and other investment funds can offer the prospect of good growth. But as mentioned above there are risks and they need to be appreciated. Tracker bonds can offer at least a guarantee that you will get your money back after a set period — usually three or five years, with the promise of a return in line with some specified stock market index, or group of indices, if share values rise. Japanese shares have been in the doldrums for some time so they have more upward potential than European or American shares. But the recovery could take some time to emerge.

Saving Certificates: These provide a fixed, safe, tax-free return with the flexibility that they can be cashed in at any time but you can lose up to six months interest if you withdraw your money at the wrong time.

Government stocks: Some Government stocks offer relatively low dividends but also the prospect — or certainty, if held to maturity — of tax free capital gains.

Lump sum for growth

Business Expansion Schemes: Significant tax relief is available to people who invest in new or expanding manufacturing, tourism, international traded service companies. and certain music ventures. There is always some risk involved but the scheme is still attractive particularly for someone with a direct interest in the project. Full tax relief is available on up to £25,000 invested each year. You have to wait at least five years to get a return.

Budget changes in December 1997 will restrict the range of projects eligible for this tax relief. They are likely to be smaller and riskier. Details of this scheme are given in Chapter 14 on page 258.

3.2 Post Office investment

In addition to its normal savings bank activities An Post also offers a range of medium to long term investment outlets. These include Instalment Savings; Saving Certificates; and Savings Bonds. They are all State guaranteed so there is no worry from the security point of view. They all offer tax free returns — indeed the returns are not even considered to be income. The return on An Post schemes is guaranteed over three to five years with the annual rate going up significantly in the latter years. In the short-term some bank and building society deposits offer higher returns but usually not on a guaranteed basis over three to five years particularly when DIRT tax is taken into account.

These Bonds are a three year investment with guaranteed returns each year. It is possible to withdraw money at any time without penalty other than the fact that no interest is payable if the money is withdrawn during the first year.

The rates of return are as follows: money left in for one year, 3.6%; two years, 7.5% which is 3.7% a year; three years 14.0% equal to 4.46% a year.

The minimum investment is £100 and seven working days notice is required for withdrawal. No interest is paid on money withdrawn during the first year. Thereafter the guaranteed annual rates apply together with the normal Post Office Savings Bank rate for each complete calendar month — with no DIRT tax or other tax stopped. No tax indeed is payable.

The money can be withdrawn at any time through any Post Office or by post from the Post Office Savings Bank, FREEPOST, Townsend Street, Dublin 2. Withdrawals are subject to seven working days notice.

The return is guaranteed for three years at the end of which you can leave your money in at rates determined from time to time by the Minister of Finance. At one time it made sense to take your money out at the end of each term even if it was only to reinvest it again. But in recent years the continuation rates have

Savings bonds

Getting an income from saving certificates.......

The only way to get an income from savings certificates is to cash them in. So to get a regular income it is necessary to cash some of the initial investment in from time to time. This should be done at six-monthly intervals or at longer periods which are multiples of six months i.e. a year, eighteen months etc. You do not have to decide in advance how many units to cash in but it is as well to have a plan.

Constant Income

In this first example the aim is to get a fairly constant six-monthly income while maintaining the lump sum. It is achieved by cashing in 23 of the initial £10 units after six months and 23 after a further six months and gradually reducing the number encashed every six months. The income stays relatively constant. Although the capital sum does dip slightly as low as £9,681 during the period, by the end of the five and a half years the remaining units are worth £23 more than the initial £10,000 invested.

	Number of units cashed in	Value of units cashed in	Number of £10 units left	Value of units left
Initially			1,000	£10,000
6 months	23	£234	977	£9,936
one year	23	£238	954	£9,883
18 months	22	£232	932	£9,833
two years	22	£237	910	£9,783
2½ years	21	£230	889	£9,735
three years	21	£234	868	£9,687
3½ years	21	£240	847	£9,681
four years	20	£235	827	£9,709
4½ years	19	£230	808	£9,801
five years	19	£240	789	£9,949
5½ years	18	£234	771	£10,023

The tables give two possible examples of how a regular income can be achieved while still leaving the nominal value of the remaining investment untouched. In both cases the assumption is that £10,000 is invested initially in units of 10. Simply divide or multiply all the figures to suit your own investment. For instance if you only have £1,000 to invest divide all the figures by 10. If you have £5,000 divide by 2.

Rising Income

In this example a constant twenty-one £10 units are cashed in each six months. Since the value of each unit is going up the income rises as well — from £214 after the first six months to £273 after five and a half years. The value of the remaining investment dips to a low of £9,750 during the period but finishes the five years six months at £9,997. Different combinations are, of course, possible. Some people may prefer to take an irregular income while others may postpone taking an income for an initial period.

	Number of units cashed in	Value of units cashed in	Number of £10 units left	Value of units left
Initially			1,000	£10,000
6 months	21	£214	979	£9,956
one year	21	£218	958	£9,925
18 months	21	£222	937	£9,885
two years	21	£226	916	£9,847
2½ years	21	£230	895	£9,800
three years	21	£234	874	£9,754
3½ years	21	£240	853	£9,750
four years	21	£247	832	£9,768
4½ years	21	£255	811	£9,837
five years	21	£265	790	£9,962
5½ years	21	£273	769	£9,997

been set at a level which removes any incentive to do that. It is no harm to check, however, what rates are being offered.

The maximum investment in the current issue of Savings Bonds is £60,000 per individual. That is in addition to any investments held in earlier issues or other schemes. Up to £120,000 may be held in a joint account. Anyone over seven years of age can invest either on their own or jointly with others.

Saving certificates

An alternative to Index Linked Savings Bonds are Saving Certificates. The current issue (fourteenth issue) is offering a tax free return of 4.89% a year if held for five years and six months. An initial investment of £1,000 grows to be £1,300 over that period.

There are no regular interest payments on Saving Certificates — you get your return when you cash them in. But even after six months their value will have increased by 1.7% and by 3.6% after a year. And it is possible to get a regular income from your saving certificates by cashing them in at regular intervals. The return on saving certificates is completely tax-free. There is no provision for the actual payment of interest. The value of the certificate simply grows by a set amount at the end of each six months. It is important to understand this factor. Interest is only added in at six monthly intervals so, if you cash in a day before a six monthly period is up, you can lose almost six months interest. The minimum investment is £50 and the maximum is £60,000 (£120,000 in a joint account). That is in addition to any money in earlier issues or in other An Post schemes.

The annual rate is low in the initial years — 3.6% in the first year and 3.8% in the second. But it rises to 7.2% in the final twelve months. You should be thinking of leaving your money for the full five and a half years and certainly try to avoid withdrawing money in the final couple of years when the returns are greatest. The value of each £1,000 goes up as follows:

6 months	£1,017	**One year**	£1,036
1½ years	£1,055	**Two years**	£1,075
2½ years	£1,095	**Three years**	£1,116
3½ years	£1,143	**Four years**	£1,174
4½ years	£1,213	**Five years**	£1,261
5½ years	£1,300		

Money may be left in after the initial five and a half year period at a rate usually fixed by the Department of Finance for three years at a time. It is based on the rate applicable to new certificates at that time.

With the interest only added in every six months, it is important — if you have to cash in — to do it as soon as possible after a six-monthly anniversary. That way you lose the least amount of interest. Only the registered owner of the certificates can cash them in. They can be cashed in either in whole or in part, with seven working days required. This facility for partial encashment can be used to provide the saver with a regular income.

The accompanying tables show how this might be achieved. The examples assume that an investment of £10,000 (1,000 units of £10 each, although with the latest issues An Post doesn't think in terms of units anymore). They may all appear on the one certificate but that does not prevent the saver from making partial encashments. They are simply written on the back of the certificate.

By varying the rate of encashment, the saver can get either a fairly static income every six months or alternatively a rising or even a declining one. As the tables show the saver can get a rising income by cashing in an identical number of units every six months. The units are, of course, going up in value so while 21 units are worth £214 after six months, they are worth £265 after five years. In all cases, it is important that the Certificates be cashed in as soon as possible after a six-monthly anniversaries of the initial investment. Otherwise interest will be lost.

There is, of course, no need to keep to a specified plan. Units can be cashed in at any time. The rate on Saving Certificates is particularly attractive in the last two years so it is best to leave the money in for the full term. The return in the early years is far less attractive but with interest rates expected to fall in the years ahead if the European Monetary Union gets up and running, Saving Certificates offer a way of locking money into a reasonable return over five and a half years.

It is possible, of course, to cash them in at any time. Seven working days notice of withdrawal is required.

An Post also has an instalment savings scheme aimed at the person who can put some money away regularly with the

Instalment savings

intention of leaving it for some years. This National Instalment Saving Scheme is primarily aimed at those savers who can save a fixed amount each month for a year. The saver — who must be over 7 years of age — agrees to save a stated amount each month for twelve consecutive months. The minimum monthly saving is £20 and the maximum £300.

At the end of the 12 months period, the total amount saved is left on deposit. After that interest starts to accrue at a guaranteed rate which rises over the years and averages 5.6 per cent over five years. The annual returns are as follows:

year one	4.0%	**year two**	3.7%
year three	5.1%	**year four**	5.7%
year five	8.3%		

So once started there is obviously a growing incentive not to withdraw the savings until the end of the five year period. The returns in the final three years are particularly attractive.

The Instalment Savings Scheme is ideal for those wanting to save a fixed amount regularly each month.

The instalment saving scheme is about the most attractive of the An Post schemes. But, of course, it is not suitable for those with lump sums to invest. As a way of guaranteeing a good tax-free return on regular savings, however, there is little to beat it. While the idea is that you would save the agreed amount each month, there is no penalty for skipping instalments.

If the savings are left for five years after the initial year's saving period you are guaranteed your money back plus 30% — that works out at about 4.9% a year.

A number of points to bear in mind:-

If you fail to keep up your twelve monthly payments and withdraw your money before the end of the year, you get no interest at all. If you miss a monthly payment you can continue on with the scheme. Interest will start to accrue on whatever you have saved during the twelve months from the beginning of the month following your final instalment.

Under previous schemes you had to make twelve instalments but could spread them over fourteen months. That's no longer the case under the new scheme. Now you save for twelve months and can miss instalments if you want to. You can make instalments at any time during the calendar month. If you don't make an instalment during that period you can't backdate one.

It simply means you have less money in the scheme to start earning interest.

If you withdraw your money after the initial twelve months you get the guaranteed bonus for each complete year together with the Post Office Savings Bank rate of interest for each additional full calendar month.

The guaranteed rates cover the first five years. Extension terms are then offered based on market interest rates at the time.

3.3 Special Savings Accounts

DIRT tax is levied at the standard income tax rate on most deposit interest. The rate is 26% up to April 1998 and after that it falls to 24%. No further tax is due on deposit interest even if the recipient is liable to a higher rate of income tax. A lower rate of DIRT applies to special savings accounts. It is 15% up to April 1998 and then rises to 20%. It was only 10% up to April 1995. People who are not liable for income tax and who are either over 65 years of age or disabled can claim back the tax.

The low rate of DIRT tax only applies to special savings accounts which meet with the conditions laid down by the Revenue Commissioners. Depositors must be over 18 years of age and can have only one special savings account at any one time. There is an upper limit of £50,000 which may be kept in the account and that includes any interest earned. A married couple may have two accounts with up to £50,000 in each. They can either be single or joint accounts. A single person will not get the concession in respect of a joint account.

To qualify for the concession certain conditions have to be met. No withdrawals can be allowed within the first three months of the account being opened and at least thirty days notice is required for any withdrawal thereafter. Some accounts will guarantee fixed rates for a set period but the rules stipulate that the rates cannot be fixed in advance for a period of more than two years.

Low DIRT Accounts

On opening a special savings account, the depositor is required to give a signed declaration which is kept by the financial institution for at least six years and may be inspected by the Revenue Commissioners. The declaration must state that the conditions of the scheme are being met; give the full name and address of the individual who is entitled to the interest on the account; and contain an undertaking that the individual will immediately notify the bank or other financial institution if he or she ceases to meet the requirements of the scheme.

All types of deposit accounts can, of course, meet those conditions. So a whole range of alternatives is available not only in terms of interest rates. Some financial institutions require a minimum deposit, others do not. Various income options are also available.

Reclaiming DIRT tax

If you are not liable for income tax and you are either over 65 years of age or permanently incapacitated, then you are entitled to claim back any DIRT tax stopped on deposit interest you have earned. In the case of a married couple, it is sufficient for either partner to be over 65 years of age.

The claim has to be made on a simple form which can be got in any tax office, at larger post offices or from wherever you have your savings. You also need a certificate from the bank or building society giving details of the DIRT tax stopped. Fill out the form, attach the certificate of tax stopped, and send it off to the tax office — the address is on the form.

3.4 Investing in stocks and shares

Stock market investment

INTEREST in the Stock Exchange has been boosted in recent years by the flotation, and pending flotation, of building societies and mutual insurance companies. It will get another boost from the cut in capital gains tax. But the marked setback suffered in October 1997 has once again revived memories of the crash of 1987. At first it seemed that history was going to repeat itself almost exactly ten years later but the stock markets rallied again and much of the initial losses were regained. The crash didn't happen but there is still a feeling that it might. Share values have risen sharply on most western markets over recent years and some commentators believe that they are overvalued.

Small individual shareholders tend to jump on bandwagons only to have their enthusiasm dampened again when the seemingly unending boom does come to an end and share values plummet. While October 1997 may be a warning there is no doubt that most share punters have done very well since the 1987 crash. The 1990s has been a good decade for stock market investors. There was a sharp 60% jump in overall share values on the Irish Stock Exchange between October 1992 and the end of 1993. That rise ran out of steam during 1994 but there was a renewed upturn in 1995 fueled mainly by a sharp 37% rise in the average value of financial shares. Share values have jumped by a further 70% over 1996 and 1997 — that's after allowing for the downturn from the high reached before the October 1997 setback. There will be renewed interest in the stock market during 1998 with the expected flotation of the First National Building Society but no one is predicting that share values will continue to spiral upwards.

The small investor may be better spreading the risk by investing in shares indirectly through a managed fund.

Taking a long term view Irish shares have performed very well in the past — outpacing most other investments. There can be sharp swings but provided you don't buy at the very top of a cycle and can take a long-term view it is possible to achieve very good returns. There can, however, be no certainty. Irish investors are not, of course, restricted to investing on the Irish stock exchange. But investing abroad involves an extra risk. The foreign shares have to be bought in foreign currency and there is

The stock market — understanding the jargon

Par Price: Every share has a par price fixed at the time of its issue. Thereafter it ceases to have very much meaning. The price at which a share is bought or sold is determined by what people are willing to pay, and the par price has no bearing on this.

Dividend Yield: Dividends are declared in pence per share — the amount being after a charge of income tax. However, most sources still calculate dividend yield as a before-tax figure. In effect, the dividend yield tells you the rate of return you can expect on the amount of money you have invested in the company if it continues to pay dividends at its current rate. For example, if the dividend yield of a company is 3.5% at the current price of the shares, then if you laid out £100 in purchasing shares at the current price the dividends would provide you with an annual income of £3.50.

Earnings Per Share: The dividend is only one part of the story. Investors are hoping for some rise in share value in addition to the dividend income. And share price is as much determined by profits as by dividend pay-out. But profits can be distorted in any year by extraordinary, once-off, losses or windfall profits. These are ignored in calculating the earnings figure. It is an indication of underlying profits. It can be divided by the number of shares on issue to give an earnings per share figure.

Cover: This is the number of times the dividend pay-out is covered by earnings. It is a guide to the likely stability of the dividend pay-out. If earnings per share are twice the dividend — a cover of two — then the dividend could be maintained even if earnings were to halve in any one year.

P/E Ratio: This is the price earning ratio. Usually given as a net (after tax) figure, the P/E ratio is the price of the share divided by earnings per share. It is much the same as a "years purchase" figure, i.e. how many years of earnings does the current price represent. A sound secure company will normally be standing at a high P/E, while a more doubtful one will stand at a low P/E.

always the risk that the Irish pound will devalue against that currency.

Whatever the prospects, small investors must always be wary of investing in shares. They cannot spread their money over a wide range of shares in order to spread the risk and they must realise that share values can go down as well as up. But for those willing to take a gamble there is money to be made provided they realise and accept that there can be no certainty.

It can be argued that the small investor is better advised to invest indirectly in shares on the stock market through unit trusts or equity linked bonds. That way he gets the benefit of skilled management for his investment. However, it can be expensive to invest indirectly. The setup costs of investing in a unit linked fund are often higher than the commission payable on a share purchase. The funds do provide a spread of investments, of course, but it can be interesting to play the market yourself provided you appreciate the risks you take and can afford to accept some losses.

Whether you go it alone, or invest indirectly, some knowledge of the stock market will not go amiss. Investing in a company on the Stock Exchange gives you a part ownership in the company concerned. The return on this part ownership depends on the performance of the company, so together with the prospect of a high return, goes the risk of no return. The degree of risk varies with the type of share and with the company.

There are debentures and preference shares which carry a fixed rate of interest and have first claim on a company's profits, and then there are ordinary shares, which are the real ownership shares, and carry with them full risks of ownership and the full prospects. If the company makes no profits, they get no dividend; if it prospers, they get all the cream. To the outsider a certain aura of mystery surrounds the Stock Exchange, but the fact is that one can buy shares as easily — perhaps more easily — than lodging money in the bank. A number of stockbrokers now have walk-in shops where it is possible to buy shares at the counter — and sell them just as easily.

How to buy the shares

The first question which enters the heads of most potential Stock Exchange investors is: "How much do I need?" There is no hard and fast answer. Some stockbrokers would put the minimum at about £1,000: some would accept a lower figure but with a minimum commission of at least £20 per transaction it does not make sense to invest very small amounts.

It is best to deal directly with a stockbroker although you could use your bank manager as an intermediary. A list of stockbrokers may be obtained from The General Manager, Irish Stock Exchange, Anglesea Street, Dublin 2. In addition to buying or selling your shares for you, the stockbroker will also give advice on what and when to buy and sell. His commission is relatively small — about 1½% of the sale or purchase price subject to a minimum. There is also a Government stamp duty of 1% on all purchases.

Brokers may not get over-enthusiastic about small investors, but a potential investor who can give a brief outline of what he requires will normally get a sympathetic hearing.

Since the abolition of all exchange controls on January 1, 1993, there are no restrictions on investing in shares abroad.

Government stocks

Government stock, or gilts as they are sometimes known, can be an attractive investment for the ordinary investor. They are not something solely for the high flier. There is nothing mysterious about them. One of their attractions is that no DIRT tax is stopped on the interest so they can be particularly attractive to the non-taxpayer who, being under 65 years of age and not incapacitated, is unable to reclaim the DIRT tax stopped on normal deposit interest. This attraction has been reduced somewhat by the introduction of the new low DIRT tax deposit accounts.

Although the price of Government stock can move up and down, the investor who can hold on until the redemption date of the particular stock takes no risk. So it is possible to invest on a no-risk basis. Unfortunately many people are put off by the very idea of investing on the Stock Exchange — either in shares or gilts. But there is no need to be. It is all quite simple. First an explanation of what a Government stock is. When the Government borrows from the public, the financial institutions, or the banks on a long-term basis, it does so by "selling" new Government stock. The stock can be thought of as an IOU. In return for the loan the Government gives out this IOU promising to pay the lender so much interest every six months and to repay the full amount of the loan at some time in the future. Usually the repayment date is left a little flexible. It may be set as between the year 2000 and 2005, for instance. In such a case it is usually assumed that the loan will be repaid at the later date i.e. 2005.

The person, or institution, who initially gave the loan, now owns a valuable IOU which gives the bearer the right to an interest payment every six months and a lump sum at some date in the future. It is those IOUs which are sold on the Stock Exchange. But their value can vary from day to day and from week to week. Let us see why that should be the case.

You can buy government stock at no risk if you are willing to hold them until they are redeemed by the government. You know exactly how much you will get and what interest you get in the meanwhile.

Suppose someone lent the Government £100 some years ago, say by buying a 6 per cent Stock redeemable in 2005. What he got was one of the IOUs promising to pay him 6% a year up until 2005 and then to give him back £100. How much is that IOU worth now? It only entitles the bearer to £6 a year in interest payments but with interest rates at about 12%, a would be purchaser can get an annual income of £6 by investing £50 in a bank. Of course, he also knows that he will get £100 in 2005. But that is a long way off.

So the purchaser may not be willing to pay much more than about £55 for the IOU at this time. If he buys it for £55 he will get an interest return of a little under 11% on his investment (£6 interest on £55 investment) and he also has the certainty of getting more than his £55 back in 2005.

If he holds the Government stock — or the IOU as we have been calling it — until 2005, he knows for certain what his return will be and he takes no risk. If he has to sell the IOU before then, he cannot be sure what it will fetch. Its price will always be determined by the alternative investments available and that, in turn, will be determined by the general level of interest rates.

There are so many government stocks, however, that the small investor should always be able to pick one with the right number of years to go until redemption to suit his particular requirements. It can be an ideal investment for someone with a redundancy lump sum who knows that he is not going to be in the income tax net and wants to get a good income on his money which is not going to be subject to DIRT tax. The new low-DIRT tax accounts are another alternative.

In addition to their attractions for non-taxpayers, government stocks may also be attractive investments for high taxpayers.

When interest rates are rising the value of government stocks goes down. But when interest rates are falling, their value rises. So they are a particularly attractive investment when interest rates are high and expected to fall. At the end of 1997 interest rates are low and are likely to remain so. Indeed they are expected to fall further if Ireland joins the single European currency but the decline won't be all that great. And there is always the danger that rates could rise sharply if the single currency doesn't develop as expected. So there is uncertainty but those willing to wait until the a stock matures needn't worry about interest rate trends. Whatever happens to the value of the stock in the interim, he knows that it will be redeemed at the par price when it reaches maturity. As long as he is willing to wait until maturity to get his money back, the investment is risk-free.

In addition to their attractions for non-taxpayers, government stocks may also be attractive investments for high taxpayers. The return can come in two ways: there is the annual interest; and there is the capital gain which can be made if you buy stock at one price and sell at a higher price. As mentioned above, if interest rates in general fall, the price of stock goes up. While the interest is liable to income tax, the capital gain is not. It is not considered income and it is exempt from capital gains tax. This provides some attractions for the high tax payer.

A person paying tax at more than the standard rate finds any tax free return attractive. If he can buy a stock which comes up for repayment in the near future, he can be sure of making a capital gain without any risk, and his after-tax return can be relatively high. He will not be paying tax on a large portion of that return. For that reason this type of stock is much in demand by high income tax payers to whom they are worth more than to a standard taxpayer or someone who pays no tax at all. Because the price is bid up, they are generally less attractive to low income tax payers. Very often, indeed, they are unobtainable since there are no sellers.

Buying stocks

Government stocks can be bought through a stockbroker or, indeed, a bank manager. A number of the larger stockbrokers now have walk-in shops which makes the whole operation a little less mysterious. The cost of buying stocks is very low although there is no fixed rate of commission. Stockbrokers charge a commission of about 1% on buying or selling government stocks and there is no stamp duty. But they would expect you to be investing a few thousand pounds at the very least.

Bed and breakfast

If you buy shares at one price and sell them later at a higher price you have made a capital gain and may be liable for Capital Gains Tax. That tax is completely separate from income tax and levied at a standard rate of 20p in the pound. A full account is given in Chapter 14, page 256. The tax is not quite as onerous as it seems since allowance is made for inflation and there is no tax payable on the first £500 of gains made by an individual in any tax year. Up to April 1997 it was £1,000 per individual and £2,000 for a married couple. The new £500 exemption cannot be transfered between spouses.

The inflation adjustment comes automatically but you need to take action to ensure that you make the maximum use of the annual exemption. You only benefit from the exemption when you actually make a gain so the trick is to make gains up to the exemption limit every year even if that means selling your shares and immediately buying them back again.

This type of "bed and breakfast" deal, as it is sometimes known, is not as complicated as it sounds. Stockbrokers are used to looking after the mechanics. The annual exemption only applies when gains are actually disposed of. So if you hold shares for one year, five years or ten years before selling them you only get the benefit of one annual exemption limit.

Suppose you have made a gain of £1,000 on an investment and have no other capital gains it makes a lot of sense to do a 'sell and buy' deal with yourself. In effect you sell the shares to yourself. You end up with the same shares that you had but the benefit comes in raising the base value of your shareholding for tax purposes. Support you originally bought the shares for £3,000 a few months earlier and they are now worth £4,000. By selling and buying them you raise the base price for tax purposes from £3,000 to £4,000. The £1,000 gain you make is exempt from tax and for future tax calculations you are assumed to have acquired the shares at £4,000.

That's the case up to April 1998 and while it may not be worthwhile to bother making annual use of the lower exemption it is worthwhile making use of the exemptions available in the 1997/98 tax year.

Investment funds

The range of investment funds has grown dramatically over recent years far beyond the traditional unit linked products offered by life insurance companies. Those traditional products are considered in greater detail in the next section which examines their uses for regular savers. This section is concerned with the outlets available for lump sum investors.

Investment funds can be viewed as pooled investments. Each individual investor's money is pooled with that of the other investors and the whole fund is managed on their behalf by professional managers.

With unit funds the managers generally charge an annual management fee and also impose a spread between 'offer' and 'bid' prices for the units. That simply means that at any one time there is usually a 5% spread between the price at which units are sold to investors and the price at which they are bought back from investors wanting to cash them in. So if you invest and cash in later the same day you'll have lost 5% of your money.

Some funds offer units at a discount to large investors while others operate a smaller spread and a higher annual management fee. But for the most part investors can assume that the investment is costing them an initial 5% of the sum invested plus a small annual management fee. So obviously he or she should be thinking of investing for the medium to long term — say three, or preferably five years as a minimum.

> You should be thinking of leaving your investment untouched for at least five years to make the setup costs worthwhile.

But the range of options is immense. The investment period may be fixed or open ended. A minimum return may be guaranteed. There may be a maximum return laid down. Some include life insurance cover, others don't. What they all have in common is that your money is invested for you and managed on your behalf. But there the similarities cease. Even similarly named funds can be completely different. PEPs and PIPs may mean different things to different companies, for instance.

We can look at the options under a number of broad categories: First, there are the open ended funds which may give some guarantees with regard to return but which have no fixed term. Then, there are the Tracker Bonds where the return is linked to the performance of some outside indicator such as a stock market and where the investment term is fixed. And, finally, there are Special Investment Accounts, which benefit from special tax relief. So let's look at those in turn.

Open-ended Funds: These funds are operated by banks, insurance companies, building societies, and other financial institutions. Investors' money is pooled and managed on their behalf by professional fund managers. There is every conceivable type of fund. You can choose to have your money invested in almost any category of shares in a range of markets. So you can have all your money invested on the Japanese or Australian stock exchange or you can choose a wider option. There are also funds invested solely in property and others invested solely in government funds. You take your pick and usually you can switch to a different fund at a later stage, if you like.

Each investor is allocated so many units in the total fund. Their value changes daily or weekly as the value of the underlying investments change. With most funds the movement can be down as well as up but some funds put a floor under your potential losses by guaranteeing a minimum return. Returns are taxed at the standard rate. It is stopped at source similar to the DIRT tax on deposit interest.

The earliest funds of this type were managed by life assurance companies and had life assurance attached. That was partly because there was tax relief available on life assurance premiums at the time and the investment could be categorised as a premium. That's no longer the case so most funds now stand alone. Indeed life assurance is best seen as a completely separate decision. There are, however, 'with profit' funds which are linked to the performance of mutual insurance companies. Unlike unit funds where gain made one year may be lost the next if the value of the underlying investment falls, bonuses on 'with profit' policies cannot be taken back once they are declared. They are worth a consideration by those adverse to risk.

Tracker Bonds: These are fixed term investments generally over three or five years. There are a range of different options. Most offer a guarantee that the investor will, at least, get his or her money back at the end of the agreed period. Some offer a minimum return on top of that basic guarantee. The maximum return possible is usually based on the performance of some stock exchange index or mix of indices. For instance the return may be linked to the performance of the FTSE100 index of British stock market prices.

So for example a person making an investment of £2,000 might be guaranteed the return of that money at the end of three or five years. That's the worst outcome. If the bond is linked to the FTSE100 index and it happened to rise by 25% over the period then the return would be 25% of £2,000, so the investor would get back £2,500 less tax at the standard rate. In most cases there is a cap on the maximum return just as there is a floor under the potential loss.

Bonds are opened for investment from time to time. But there is usually a wide range to choose from at any one time. They should be viewed as a fixed term investment. There can be heavy penalties for withdrawing money within the fixed term.

Special Investment Accounts: These are investment funds which benefit from special tax concessions because at least 55% of their assets are invested in Irish equities. Tax is charged at only 10% on any gains instead of the full standard rate. Otherwise they are similar to the open-ended funds considered above.

Which is best for you?

With all of these investments it is important to take a medium to long term outlook. It can be costly to withdraw too early. While the setup costs for lump sum investments is not too great, it is sufficiently high that the investor should be thinking of leaving his money for a reasonably lengthy period. Most companies allow investors to switch from one fund to another within their own stable — usually at least once a year. But there can be a cost involved and switching from one company's funds to another always entails a significant cost — the full 5% again. And that is something to watch.

Some financial advisers have been known to encourage such switching, more in the interest of maximising their commission than in the interest of the investor.

Normally, any income earned on the fund is reinvested to the benefit of the investors — although there are provisions in some plans for the investor to get a regular income. This is arranged, however, by the sale of units and there is no guarantee that the remaining units will continue to be worth as much as

Be wary of an investment adviser who does not spend some time asking personal questions about your tax position, your financial position, your needs, pensions entitlement etc. Unless he knows your requirements he cannot weigh up all the options and be sure of giving the best advice.
 Always make the cheque out to the company running the fund and not to the broker.

the initial investment. In other words, the income could, in some cases, be paid out of capital.

Units can normally be cashed in full at any time, although there is often a small expense deduction made on the amount of any partial withdrawal of funds. The performance of each fund may be subject to short-term fluctuations so it is best judged over a period of a few years. But the past performance of a fund may not be a good guide to future prospects. The sophisticated investor will also want to look at the mix of investments within each fund. This can vary greatly from one fund to another.

There is no single answer to the question "which is best?" It all depends on the individual, his or her personal circumstances and attitude to risk. Before seeking advice or making a decision ask yourself what you are investing for, how much risk are you willing to take, and what are the chances of you needing speedy access to your money. Having the answers to those questions in your head will help you to make the right decision.

Most unit funds, but not tracker bonds, are open for regular saving as well as lump sum investment.

Unit linked saving

THIS type of savings vehicle is too often referred to as life assurance and, of course, there is an element of life assurance in it, but it is basically a way of saving for the future. Indeed, there are similar saving schemes available, even from life assurance companies, with no life assurance element attached. More money goes into the savings that way since there are no life assurance premiums being deducted. In most cases the actual assurance cover is relatively small, considering the premium, and such policies are best viewed simply as saving vehicles. The investor undertakes to pay a regular premium either monthly, half-yearly, or annually and at some date in the future he gets a lump sum. If he dies in the meanwhile his dependents get a lump sum benefit which is relatively small.

The actual savings type policies are sometimes sold alongside other policies which do provide a higher life assurance cover but they are separate. Life assurance is dealt with in chapter 4 on page 83. Here we are concerned simply with the policies aimed mainly at saving for the future. They usually involve just the minimum amount of life cover. These policies are grouped under the general description of endowment insurance. And like all insurance and long term investment decisions, they should not be entered into without some thought.

Remember that, although the monthly or annual premiums may seem reasonably small, you are committing yourself to investing quite a large sum of money over the course of the policy. Remember also that with some schemes well over half of the first year's premium may be going to the broker in commission and not really earning any return for you. There are other charges as well. There are a wide number of different schemes offered by the various assurance companies. Performance, i.e. the rate of return, can vary considerably. Basically, there are three main types of schemes: unit linked schemes; with profits schemes; and without profits schemes.

Unit-Linked: Lump sum investment into this type of fund was considered in the last section. After paying the commission and the cost of the life cover the remainder of the premium goes to buy units in one or other of the life assurance company's funds.

Do not be fooled into thinking that endowment insurance is providing anything but the minimum of life cover. Think of them simply as investments.

Setup costs are very high so you are almost certain to lose if you cash in during the first few years.

The investor picks which one. The yield depends on the performance of the underlying investments. The value of the policy at any time is simply the current value of the units bought. And it is possible to cash them in at any time. But because of the heavy setup costs, there is little chance of getting even your own investment back if you cash in during, say, the first five years.

With regular premium policies, the commission is an initial 2.5% of annual premium for each year of the policy up to a maximum of 50% and there is also an annual commission of 4% of the premium paid each year.

Unit values can, of course, move down as well as up, so it is better not to be faced with a situation where you have to cash in at some particular time when values are at a low ebb.

With Profits: These schemes are linked with the assurance company's own internal funds and, unlike the unit linked policies, offer a minimum guaranteed return plus bonuses. The level of bonus can differ greatly from year to year and from company to company. The biggest bonus usually comes at the end of the term when the policy matures.

Without Profits: Here the amount payable on death or at the end of the term is fixed. There are no bonuses and no participation in profits. The premiums are, of course, cheaper than with unit-linked or with-profits policies but the returns are also relatively small.

Which is best for you?

The type of policy to choose depends very much on the person's own circumstances and attitude to risk. Unit linked policies offer the best chance of high return, but there is a risk that it will not materialise. If, for instance, the fund is invested in equities, the amount eventually paid out will depend on the state of the stock market at the time of the payment. And who is to say what market conditions will be like ten years hence.

With-profit policies offer a chance of participating in the insurance company's own profit and usually once bonuses are declared, they can't be taken back. But many of them declare their largest bonuses as 'terminal' ones i.e. at the end of the policy period. And some of those terminal bonuses have been cut back in recent times. So there is a risk of getting a lower return than expected but the risk is less than with unit-linked policies — although the chance of a really high return is also less. Endowment policies without profit carry a certain fixed return and there is practically no risk involved. But the rate of return is relatively small.

Endowment policies have a lot of uses. They are most often used as a way of saving for the future with the investor deciding, by his choice of policy, what degree of risk he is willing to take. They are also used as a way of repaying loans. The borrower only pays the interest on the loan but also takes out an endowment policy designed to pay off the loan when it matures. There is more about that in chapter 5 on general borrowing and in chapter 6 on borrowing to buy a house.

Endowment policies may be used to provide a lump sum on retirement which can then be used to buy a pension but it's usually better to save through a special pension scheme. You won't be able to get at your money but tax relief may be available on the contributions — see chapter 10. Endowment policies can also be used to provide cash for educating children or even for providing a lump sum on marriage. The policies in all cases are basically the same although the sales pitch may be different.

As outlined above, however, not all policies are the same when it comes to performance and risk. Care must be taken in choosing the right policy to suit your particular needs. This requires shopping around or going to a reputable broker who will give you independent advice. These matters are dealt with in the next chapter.

Those saving for retirement should consider a pension scheme rather than an assurance scheme. It may be possible to claim full tax relief on all the contributions made.

3.7 Getting income from annuities

BUYING an annuity is one of the safest ways of providing an income during retirement. The main appeal is to those who have limited capital which they want to spread out as income over the post-retirement years. The money is simply used to purchase an income which is guaranteed to continue until death. Around that central idea there are a fair number of options. In all cases the income is guaranteed for an uncertain period. The assurance companies which sell annuities do not know when the person is going to die. But they have an idea of the average life expectancy of annuity purchasers. In money terms those who live longer get a very good return while those who die younger get a relatively poor return. But in all cases there is the security of knowing that the income will continue until death.

Annuity rates can vary. It is worthwhile shopping around for the best rate.

There are various options available. Usually the first interest payment is made six months after the annuity is purchased and the payments are made at six monthly intervals. If the first interest payment is required straight away the rate of return is slightly lower. It is usual to guarantee at least five years payments whether the purchaser dies during that time or not but if you do not want the guarantee the rate is slightly higher.

There are also annuities suitable for couples. Known as "joint survivor annuities" they are taken out on the joint lives of the couple. On the death of one the income continues at a reduced rate until the death of the other. The rate of return on joint survivor annuities is, of course, lower than on a single life annuity — about 20% less in the case of a husband aged 65 whose wife is 61 when the annuity is taken out. This 20% reduction also assumes that the income is halved on the death of one partner.

Rates of return offered on annuities vary from week to week but, of course, once the annuity is bought the income is guaranteed at that level. The return offered does, of course, vary with the age of the person or couple involved. But the returns are better than could be obtained by simply putting the money on deposit somewhere. And there are certain tax advantages. Part of the annual income — usually about a third — is considered to be the repayment of the initial capital sum and, as such, is not liable for tax. The amount varies with the current rate of interest, and it is constantly changing. On the non-capital element of the payment — approximately the other two-thirds — the recipient is liable to pay income tax if he or she is in the tax net. If they are on a relatively low income, they may be exempt from income tax entirely — see chapter 13 or Appendix 1 for tax exemption levels.

To sum up, annuities are a good way of getting a guaranteed income during retirement from limited capital. The drawback is that you use up your capital in the process, leaving nothing when you, or both you and your spouse, die.

Assurance

Insurance for life and death

4.

AN essential part of any family finance plan must be the protection of one's dependents against the financial loss which inevitably results from the death of a bread winner. One thinks usually of the death of the husband in this regard, and the loss of income which will result. But the early death of a wife, even if she is not an income earner, can also impose a financial burden on a widower trying to keep a family together. Life assurance offers a way of easing these financial burdens caused by death.

The provision of protection for family and other dependents is the first and primary role of life assurance. But, as outlined in the chapter on medium and long-term saving, life assurance can also be viewed as a way of saving for the future — for retirement, educating the children, or even marriage. Most assurance policies satisfy both needs to some extent. Some are aimed more at protection while others are aimed more at saving. Some, of course only offer protection with no monetary return if the insured person lives beyond a certain age.

It is important for the person taking out the insurance to be clear on what he needs from the policy and to keep the distinction between protection and saving in mind. The insurance industry is pledged to emphasise the differences in the future, in response to the complaints over a lack of clarity in the past. Let's first have a look at the type of policies generally available, and then examine how they can be used to satisfy the average family's needs.

There are four basic types of life assurance.

- Term or temporary insurance.
- Whole of life assurance.

- Endowment assurance.
- Disability and illness assurance.

Term insurance

Pure life assurance which pays out only if death occurs during a fixed period of years is relatively cheap.

A man aged 30 can ensure that his dependents receive £100,000 if he dies within the next ten years at a premium cost of £11 a month. That is not bad value. Mind you if he goes to the wrong insurance company he could pay twice that for the same cover. The very big difference between the cheapest and the dearest highlights the necessity of shopping around either by getting a range of quotes yourself or by getting an independent broker to do the job for you.

This type of insurance is called term insurance and all too little of it is sold. We tend to spend a lot on life insurance compared to our counterparts in other countries but we favour savings type policies which are really geared towards saving for the future and which only pay out a relatively small amount in the event of early death.

Term insurance pays out nothing if the insured person lives for the set term of years. Suppose like our example above, you are thirty years of age and take out a ten year policy. If you live until you are forty, the policy ends and you get nothing back. But it is not a complete loss. Indeed it is no loss. What you have bought during the ten years is peace of mind: the knowledge that should you die your dependents will be that little bit better off financially. That peace of mind is worth buying.

Not everyone needs term insurance. But there are certainly a lot of people who need it and do not have it. If you are in a company pension scheme you are possibly covered fairly well for life insurance within the scheme. But it is worth checking out how high the cover is and considering whether or not you should take out a little more. Then what about insurance on the stay-at-home spouse. The financial cost of keeping a family together following the death of a wife and mother can be substantial. A lump sum can certainly make living more bearable. It has been estimated that employing someone to carry out all of the duties of a housewife would cost in the region of £350 a week.

Term insurance may also be important for people who lose their jobs. The loss of the job may also mean the loss of the insurance cover provided within the pension scheme. In some cases employers will keep the insurance cover in place for a short time, or it may be possible for the redundant worker to keep up payments himself. There are a wide range of term insurance options. You can pick the term of years and the size of the cover. The older the person is when the policy is taken out, the higher the premiums. Term insurance is the cheapest way of providing real financial protection for dependents and it is the first type of policy a young family man on slender means should consider. Within this general category there are a number of different possibilities.

Level Term: In this case the sum insured remains fixed for the term of the policy. If the person insured survives the term no payment is made by the insurance company. If he or she dies during the term, then the sum insured is paid out. Even if there is no pay-out, and hopefully that will be the case, the policy offers value for money in the peace of mind it provides.

It could cost up to £350 a week to employ someone to carry out the duties of a housewife.

Convertible Term: This provides the same basic insurance cover as level term assurance, but there is an option to convert the policy into another type. Usually the assurance company allows conversion at any time during the life of the policy and agrees not to require any further medical test or proof of good health. The policy into which you convert will operate from the date of conversion and will be at the normal premium rates applied to such policies given the insured person's age at the time of conversion. A convertible term assurance policy need not cost much more than a level term policy — particularly if it is a relatively long term policy.

Unless your means are very slender and unlikely to improve over time, convertible term assurance makes much more sense than level term. It provides flexibility in the future when life cover may be less importance.

Decreasing Term: This type of policy is often referred to as a mortgage protection policy since they are often taken out for this purpose. The life cover gradually decreases over the term of the policy. For instance a policy may provide initial cover of £10,000 declining over twenty years. If the insured person dies in the first year his family would get the full £10,000, but by year ten it has reduced to £7,950 and in the last year the cover is only £1,200. This, of course, is an ideal way of providing for the repayment of a house mortgage in the event of death. The sum owing to the building society is decreasing year by year as

Mortgage protection policies are an example of term insurance.

repayments are made and the sum payable by the insurance company will more or less keep pace.

Some decreasing term policies simply guarantee to pay off the mortgage in the event of death — less any arrears — provided interest rates remain within set limits.

Banks and building societies make it a condition of granting a mortgage that the borrower takes out a mortgage protection policy. Indeed it is a legal requirement on building societies. You don't have to take out the policy with the lender's own insurance company but it is usually cheaper and easier to do so since the premium can be collected with the repayments and some lenders make it expensive to switch by imposing an additional fee on borrowers who take out the insurance elsewhere.

Family Income Benefits: This is another type of term insurance which provides, instead of a lump sum, a regular income for the family or dependents. For example, the policy on a married man might provide for the payment of £5,000 a year every year between his death and the end of a twenty year term. The payment made by the insurance company would not be liable to income tax.

Endowment assurance

With this type of policy the saving element is uppermost. They provide the minimum of protection. The actual sum payable on death is relatively small per premium pound compared with term or whole life assurance. They are best viewed as a method of saving or investing and for this reason have been dealt with in the chapter on medium and long-term saving.

Disability insurance

Disability benefits are often included in company pension schemes. About three-quarters of all private pension schemes provide for income continuance where a member is unable to continue working due to disability or long-term illness. For those who are not covered through a member scheme there is always the option of providing the cover through what are known as Permanent Health or Income Continuance policies. Self-employed people can be particularly vulnerable to loss of income in the event of illness or disability.

As with all insurance it is well worthwhile shopping around or getting a broker to do it for you. It is important to compare not only the price but also the extent of the cover and, most importantly, what is **not** covered.

As an example of the type of cost involved one company is quoting a monthly premium of £30 a month to insure a man aged thirty for £250 a week while he is unable, because of illness or disability, to work at his usual job. The premium goes up to £47 for a man aged forty. No benefits are paid for the first thirteen weeks of illness unless the claimant is hospitalised.

While tax relief on life assurance policies has been abolished it is still allowed in full on the premiums paid for this type of policy up to a limit of 10% of income. So the true cost can be reduced by almost half for a top rate tax payer. Any benefits received, however, are taxable if the recipient is liable for tax.

We usually think of disability arising as a result of an accident but, of course, it can also arise as a result of serious illness. And serious illness can put many strains on a families' finances. Over the past couple of years the insurance companies have been vying with one another in devising ever more elaborate policies providing lump sums in the event of the insured person suffering a serious or critical illness. Payment is usually only made if the person survives for fourteen days after being diagnosed as suffering from one of a stated list of illnesses. Not all illnesses are covered so it is important to read the fine print.

This type of policy should not be seen as an alternative to medical insurance such as VHI or BUPA designed to cover the cost of medical care. Neither is it an alternative to permanent health insurance designed to pay an income if you are unable to work because of an illness or disability. It is not really an alternative to basic life assurance either.

But it does pay out a lump sum which may be used for any purpose. It may help to pay medical expenses or to supplement income. But there is no need to show that the medical expenses have been incurred or that you have lost income. The claim is allowed provided you have suffered one of the designated illnesses and survived for more than fourteen days. The vast bulk of claims in Ireland are made in respect of cancer followed by heart problems and multiple sclerosis.

With some policies premium levels are fixed and guaranteed for the term of the policy. With others the premium is reviewed from time to time and you may be called upon to increase the premium or else accept a reduction in the level of cover. With

Critical Illness Insurance

this second type of policy, part of each premium is invested and the policy may build up a surrender value. The level of future premiums, after an initial fixed period, depends on the performance of the investment fund.

There is heavy competition among the companies so it is well worthwhile shopping around for the widest cover at the cheapest price if you feel that you need this cover.

It pays to shop around. Products are changing. But by way of illustration, a man of 45 should be able to get cover for £50,000 in respect of serious illness or total permanent disability for a monthly premium of about £27 but some companies quote premiums as high as £48 a month. Conditions vary between the various policies so you can't compare on a strictly like-with-like basis. You can shop around, however, by yourself or through a broker. If you do use a broker he or she should be able to justify his or her recommendation.

Whole of life assurance

Term assurance is pure protection. There is no element of saving since no payments are made if the insured person survives the term. With whole of life assurance there is an element of saving, although it is saving for your dependents after your death. The insurance company undertakes to pay the agreed sum — plus bonuses if you go for a with-profits policy — whenever you die. So unlike term assurance, the payment is made at some time.

Obviously the premiums payable for a given life cover are higher in this case than a similar term assurance. You can opt to pay premiums up to death or else elect to stop paying premiums at a certain age. For most people, whose incomes fall after retirement at 65, it is a good idea to have premium payments stopping then.

What to choose

No family should be without some form of life assurance. As mentioned in the introduction to this chapter the early death of husband or wife can impose severe financial burdens on the surviving spouse. And for a relatively small sum, life assurance can provide some protection and a certain amount of peace of mind. Remember, that even if you live to pay all the premiums on a term assurance, and therefore get no monetary gain, you have still got a return in the peace of mind you have enjoyed over the years knowing that your family has some protection against the financial loss they would suffer through your early death.

It is important, however, to get the right type of assurance geared to your own particular circumstances. There can be no hard and fast rules. Every family's circumstances are different, but here are some guidelines to follow. Protection is obviously the first consideration. And the newly married couple on a tight budget can get this through term assurance. Unless the budget is extremely tight, convertible term assurance offers the best bet providing the flexibility to convert into other types of assurance as the family circumstances, and possibly budget, improve.

So the first policy should be a convertible term assurance either providing a lump sum on the death of the husband or else the guarantee of a regular income over a set number of years. It may be that the husband is in a pension scheme at work which provides adequate protection. In that case he may not need term assurance but should go first for either a whole life, or endowment type policy.

So, first check if there is adequate cover through an occupational pension scheme. If not, then term assurance is the cheapest way to get protection. A 25 year old might take a policy over a 30 year term — the cover ceasing at age 55, by which time other policies will have been taken out.

If a house is being purchased on a mortgage, it makes sense to take out a special kind of term assurance, called a mortgage protection policy. For a very low premium this will provide enough funds to pay off the mortgage should the breadwinner die within the set term. Basically it is a declining balance term assurance i.e. the amount paid out on death goes down each year in line with the reduced indebtedness to the provider of the mortgage. In practice lenders will require you to take out such insurance.

It is also possible to get a term assurance to cover the full value of the house without any decline in the amount payable on death, but this is more expensive.

If money is not so tight, a whole life assurance policy — preferably with profits — can be used to provide protection. As already mentioned this is more expensive than term insurance but the sum assured, plus bonuses accumulated over the years, is

Life assurance is primarily concerned with providing protection for your family and dependents in the event of early death.

paid on death. So there is an element of saving. But they are savings which the person assured will never see since they are only paid out on death. A variant of this type of policy may be used to cover the expected cost of inheritance taxes. There are special policies for this purpose where the proceeds are not considered to be part of the estate for inheritance tax purposes.

The next thing to consider is a policy on the wife's life. Few people think of the costs imposed on a family by the death of a wife and mother, even if she is not wage-earning. The husband who wishes to keep his family together might need to employ a housekeeper and will certainly be involved in some expense in looking after the children. Such cover might take the form of an endowment policy say over ten or fifteen years. By the end of such a period the children will be older and the costs of keeping a family together would be a good deal less. If the wife survives the ten or fifteen years, as hopefully she will, then the policy will pay out a useful lump sum which can be put towards the children's education.

When these protection needs have been taken care of it is time enough to start looking at the attractions of endowment assurance as a method of saving.

These are just some general guidelines for deciding what type of policy you need. So how best to go about taking them out and what about the fine print? Let us look first at the usual conditions applying to life assurance.

Commission — the cost

It is important to shop around for the best policy. There can be a wide variation in the cover and cost. A good independent broker can help you in making the choice and can provide information on what is available and why one policy may be better suited to your needs than another. He or she can also help you to decide on the type of policy you need. The broker gets paid for those efforts by way of a commission and is worth the price if the job has been done well. The customer should be aware of that cost, however. It helps to bring a little more realism into the buying process and should reduce the number of policies which are prematurely cashed in.

Having remained unchanged for many years the life assurance companies have jointly agreed to a number of changes in the commission rate structure in recent years. The latest change was introduced late in 1996.

Commissions on Life Assurance Policies

Policy type	Commission
Savings type policies.	An initial 2½% of first year's premium for each year of the policy subject to a maximum of 50%, plus an annual commission of 4% of each year's premium payable thereafter.
Protection policies — term, permanent health and critical illness.	An initial 10% of the first year's premium for each year of the policy subject to a maximum of 90%, plus an annual 3% payable on each annual renewal.
Pension policies.	An initial 2½% of the first year's premium for each year of the policy subject to a maximum of 50% plus 4% of annual premium pay on each renewal.
Single Premiums.	5% of the premium paid on pension policies. 3% of the initial sum on life assurance bonds plus ½% of the fund value each year.

The overall impact of the 1996 changes was to reduce the commission paid up front while increasing the annual renewal commissions. The cut in the initial commission rates on savings type policies can be seen as an attempt to boost demand for flagging products. Sales of unit-linked and endowment policies have fallen off dramatically partly as a result of a movement away from endowment mortgages. The initial commission on savings type policies and regular premium pension plans is now capped at 50% of the annual premium with an annual renewal commission of 4%. That commission, of course, goes to pay the broker for his advice and administration of the policy so it can be money well spent if the broker has been doing his or her job.

There is also commission, of course, on single premium products. These include both pensions and investment bonds. The commission on single premium pension plans was raised to 5%

late in 1996 while the rate of other single premium investment bonds was set at 3% with an extra half per cent coming out of the fund value each year.

Commission has been the traditional source of income for insurance brokers and financial advisers but there are some who operate on a fee basis and take no commission. The end result for the client may be much the same in either case. What's saved on commission may well go on the fee. An argument in favour of fee based charging is that the adviser cannot be influenced by commission considerations. He gets the same fee whatever he advises so the advice wouldn't be coloured by any desire to maximise commission.

The counter-argument is that the commission agreement between the insurance companies is aimed at reducing that type of abuse. All companies provide the same commission to the broker but, of course, commission rates can differ between products so the commissions agreement is not the complete answer.

There is a different commission arrangement for protection type policies — the type which only pays out on death or for illness or disability. The initial commission is calculated on the basis of 10% multiplied by the term of the policy subject to a maximum of 90%. So a five year policy pays a commission of 50% with an ongoing commission each year of 3% of the annual premium.

The fine print

The first point to bear in mind with all assurance policies is the condition of 'utmost good faith' implied in all contracts. This simply means that you are required to tell the assurance company all the facts relevant to its assessment of the risk it is undertaking in assuring your life. If you withhold a relevant fact then the policy can be declared null and void and no payment will be made.

There was a case in Ireland where a man taking out a policy described himself as a packer in a quarry on the assurance proposal form. In fact his job was packing the explosives for the blasting operations, but he did not explain that fact. Had the policy been issued and the man killed in an explosion the assurance company would have been within its rights not to pay out on the policy. It would not be sufficient to claim that the company had never asked what his job entailed. It was up to the man taking out the policy to give all relevant details and the fact that he was dealing with explosives was obviously relevant.

Recent court judgments have made the law less clear on this matter and the insurance companies are taking more care in asking the right questions and stressing the need for full disclosure of relevant details. But it is obviously important to give full details of past illnesses etc.. There is no need, however, to get unduly worried if you forget to declare some minor point.

A further point is that you can only take out a life assurance policy on someone whose death will clearly involve you in financial loss. You must have an insurable interest in the person's life. A husband or wife is considered to have an infinite insurable interest in the life of his or her spouse and a child, of course, has an insurable interest in its parents. But the insurable interest of parents in their children is considered to be very small. This last point was written into law many years ago to prevent unscrupulous parents from taking out large assurance policies on their children and then being tempted to murder them.

Only surrender assurance policies as a last resort. There are various other options worth considering if you can no longer afford the premiums or need to get some money.

With life assurance the other sections of the policy are usually straightforward enough. They contain details of who is insured; conditions on the payment of premiums; how claims are to be made and paid. A point to bear in mind is that the name on the policy should coincide with the person's name on their birth certificate. Otherwise problems can sometimes arise. There will also be provisions on surrender values, conversion rights if applicable, and options available should you be unable to keep up your premium payments.

Let's have a look at these in more detail as they can sometimes lead to difficulties and misunderstandings.

Surrender Values: Most policies provide for an early cashing in. But it is not something to be considered except as an absolutely last resort. The surrender value of a policy is usually less than the amount of premiums already paid so that an early cashing in involves you in a definite loss. In a way this is understandable. An assurance policy is rightly viewed as a long-term contract — a good reason for making the right decision in the first place — and the assurance company is involved in some heavy costs in preparing the initial contract. On term assurance there is often no surrender value and certainly in the early years of a whole of life or endowment policy the surrender values are very small. So if at all possible forget about surrendering your policy. There are other options if you are unable to keep up your premiums.

Paid-Up Policy: If you find that you can no longer meet the premiums it is usually possible to convert the policy into one that is 'fully-paid up'. Suppose you have a twenty-year endowment policy on which you have paid premiums for ten years and the life cover is £2,000. It is usually possible to stop paying premiums and continue to have a policy covering you for half (ten-twentieths) of the original sum assured.

Conversion Rights: If you have a policy carrying conversion rights — say a convertible term assurance — bear it in mind when you come to take out fresh assurance. You may have reached the stage where you can afford higher premiums — and could benefit from the tax relief involved — so consider first whether it is better to convert an existing policy rather than take out a new one. If your health is failing this option may be particularly valuable as you will not usually have to undergo a new medical test.

A policy with a surrender value is good security for a loan. In some cases insurance companies themselves lend money on them.

Loans: If you find yourself unable to meet the premiums on a policy or if you have a need for ready cash, it is usually possible to obtain a loan from the assurance company on endowment policies. Some companies give loans up to the full surrender value of the policy. Others draw the line at 90%. Interest rates on these loans are normally very competitive and, very often the interest does not have to be paid as it is taken out of the benefit due at the end of the term. Since term assurance does not generally have a surrender value, it is not possible to get loans on these. Loans are not given on unit linked policies either. The facility to get loans and the conditions on which they are given, vary from company to company, and it is no harm to get details when taking out a policy.

Selling a policy: If you have a with-profits policy which you have to surrender it may be possible to sell it to an investor for rates up to 25% higher than the surrender value. That's because the return on some policies is likely to be far better than the returns available on other investments. There are companies specialising in arranging this type of sale.

How to buy assurance

Buying life assurance can be a far bigger financial decision than many people realise. It is a long-term contract which can cost a lot over the years and can involve considerable loss if cancelled too soon. So it is essential to make the right decisions at the start. Don't be afraid to shop around, ask questions, and take your time over decisions. Take advice from more than one person before committing yourself.

The earlier part of this chapter provides some guide to the type of policy you may need to suit your particular circumstances. Work out for yourself the type of policy you think you need and have your reasons clear in your mind.

Only then approach the insurance sellers. They fall into three broad categories and by law they must declare which category they fall into. There are "tied agents" who only sell the products of one assurance company; "agents" who sell the products of up to four companies; and "brokers" who should give independent advice and write policies for at least five different companies.

Let us have a look at these three in more detail.

Tied Agents: In general tied agents are trained to sell the products of their own company and may or may not know all that much about the global technicalities of assurance. They are, of course, out to sell their own company's products and they may have an incentive to sell a particular type of policy because it provides them with a higher commission or the company simply wants to sell that product. But they can only do this to a limited extent. Most companies are jealous of their good name — looking to ongoing business — and would quickly weed out any agent who was obviously misselling policies in order to boost his commission.

Agents: Some of these are part-timers who may be expert in their own fields of law, accounting, or what have you, but can only have a limited knowledge of assurance. But their expertise may be more than adequate and they have to be able to choose from at least two companies' products.

Brokers: By law brokers must either be members of a recognised broker organisation or else registered with the Irish Insurance Compliance Bureau — an overseeing body run by the insurance companies. If good, he is in an ideal position to advise you, given the fact that he is independent of the assurance companies and can pick from the policies offered by at least five companies. But care must be taken in picking your broker. Be particularly wary of brokers who advertise one particular policy to the exclusion of others. Remember, the broker can only be good if he takes stock of your personal circumstances first before trying to sell you a policy. There is no easy guide to picking the right intermediary. For preference go to a reputable firm which can obviously provide sound back-up service. Ask around for advice about who other people have found reputable. If in doubt, seek the advice of more than one broker or agent. Get details of policies direct from the companies concerned. Write to other companies asking for details of their similar type policies. In all cases, take your time before deciding.

With life assurance, a good broker or agent will want to know details of your financial position; any other assurance cover you have; your prospects for the future; the size of your family; and your plans for them. If he does not ask for such details, be wary, since he cannot possibly give sound advice without knowing details of your personal circumstances. Under the 1990 Insurance Act the industry has accepted new codes of conduct and set up systems for dealing with complaints —see chapter 11.

Medical Insurance

While every Irish citizen is entitled to a basic health care free of charge it is possible to get speedier treatment if you are able to pay your own way. You also have a wider choice of consultant and of hospital accommodation. Private medical care can, however, be very expensive and would be beyond the reach of most people in the absence of an insurance scheme. The VHI (Voluntary Health Insurance) had a near monopoly of the provision of medical insurance up until January 1997 when the law was changed allowing for competition. At the time a restriction of 'community rating' was imposed on all new entrants. This requires that insurers in this category provide cover at the same premium rates to all adults seeking it.

The British based BUPA subsequently entered the Irish market and during 1997 developed a range of products similar, but not directly comparable, with those offered by the VHI. Late in 1997 the VHI extended its range with the introduction of optional enhancements to its existing plans. As a result the consumer is left with a confusing range of options. VHI has five basic plans to each of which may be added extensions giving ten different options. BUPA offers three basic plans.

The VHI provides various levels of cover depending on the type of hospital accommodation required. Plan A covers semi-private accommodation in public hospitals while at the other end of the scale Plan E covers accommodation in the Blackrock Clinic and Mater Private Hospital. VHI does not guarantee to cover all the medical costs involved in all procedures but it does supply a list of medical consultants who do accept VHI rates as full settlement of their fees. Other consultants may charge more than the VHI payment rates. Your doctor will be able to tell you whether a consultant is in the VHI scheme. Don't be afraid to ask.

There are limits to the amount of cover. Under the five basic plans, A to E, hospital stays of up to 180 days per year are covered. Any excess above that is not. The first £400 per family or £250 per person of medical costs outside of hospital are not covered. There is an upper limit of £2,500 per family on such cover. The outpatient cover includes the cost of visiting a doctor, casualty treatment, X-rays, physiotherapy, etc.

Those excesses are reduced for those paying for the an additional *option* premium.

Specifically not covered are routine dental or optical care; long term nursing care; cosmetic treatments; treatment for eating disorders or weight reduction; midwifery fees for births at home; alternative medical treatments such as acupuncture. BUPA does provide some cover for alternative medicine.

There are also time limits on pre-existing ailments which apply both to new members and those rejoining after a lapse of membership. If you do not pay your subscription within fifteen days of the due date your policy can be lapsed — so be careful.

Those under 55 are not covered for pre-existing ailments for the first five years after joining and get no benefits for ailments arising in the first thirteen weeks. Those aged between 55 and 60 on joining are not covered for existing ailments for seven years and get no benefits for ailments arising in the first 18 weeks. For those joining over the age of 60, there is no cover for pre-existing ailments for ten years and no benefits for ailments arising in the first 26 weeks.

VHI and BUPA compared

The following is a comparison of some of the main features of the most popular of the VHI and BUPA plans. It is based on the situation as at the end of 1997. It doesn't cover all the fine print.

	BUPA Ireland Essential Plus	VHI Plan B Option
Full cover in participating hospitals	Yes	Yes
Inpatient excess[1] (can be bought out)	£50 per claim	None
Outpatient cover		
Annual limit	£5,000	£5,000
Excess[1] — individual[1]	£200	£175
Excess[1] — family	£350	£300
Cover abroad		
Days	180	90
Maximum amount	£13,500	£15,000
Repatriation costs	Unlimited	£1million
Home nursing		
Annual maximum	£1,000	£600
Daily allowance	£25	£30

(1) The excess is the amount of any claim or, in the case of out-patients claims, the amount of claims made each year, that you have to pay yourself. For instance with BUPA the first £350 of a family's outpatients costs each year are not covered.

BUPA offers three alternatives, Essential, Essential Plus, and BUPA Gold. The Essential Plus plan is pitted against the most popular VHI alternative, Plan B plus options. The plans are not directly comparable. The BUPA plan, for instance, has a slightly higher excess for outpatient care i.e. the claimant has to pay the first £200 a year with BUPA while the VHI figure is £175. BUPA also requires the claimant to pay the first £50 of private hospital bills while VHI pays in full. But, on the other hand, the VHI provides a lower cover for home nursing — £600 a year against BUPA's £1,000 and at the time of writing (December 1997) BUPA's cover is 18 per cent cheaper .

There is, of course, no guarantee that relative premium levels will not change in the future. VHI increased their premiums by 9% from September 1997. BUPA may well increase their rates at some future date.

The tax relief on medical insurance contributions has been restricted to the standard rate since April 1996. Before April 1995 it was granted at the taxpayer's highest tax rate. It was reduced in the 1995/96 tax year so that higher rate taxpayers only got the benefit of half the relief at the higher rate.

There is a 10% reduction in premiums for those in group schemes. Many credit unions operate group schemes which are open to self-employed people provided they join the credit union. Not only do they get a 10% saving on the premium but the credit union may also provide them with a cost-free facility for paying the premium in monthly instalments.

Borrowing

Borrowing — the best deals

5.1

SENSIBLE borrowing has always had an important and beneficial role to play in family finance. But there is a cost involved. Interest rates have remained low for some years and they are expected to fall further during 1998. That's assuming the movement to European Monetary Union doesn't go off the rails. If it does anything could happen. But when looking at interest rates don't forget that inflation is also low so the real cost of borrowing is as high as it ever was. However it can often make sense to borrow. Against the cost there can be offsetting benefits i.e. the benefit of buying something now rather than having to wait until you have saved up the money. Tax relief can reduce the cost of some loans such as those used to buy, maintain or improve your principal residence or to buy shares in your own company. Mortgage tax relief is detailed in Chapter 6.3 on page 136. But in all cases you should be aware of the cost; be clear that you can afford the repayments; and, of course, shop around for the cheapest possible loan.

Be clear in your mind what the repayments are and when they are payable. Are you sure you will be able to meet them as they fall due? What is the likelihood of you hitting a bad patch — an unforeseen expense or drop in income — which might make repayment of the loan difficult or impossible? Each individual will exercise a different degree of caution, but there is no need to be cautious to the point of not borrowing at all. Most reputable lenders will allow a degree of flexibility to help a borrower over an unexpected bad patch.

There is a wide range of options open to the would-be borrower: bank loans, finance houses, credit sales, budget accounts, H.P. etc.. And the cost can vary greatly. All those providing credit, either by way of loans or by way of credit sales, are required to show the true rate of interest being charged on their loans. All but the most general advertisements for loans are required to show interest rates. So it is possible to shop around by just keeping your eyes open and comparing rates. The difference between the dearest and cheapest loan can be significant. Getting the cheapest available can save you a lot of money and remember that the lender really wants to lend money. That is how they make a profit. If nobody borrowed they would go out of business.

Shopping around

Borrowing is a normal business transaction, in which the buyer is buying a commodity from the seller. The commodity in this case is money. It might be more correct to say that the borrower is hiring the use of the money for a period and will be paying a rental — the interest — for the use of it. The lender has one thought in mind — will he get the money back? This is the risk factor, and the higher the risk he considers he is taking the higher the interest he will charge. The longer the period of the loan, the greater is the risk he foresees: so normally the longer the term of the loan, the higher the interest rate. The major exception to this rule are mortgage loans on which rates are relatively low because of the security provided.

Most lenders, of course, have their interest rates fixed at any particular time and, as a result, have a set idea about the risk they are willing to take, or, in other words, the type of person they will lend to. So the would-be borrower should be ready to fortify the lender's faith in his ability to repay. As we said, the lender wants to lend the money — he just needs convincing that you are a good risk.

Lenders, be they banks, finance companies or pawnbrokers, want to lend money. That is their business and that is how they make their profit. There is no need to go out with the begging bowl.

Obviously, you want to pay the lowest interest rate possible, and as a rough guide the rates will go up as you move along the following list: building societies (for mortgages), credit unions, the major banks, finance houses, credit accounts, hire purchase, money lenders. It used to be very difficult for the uninitiated to compare the interest rates being charged on alternative loans but this difficulty has been overcome with the requirement that all lenders show the annual percentage rate (APR) charged on their loans. This may be considered the true rate of interest and can be used to compare alternatives. The APR shown on loan advertisements, shop notices and loan agreements has to be based on the global cost of the loan — interest and other charges. So it is ideal for comparing one source of finance with another — the lower the APR, the cheaper the loan. New laws are in the pipeline which will require lenders to provide even more information in more easily understood terms.

In the past lenders declared their interest rates in all sorts of different ways which were not comparable. Some quoted rates close to the true annual rate of interest; others quoted monthly rates; others a rate on the initial sum borrowed; or some other such device aimed at making comparison almost impossible.

It is no harm having some understanding of what a true rate of interest is. Suppose you get £100 now and repay £110 this day next year — i.e., the initial £100 plus £10 interest — that is a true rate of interest of 10% — £10 on £100. But suppose that instead of repaying in a lump sum, the repayments are spread over the full year and you still repay a total of £110, that is nearer a 20% rate of interest, since you did not have the use of the £100 for the full year. Indeed, you only had, on average, the use of £50 for the full year, since you had more than £50 for the first six months, but progressively less than £50 for the second six months.

It does not matter a lot how the rate of interest is actually calculated as long as they are all calculated in the same way so that the borrower is comparing like with like. The APR allows you to do this since it has to be calculated in the same way by all lenders. Some of them may still be quoting rates calculated in different ways but they have to quote the APR as well. The best advice is to ignore any other rate except the APR.

As mentioned above the borrower has a wide number of options open to him and the cost difference between the cheapest and dearest loans can be considerable. So it pays to consider carefully the various options and to try the cheapest first.

Associated banks

This is the term given to the four largest banks — Allied Irish Banks, Bank of Ireland, National Irish, and Ulster Bank. They are the largest lenders of money in the country and offer the greatest range of loans. Their interest rates are among the lowest available. But be careful — not all of their loans are given at the lowest rates.

Banks will obviously take a more favourable view of loan applications from existing customers but they will consider requests from non-customers. Remember they make their profits by lending money. They do like to see a borrower's pay coming directly into the bank although they are obviously flexible in this.

Let's have a look at the type of loans available:

- **Overdraft** This is usually the cheapest type of bank loan because of its flexibility. But it can prove expensive in some circumstances. Running up an overdraft will usually lose the customer the benefit of free banking. Someone who keeps his current account in credit may be exempt from bank charges on his transactions but once the account runs into overdraft — even for a short period — it can mean having to pay bank charges for a full three months. Those charges must be considered as additional to the interest in working out the true cost of an overdraft. In the case of Allied Irish Banks and Bank of Ireland there is also a fixed annual fee of £20 for having an overdraft permission. But an overdraft does allow greater flexibility.

Once an overdraft permission has been granted, it can be drawn on at any time without fresh recourse to the bank. That convenience has some value and there is a very tangible gain as well. Every penny put into the account immediately reduces the amount of the loan and since interest is charged on the amount outstanding each day there can be a significant saving.

Suppose, for instance, the borrower has his or her wages paid into the bank each month. Let's suppose that a net £1,000 is lodged. If that money is spent evenly over the month the customer has a net £500 on average in the account over the year — more than £500 early in the month and less than £500 later in the month but an average of £500. That's automatically reducing the size of the overdraft. At 11% a year the interest saving would be £55 to help offset the extra charges which might be incurred.

To avail of an overdraft you need to have a current i.e. cheque book account. In effect you ask your bank manager if you can overdraw your account to a specified sum. If he agrees you can then write cheques for that amount over and above the funds you have in your account. You only pay interest on the actual amount you have drawn and, as mentioned above, interest is calculated on a day-to-day basis. If you don't make use of the overdraft permission you pay no interest.

Overdrafts are the most flexible way of borrowing and they can be one of the cheapest.

Overdraft permissions, however, are only given to cover short-term borrowing requirements. There are no set repayments, but the account has to be back in credit at least within a year and the bank manager will want some assurance that you will be able to clear off the debt within that period. So overdrafts generally have a limited use. They are particularly useful to cover the odd bad month when a number of large payments fall due. In other words it should be viewed like an advance, or a "sub" on your salary or wages which will have to be paid off on the next pay day or at least over a few pay periods.

Repayments (monthly) per £1,000 borrowed

Interest rate	3 years	5 years	7 years	10 years
10%	£32.17	£21.14	£16.49	£13.10
10.5%	£32.39	£21.38	£16.74	£13.37
11%	£32.62	£21.62	£16.99	£13.63
11.5%	£32.84	£21.85	£17.24	£13.90
12%	£33.07	£22.09	£17.49	£14.18
12.5%	£33.29	£22.33	£17.75	£14.45
13%	£33.52	£22.57	£18.00	£14.73

- **Budget Accounts:** Some banks also run budget type accounts where the customer sets out his spending requirements in advance. The spending needs will not, of course, be spread evenly over the year but the bank allows for overdraft type loans to cover the lean periods while requiring fixed regular payments. It is simply a way of balancing out one's cash flow. But it is fixed and formalised — unlike the normal overdraft.

Three of the big four banks offer budget accounts which are a sort of formalised overdraft. Allied Irish Banks has "Masterplan"; Bank of Ireland has "Budget Saver" and National Irish has "Home Management". In all three the borrower makes out a budget for the year ahead listing the bills which he wants covered. Those are then totalled up, divided by twelve, and he pays that much into the account each month. As bills fall due, he can draw out sufficient money to pay them, borrowing automatically any excess needed when his savings fall short of what has to be paid. There are charges to pay in addition to the interest on the amounts needed to be borrowed but they are relatively small.

- **Term Loans:** Unlike overdrafts, term loans have fixed repayment commitments. Also, unlike an overdraft, the agreed amount is given to you or transferred into your current account and interest liability begins to accrue immediately. The interest rate is the same as that on overdrafts but ignoring the impact of bank charges — as mentioned above — a term loan may prove more expensive for short term borrowing since you do not have the flexibility of drawing down only what you need. Repayments are normally set in monthly amounts extending over a fixed period.

Interest rates can differ from bank to bank and, of course, from time to time. So it can pay to shop around although there is no certainty that the bank offering the best rate today will still be charging the lowest rate when you get to the end of your repayments. The interest rate is not fixed for the period of the loan but moves up and down as rates in general change.

The larger banks also have finance houses which give term loans. But these are at higher rates of interest than charged by the banks. The differences between the two are being blurred in some banks now and it is possible to end up getting the loan from the more expensive finance company anyway. The banks make more profit that way. The only advice is to stand your ground and try to get a bank loan.

Interest rates can vary greatly so it pays to shop around. Remember you are doing the lender a favour by borrowing.

Some banks also offer what are known as endowment loans although they are less popular now and seldom actively marketed. These are usually for longer periods — say ten years — to be used for home improvements or education. Basically the idea is that the borrower only pays the interest on the loan during its term — say ten years. He also takes out an insurance policy which matures at the end of the ten years hopefully providing enough funds to pay off the loan and maybe even leave something over. The poor returns on many insurance funds in recent years have made such loans a doubtful proposition.

- **Other Loans:** All of the big four banks can provide more flexible loans to suit special circumstances. There are also "loan accounts" on which there are no fixed repayments. Such loans are negotiated on a personal basis with the repayments geared to suit the circumstances. The interest rate is no higher than that on an overdraft or term-loan.

All four banks also give loans secured with mortgages on the borrower's house or other property. They are, of course, mainly used for house purchase but need not be. The interest rate is lower than on other loans but there are usually set-up costs involved in taking out the mortgage — see chapter 6. National Irish Bank has a flexible mortgage type loan scheme which differs from other mortgage loans in that there is no set up charge and interest is only charged on the amount actually drawn down at any one time. The interest rate is slightly higher than the rate on overdrafts or term loans.

Trustee Savings Banks

The TSB Bank has been growing rapidly in recent years and extending its range of services. They now provide a full range of saving and loan facilities for personal clients and are expanding their range of services for business customers. It offers the same options as other banks including:

Cheque Book Accounts: Cheque books and cheque cards are provided. Overdraft facilities can be agreed on the same basis as those described above.

Term Loans: Loans for three, five and seven years are provided to regular customers.

Mortgages and Bridging Loans: Finance is normally available for mortgage and bridging finance for house purchase.

Building societies

The major building societies have been expanding their range of lending facilities beyond mortgages for home purchase. They can offer the same range of unsecured loans as the major banks do in addition to the traditional mortgages secured on property. Most will also provide business loans and loans for buying commercial properties. The personal borrower has the choice of getting an unsecured term loan just like a finance company loan or else a loan secured by mortgage on his or her house. That can either be a new mortgage or a top-up mortgage where the value of the property exceeds the outstanding loans on it. The usual way is to take out a new increased mortgage and pay off the existing one. But it is possible to take out a second mortgage while leaving the existing one. This type of loan is also available from the banks, of course, and it pays to shop around to get the cheapest deal. Apart from differences in in-

Doing a wealth check on your borrowings — it

Financial decisions, once made, are all too seldom reviewed. This is particularly the case with personal borrowings. Built up over time for various different reasons, it is very easy to let each loan run its course. Yet personal circumstances change, interest rates vary, and the need for the debt may diminish as other assets become available.

So it's worth doing an occasional wealth check on your borrowings. It is possible to refinance debt in order to alter repayment schedules or avail of lower interest rates. It may be worthwhile using savings to reduce or pay off a loan. The biggest interest savings can be made by rolling up a number of loans into a mortgage top-up. The interest rates are the lowest available and the repayments can be spread over as long as twenty years. It's an option which needs very careful consideration and it's not the only change which can produce savings. Before you can make any decisions, of course, you need to take a little time to itemise your current loans and work out what they are costing you. Then you can start looking at the alternatives.

But first list your loans. They are likely to fall into three main categories.

Mortgage: You know how much you initially borrowed but how much do you owe now. If it was an endowment mortgage you still owe as much as you did on the day you took out the loan but your endowment policy should be worth something. Find out how much it is worth. It's seldom worth cashing in a policy on which you have already incurred heavy set-up charges but it's nice to know where you stand.

How much equity do you have in your house? If it is worth at least 10 per cent more than the outstanding loan you should be able to get a top up mortgage. What rate of interest

terest charges there may also be differences in set-up costs. A bank or building society with an existing mortgage on the property should be able to set up a new mortgage at a lower cost. But it is important to check interest rates as well.

Because of the cost of setting up the mortgage this type of loan does not make much sense unless a fairly sizeable amount is being borrowed — say upwards of £3,000. And it is important to appreciate that the loan is secured on the property. The bank or society has the right to sell the property to get its money back if the borrower defaults on payments. It is that security which allows them to charge a lower interest rate. So in return for a cheaper loan the borrower is putting his home or other property on the line.

are you paying? Is it fixed or variable? How does it compare with the competition. It can be worth switching mortgages although it is a big step and likely to require a heavy up-front cost. See page 130.

Bank Loans: We can include credit union and finance company loans in this category. You should check what rate of interest you are paying. There isn't a lot of variation at this time between one institution and the other but if you have a loan that's a few years old you may discover that you are still paying a fixed rate that's a little over the odds. If so you need to find out if you can pay it off without penalty.

Also check your overdraft. An overdraft can be the cheapest form of bank borrowing since you only pay interest on the amount outstanding each day. So when your pay cheque is lodged to your account, your interest liability immediately goes down. A well used overdraft can be cheaper than a term loan even though the interest rates are the same on both.

But running up an occasional overdraft can be very expensive since it usually makes you immediately liable for bank charges during the relevant quarter. Running up an overdraft for just one day can prove very costly.

Credit Cards: Credit cards should ideally only be used to secure free credit by paying the bill in full each month. Occasionally letting some of the bill run on for a month or two is not too costly but on-going debt should definitely be avoided. The interest rates can be penal - up to 26 per cent. It's easy to get into the habit of letting the credit card debt run on and on paying only the minimum requirement each month. The answer is to get a term loan to pay off the debt. If you then let the credit card debt run up again it may be time to bring out the scissors and cut the card in two.

Borrowing on mortgage can make sense where the money is being spent on a house extension or other long term investment in real assets — that can include education. But despite the lower interest rate it may not be a good idea to borrow on mortgage simply to pay off short-term debts or finance short-term purchases such as a car or a holiday.

People have been encouraged to extend their mortgages to pay off their bank and credit card debts. Their monthly repayments can go down as a result but that is partly because the debt is being spread over a longer period. In two or three years time they will still be facing many years of higher mortgage repayments while the bank and credit card debts may have again emerged. And they have put their homes up as security.

So care needs to be taken. It is usual for mortgage finance providers to charge the normal house purchase rate for personal loans related to the house. Up to an extra two percentage points may be charged on other personal loans with business loans rating three percentage points above the basic mortgage rate.

Finance houses

The term covers a wide range of smaller banks including subsidiaries of the big four banks. And in the area of personal loans it also covers the State-owned Agricultural Credit Corporation (ACCBank) and the Bank of Ireland subsidiary, Premier Banking which operates a phone-in service. That covers a wide range of different companies offering a diverse range of loans. Most offer personal loans like term loans and these are likely to carry the lowest interest rates.

There are a couple of points to bear in mind regarding finance house loans. They sometimes provide loans through car dealers or shops, but it is usually cheaper to go direct to the finance house itself to get your loan. The intermediary often takes a commission — which you pay — and in any case you are in a stronger bargaining position when buying the goods if you arrange the loan yourself. As far as the seller is concerned, you are then a cash buyer.

Another point is that finance houses often have sliding scales of interest rates on personal loans, depending on what the loan is for. Cheapest rates are usually for things like house extensions — dearest, perhaps, for second-hand cars. They are seldom in a position to check — they just ask you.

Store budget accounts

Most of the larger stores have their own budget account facilities and a growing number of smaller stores have budget accounts run for them by finance houses. The interest rate is much the same as charged by the finance houses. The best advice is to avoid them.

While a budget account is handy, it can be relatively dear to run — it is cheaper to try to get a term loan from your bank or, cheaper still, your credit union. Budget accounts are flexible, however, allowing you to spend up to the applied maximum credit level at any time. The usual scheme is that the credit limit is eight times your monthly payment.

The worst part, however, is that you have to use it in the one store, or group of stores, so there is a disincentive to shopping around. Indeed, borrowing on your credit card is likely to be as cheap while still leaving you the freedom to shop around. But in either case, of course, you may be tempted to spend more than you should, or really want to.

The advice is to try to get a bank or credit union loan for major shopping sprees. If you want to have a store card to avail of special offers or promotions try to keep it on the basis of a monthly card. That should cost you nothing. If you actually do a lot of shopping in the one store there can be some advantage in having a card, even for credit purposes, since the card is generally free and the interest rate can be lower than that charged on a bank or building society card.

Credit Unions

C redit unions are among the cheapest providers of loans but they are, of course, only available to members. Membership is open to those who are part of a "common bond" i.e. live in the locality or work in the particular firm covered by the union. To qualify for a loan it is usually necessary to be a member of some standing having shown an ability to save. But that can be well worth the effort. There are credit unions now based in most localities and in many organisations and big firms.

With the enactment of new legislation in 1997 credit unions have been enpowered to provide larger loans over longer periods. The standard interest rate is 1% a month — an annual percentage rate of 12.6%. That is slightly higher than the rate on a term loan from one of the major banks, but credit unions offer a number of extra advantages.

Credit unions are non-profitmaking organisations. Any surplus made belongs to the members. Some credit unions use some of the surplus to give interest rate rebates to their borrowing members. Another advantage is that loan protection insurance is built-in. It provides for the repayment of the loan in the event of death or permanent disablement. Limits may apply to the size of the loan and the cover is curtailed for the over 60s and not available for the over 70s.

Another built in insurance provides for the payment of a benefit to a member's estate in the event of death. In the case of a member aged under 55 the benefit is equal to the amount on deposit or in shares at the time of death. The benefit is lower for those over 55 and not applicable in the case of the over 70s.

Hire purchase

Hire purchase is a very expensive way of buying on credit. Not only is the interest rate high, but there are also high administrative charges, all built into the hire purchase price. Most people who can buy goods on HP would be acceptable for at least a finance house loan — assuming they do not have a normal bank account. Either finance houses or banks would be far cheaper. The best alternative for most people tempted to borrow on hire purchase is the local credit union.

Insurance

It is sometimes possible to borrow against the surrender value of with-profits endowment life assurance policies. Most insurance companies will provide such loans and the interest rates are usually relatively low. In some cases there is no need to repay the loan, since the sum involved will be taken out of the final sum due on maturity of the policy. Indeed, the interest payments can also be rolled forward in this manner. But the policy does need to have a cash-in value higher than the size of the loan.

Credit cards

Credit cards are best seen as a means of getting short-term credit — they are a boon if used wisely in this way. They save you carrying cash; enable you to keep a record of your spending; and can provide you with a handy period of free credit. But used unwisely, they can be very expensive. If you exceed your permitted period of free credit you end up paying a fairly high rate of interest on the outstanding amount — up to twice the rate you would pay on an overdraft or term loan from one of the big-four banks. See the section on credit cards in chapter 2 on page 30.

Pawnbrokers/ moneylender

The best advice is not to borrow from them at all, although pawnbrokers are not all that expensive provided you do not make a habit of using them.

Tackling debt problems

IT is all too easy for debts to become a problem and when they do there is a strong temptation to bury your head in the sand and hope that the problem will go away. Of course, that just makes it worse. The only solution for those with debt problems — or heading that way — is to confront the difficulty head on. The quicker that is done the quicker the problems can be solved.

Mr. Micawber in Charles Dicken's novel "David Copperfield" well understood the problem of debt. His comment is often quoted. It goes like this: "Annual income twenty pounds, annual expenditure nineteen nineteen six, result happiness. Annual income twenty pounds, annual expenditure twenty pounds nought and six, result misery". It has been suggested that Charles Dickens arrived at this view himself as a result of his father's experiences. Mr. Dickens Senior spent some time in a debtors prison.

There is no debtors prison today and contrary to some popular notions it is not possible to end up in prison simply for being in debt. But you can get locked up for failing to meet debt repayments decided on by a court. Initially when a person is brought before a court for debt it will do no more than decide on equitable repayments in the context of the person's ability to pay. It is only if those repayments are not met, that a person may face jail - and then only for blatantly failing to pay. A court can always be asked to adjust a repayment order if circumstances change.

But there should be no need for anyone to appear in court for debt. If action is taken soon enough and creditors kept informed of any financial difficulty then it is usually possible to reschedule repayments and sometimes even have interest charges reduced. It is important to take action as early as possible.

Debt is not a bad thing, in itself. Borrowing, indeed, has an important role to play in most families' finances. But borrowing can get out of hand. Problems start to arise when a person's — or a family's — spending needs start to outstrip their income. Initially it may seem possible to handle the problem. But it is usually only being compounded. The balance on the credit card runs up. The ESB bill is missed so that something else can be paid. There is a hope that something will turn up. But it doesn't. Postponed debts do not go away. Indeed if interest is being added on, they only get worse.

The quicker you face up to debt problems the quicker they can be solved.

Swopping a number of small loans for one big one can be a big mistake too. You can, of course, reduce your monthly repayments by replacing some short-term expensive loans with a cheaper building society or bank mortgage spread over a longer period. But you may be only storing up problems for the future. If you do not meet the repayments on the mortgage you will be putting your home in jeopardy.

This is not the answer if you have major debt problems. If you see it as part of a solution you need to be absolutely sure that you will be able to meet the mortgage repayments and you also need to check that there are no heavy penalties involved in paying off your existing loans early. With many finance house loans there are such penalties. And there is no sense in replacing your loans with even more expensive ones. Overall there is no easy solution down this road.

Remember that you have to deal with the priority debts first. A building society will normally agree to reduce repayments so long as you are at least meeting the interest portion. In the early years this may, unfortunately, represent more than 90% of each repayment so that the possible reduction is not great. But if you are not meeting the interest, then the amount outstanding keeps going up. Banks, credit card companies, and finance houses will sometimes agree to reduce interest charges. Some of their rates are so high they can well afford to. If you feel unable to do the negotiating your local St. Vincent de Paul Society or credit union is likely to know of someone who may be able to help.

The Department of Social Welfare runs a money advice and budgeting advice service throughout most of the country. It's a free service of course. Ask about it at your local Social Welfare Office. Another scheme administered with help from the St. Vincent de Paul Society and credit unions also provides advice on budgeting and will negotiate with creditors on behalf of borrowers. It is not there to pay off loans but rather to help people budget their way out of difficulties. In some cases arrangements may be made to pay off expensive loans and replace them with cheaper credit union loans. The first approach should be to your local St. Vincent de Paul Society or credit union.

SIX POINT PLAN

The following six step action plan is based on a booklet prepared by the British Office of Fair Trading. It boils down to facing your problem, coming clean with your creditors and making them an offer based on a full disclosure of what you can afford. The advice is as applicable here as in Britain.

ONE: The first step is to work out exactly what your income is. Get out a copy book or a few sheets of paper and detail your income — what actually comes into the house from all sources each week or month.

TWO: Secondly, you list your total spending needs. Do not leave anything out. There are the obvious things like rent/mortgage repayments, food, fuel etc. But do not forget to include the irregular spending items — clothes, the ESB bill which only comes in every two months, insurance bills which may only come once a year etc. Bring it all down to a monthly or weekly figure.

THREE: Then compare your first list with your second. If your income exceeds your spending needs then you do not have a problem in meeting your ongoing commitments. Check your figures again. If your outgoings do exceed your income an obvious approach is to cut your spending. Divide your spending into essentials and nonessentials. Can you cut back? Is there anything you can sell to bring in money to reduce some debt — not goods that you have on HP, although if you do have goods on hire purchase and you have not paid a third of the price, the HP company may take them back.

FOUR: Examine possible ways of increasing your income. Are there any social welfare benefits you are entitled to — supplementary benefit or the family income supplement (see chapter 12). If you are on social welfare and have difficulty meeting your rent, you may be entitled to rent allowance under the supplementary benefit scheme administered by your local health board.

FIVE: List exactly how much you owe. Divide the loans into priority ones and others. The priorities would be rent/mortgage, ESB, other fuel bills. If you fall too far behind with these you could lose your house or have the electricity or gas turned off.

SIX: Lastly having gathered all that information the final step is to talk with your creditors. Summarise the figures you have listed and let them see the details of your income and spending. That way they will realise how much or how little you can afford to pay. Make an offer.

Home buying

Home buying an easy guide

6.1

FOR most families the purchase of a house represents the single largest financial commitment of their lives. The purchase of the house will require two, three or more times the average person's annual salary. And if the money to make the purchase is borrowed, the repayments will take a considerable part of the family budget. But buying a house does not simply add to household expenses. It is a major investment decision as well, and the return on the investment can be sizable. Borrowing to buy a house usually makes good financial sense even when interest rates are relatively high. Assuming that you do not pay an inflated price for the house, there is little doubt that it makes more sense to borrow and buy, rather than to rent — unless, of course, the rent is particularly low as it might be on a local authority house.

Over the longer term the value of house property can be expected to rise faster than the rate of inflation unless the economy collapses completely. Interest rates will hopefully fall even further and average out reasonably over the twenty years or so during which the loan is being repaid.

So it usually makes sense to buy a house. Even the fairly heavy costs involved in making the purchase can be more than offset for first time buyers of new houses by the State grants available. But you need some money to start off — for the deposit and expenses. You need to convince the lender that you will be able to meet the loan repayment. But there are traps along the way and a lot of critical decisions to make. And many of those decisions have to be taken on the basis of assumptions about the future rather than hard facts. So what are the options?

What are the options?

The main constraint on what you can buy is the availability of finance. For most people this means simply the extent to which they are able to borrow. The range of borrowing options open to the house buyer has widened significantly in recent years with most lenders actively seeking mortgage business. It is likely that in the not too distant future credit unions will also be offering longer term loans suitable for home purchase. And for those who cannot get loans elsewhere, local authorities offer three different types of loan.

In most cases it is now possible to walk in off the street and be considered for a loan. It is not necessary to have some minimum savings built up or indeed to have ever been a customer of the lending institution. But some lenders may charge preferential interest rates to those who have been saving with them and have built up some minimum amount perhaps over a certain period of time. Remember the benefit of the lower interest rate will be there for up to twenty years. In all cases the would-be borrower is presented with some choice. For some, it will be between the different local authority loans. For others, it will be a choice between different lenders and different types of loan and those choices are wide.

In almost all cases, it makes good financial sense to buy a house on mortgage, provided you are eligible for income tax relief on the interest paid.

It is never possible to be sure of making the right decision. Borrowing by way of a mortgage is a long term decision and who can tell what is going to happen over the space of maybe twenty years. What appears to be the cheapest and best option now may prove to be otherwise over the course of time. It may be possible to switch later but that is also always expensive although sometimes worthwhile. So it is worthwhile making the best possible decision at the outset and a well informed choice is more likely to be the right one. So an understanding of what is available cannot go amiss. Let us have a look at the options.

Local authority loans

Local authorities — county councils and corporations — provide house purchase loans for those on relatively low incomes and can also pay mortgage subsidies to tenants and tenant-purchasers of local authority houses who give up their houses to buy a private house. There is also a scheme whereby people on a local authority housing list can jointly buy a house with the local authority. Let us have a look at each of those schemes.

Rent or Buy?

Successive governments in Ireland have sought to encourage home ownership through a combination of incentives including grants and tax reliefs. The result is that it is almost always better to buy than to rent. And this has not been changed by the new tax relief of up to £500 (single), £1,000 (married) on rent paid for private accommodation. The main exception is someone who is not going to stay in the one place for too long. There are once-off costs incurred in buying which are obviously best spread over a number of years and not repeated too often.

Buying can be far cheaper than renting. A three-bedroomed house in Dublin can cost upwards of £400 a month to rent. The net monthly repayments on a £60,000 mortgage can be as low as £330.

Taking the example of a married couple buying their first house for £90,000 with a £60,000 mortgage. We can assume that the £3,000 first time grant pays the costs of purchase, legal costs, surveys etc. At an interest rate of 7.5% the gross monthly repayments on £60,000 would be £480 while the tax relief for a married couple is worth £150 a month. That brings the net cost down to £330. For a single taxpayer the net cost would be about £390. But that is still cheaper than the rental cost of a similar house.

There are other factors to take into account. Someone renting a house would not need the £30,000 deposit. If they have £30,000 they can earn interest on it. That could be worth £150 a month. That's another cost of buying. It puts the cost for a married couple to £480 — about the same cost as renting. But there's another advantage in buying. The value of the house should go up. Just going up in line with a 3% inflation puts £225 a month onto the value of a £90,000 house. New houses tend not to rise in value initially because the £3,000 grant makes new houses more attractive to most buyers than an almost new one, but the prices catch up later.

The straightforward local authority loan is only available to those who have been turned down by both a bank and a building society. Would-be borrowers have to get those refusals in writing before the local authority can consider them for loans. Just being turned down by these private institutions is not enough, however. There are other conditions to be met.

Where there is only one earner his or her income must have been no more than £15,000 in the last full income tax year if the applicant is the only earner in the household. A second income is also taken into account according to a set formula. The principal income is multiplied by two and a half and to the product is added the subsidiary income. The final figures must be no more than £37,500.

If we take the example of a couple, one earning £12,000 a year and the other £7,000, the sums work out like this. Two and a half times £12,000 is £30,000. Adding the £7,000 brings that up to £37,000. That's less than the £37,500 limit so the couple are eligible for a local authority loan provided, of course, they can't get a loan elsewhere.

That maximum income limit does not apply to "special category" applicants who are either tenants or tenant purchasers of a local authority house who are returning it to the authority, or they are on a local authority housing list for a year and the family consists of the applicant and at least two other adults or one child.

The three types of loan are as follows:

Annuity Loan: There is no minimum income requirement but the local authority must be satisfied that it is sufficient to meet the repayments. The maximum loan is £38,000. Within those upper limits, loans are given of up to 95% of the purchase price or the market value of the house (whichever is less). Loans of up to £43,000 are given for the purchase of houses on certain offshore islands.

Interest rates are variable and will not exceed the standard building society rate. Loans for new houses can be repaid over 30 years while the upper limit for second-hand houses is 25 years. Normally neither the borrower, nor his or her spouse, should ever have bought or built a house before. An exception is made for people living in substandard conditions.

Income Related Loans: With these loans the repayments are based on the borrower's income during the previous year. The basic conditions are much the same as those mentioned above. In the case of a couple, only the income of the higher earner is taken into account and loans may be given to people who have owned houses before if the move is necessitated by an employment need or in the case of marital breakdown. The maximum loan in this case is £38,000 (higher for those in the special categories of employment need or marital breakdown mentioned above), and it cannot be more than 90% of the market value or purchase price.

The options - building societies and banks

The range of mortgage options now available is very wide. The following is an outline of the various mortgage types.

Annuity: This is the old traditional mortgage where each repayment covers the interest and also pays something off the loan. The amount owing goes down each year, slowly at first and then progressively quicker. But you are fifteen years into a twenty year mortgage before you have paid off half the loan.

Endowment: With the basic endowment mortgage the loan is not repaid until the end of the term. The borrower pays interest each year on the full amount and also pays premiums on a life insurance policy which should, at the end of the term, mature yielding at least enough to pay off the loan. Their attractiveness depends on how the insurance policy actually performs and, to a large extent, on the continuation of mortgage interest relief.

Low start: The repayments are kept at a fixed level for the first number of years — usually three or five — even though they may not be enough to even meet the interest payments on the loan. As a result, the amount borrowed may go up during that initial period. The borrower then starts paying off the higher loans in the normal way. Such loans can be useful for borrowers buying a house which is a bit beyond them now but who hope to be better off in a few years time.

Fixed Interest: The interest rate is fixed for a set number of years irrespective of movements in the market so that the borrowers knows exactly what the repayments will be during those years. At the end of the set period, interest rates may be fixed for another period or the borrower may switch to normal variable rates. The borrower gambles that the fixed rate will prove lower than the market rate. Even if it doesn't there has been the security of knowing that whatever happens the repayments were not going to rise.

Pension linked: This is an endowment type mortgage linked to a pension scheme rather than an insurance policy. For a self-employed person it provides better tax relief since all the premiums to a pension fund can be allowable for tax relief. But the contributions to the pension scheme need to be quite large since the mortgage has to be paid off from the lump-sum option on retirement leaving the bulk of the savings to buy a pension.

Foreign currency: It is possible to borrow in a foreign currency at the interest rates being charged in the country concerned but the borrower takes on the additional exchange rate risk. The loan is taken out and has to be repaid in the foreign currency.

Repayments are based on 22% of the gross income in the previous year — the income of the highest earner at the time is taken into account even if that is not the person on whose income the original loan was based. Those who borrow less than $2\frac{3}{4}$ times their income can base their repayments on 20% of that income. The interest rate is fixed each July — currently at $5\frac{3}{4}$ percentage points above the annual rate of inflation up to the previous May. So if prices rise by 3% a year the interest rate is set at $8\frac{3}{4}$%. But no matter what the rate of interest is, the repayments remain at the 20 or 22% of income — whatever percentage was fixed at the beginning.

Convertible Loan: This offers a mix of the two loan types already described. The loan cannot exceed £38,000 or 90% of the purchase price except for "special category" borrowers who can get slightly higher loans. It is a low rise repayment loan with the repayments fixed as a percentage of income during the first five years, thereafter reverting to the normal annuity method. The interest rate is variable at the same level as for the basic annuity type loan.

Shared Ownership: Tenants or tenant purchasers of local authority houses wishing to give them up to buy a private house, or people on a housing list, or those who meet the income criteria mentioned above may qualify for a local authority loan to buy a half share in a private house of their own choosing. The local authority buys the other half share and charges an annual rent calculated at 5% of its value. Those with incomes below £12,000 enjoy a reduced rental. The maximum reduction is £1,200 a year for those with incomes below £8,500 while the minimum is £250 for those earning between £11,001 and £12,000.

Which is best?: There is no easy answer to that one. The convertible loans give maximum flexibility with a chance to keep repayments low in the early years when money is likely to be tight and for this reason must be better than the annuity type. The income related loans, while good value when market rates are high are relatively expensive when building society rates, on which the other local authority rates are based, are low.

Building societies and banks

Building societies and banks have been almost dragging people in off the street and stuffing loans into their pockets in the last year or so as the supply of funds well exceeded demand. It is a far cry from the long standing custom of having to meet stringent savings criteria before even being considered for a loan. Most building societies have dispensed with the requirement that borrowers have a certain sum saved for a year or so before applying for a loan. But some do still charge a higher interest rate to borrowers who do not have such savings. That is a thing to watch. Remember it can pay to shop around and the lenders are looking for your custom. So don't just pick the first option that comes along.

It is not too difficult to pick the cheapest loan. Have a look at the stated interest rate first and then at the monthly repayments. The repayments are possibly the best guide since interest rates are still being stated in different ways which are not always comparable. But remember that it is the interest rate over the full term of the loan that matters so do not be taken in for short-term catchall promotions. The following are the main choices:

- Annuity or endowment mortgage
- Fixed or variable interest rate
- If endowment, what sort of endowment?

There is no single answer to which is best. It depends on the individual. Let us have a look at what each entails.

Endowment versus annuity

The annuity mortgage is once again the most popular. It operates the same as most loans. The borrower makes a monthly repayment which includes both interest and something off the loan itself. Initially most of the repayment is interest with very little going to reduce the amount owing. But as the years pass the loan goes down faster and in the later years the interest part of each repayment gets smaller. That is the way most people expect to pay off loans and it is easily understood. But it has some implications for tax relief. Tax relief is allowed on the interest paid on loans used to buy, extend or improve the borrower's own residence. The full repayment does not qualify for relief — only the interest portion. And with the annuity type mortgage the interest portion is declining over the years. So the tax relief is going down.

The decline is relatively small in the early years and even ten years into a twenty year loan three-quarters of each monthly repayment is still interest. After that it goes down at a relatively faster pace so that by year fifteen only a little more than half the repayment is interest. With an endowment mortgage the tax relief should remain constant for the life of the loan. It should only change if the Government changes the rules or if the borrower moves into a different tax bracket. If he loses his job and ceases to be liable for tax, then there is no tax relief. But that applies, of course to both types of loan.

Endowment mortgages combine a loan with a life assurance policy. Only the interest on the loan is paid during its life. But the borrower also pays premiums on a savings type life assurance policy. That policy is designed to mature at the end of the loan — say twenty years hence — and yield enough to pay off the loan. There may even be something left over.

So there are two possible advantages to endowment mortgages. Firstly, the money being saved up to pay off the loan may yield a better return as savings over the years than the interest it would save if it were used to gradually pay off the loan. Secondly, and contributing to that hope, is the possibility of getting better tax relief over the term of the loan.

Endowment mortgages involve taking some risks. They may be worth taking but you should realise what they are.

But there can be no certainty. There is always the possibility that tax relief on mortgage interest will be abolished. If it is, the hoped for extra tax saving will not emerge. On the other hand the hoped for return on the insurance policy may not emerge. The borrower must weigh up the possible benefits and the risks. There can be no single right answer. Much depends on what view one takes of likely future developments with regard to the rate of return on insurance policies and the continuation of mortgage tax relief.

The interest rate on endowment loans is often higher than on the traditional loan although the opposite is sometimes the case. There is no logic either way. Where the interest rate is higher on endowment loans the usual addition is an extra half of one per cent. It does not sound much but over twenty years it adds up to a lot and certainly eats into some of the tax advantage.

Endowment mortgages are every bit as flexible as annuity mortgages for the person moving house. The endowment policy can be maintained and moved to the new mortgages but there is less flexibility in another respect. If the borrower runs into financial difficulties there is less scope for reducing the repayments to help tide him or her over until the cash flow situation improves. With an annuity mortgage the interest portion of each repayment goes down as the years progress. The lender is

Monthly repayments for each £1000 borrowed

The following are the monthly repayments per £1,000 borrowed on an annuity mortgage. They include no provision for mortgage protection insurance or other extras.

Interest rate	Term of loan in years			
	10	15	20	25
6%	£11.33	£8.59	£7.27	£6.52
6½%	£11.60	£8.87	£7.57	£6.84
7%	£11.87	£9.15	£7.87	£7.16
7½%	£12.15	£9.45	£8.18	£7.48
8%	£12.42	£9.74	£8.49	£7.81
8½%	£12.71	£10.04	£8.81	£8.15
9%	£12.99	£10.34	£9.13	£8.49
9½%	£13.38	£10.65	£9.46	£8.83
10%	£13.56	£10.96	£9.79	£9.18
10½%	£13.86	£11.27	£10.12	£9.54
11%	£14.15	£11.59	£10.47	£9.90
11½%	£14.45	£11.92	£10.81	£10.26
12%	£14.75	£12.24	£11.16	£10.63
12½%	£15.06	£12.57	£11.51	£11.00

usually happy, in the short-term at least, to agree to a reduction in the repayments provided the interest portion is paid. But with an endowment mortgage there is no scope for cutting repayments. Since the loan is never reduced, the interest element remains unchanged — except for changes in interest rates — and a failure to meet the premiums on the life assurance policy may result in it lapsing.

There is greater tax relief on an endowment mortgage simply because the interest payments remain high for the full term of the loan. But that benefit, if it is a benefit, comes at the end of the loan. The net repayments on an endowment mortgage are usually higher in the early years — when budgets are tightest. This fact is sometimes hidden in the examples by showing the average tax relief on the traditional type mortgage. But the average is a lot lower than the actual tax relief gained in the early years.

Picking the best endowment

Much damage was done to the image of endowment mortgages by the way they were promoted by some salesmen a few years ago. The risks were glossed over and the likely returns were inflated. Borrowers were not prepared for the downturn in fund values and the cuts in insurance policy bonuses. Endowment policies are an alternative for people who understand the risks involved and are willing to take them. But careful selection is essential. The difference between the best policy and the worst can be immense. There may be thousands of pounds at stake in that decision. Yet it is one which few people give much thought to. That is what we have to look at now. Remember the purpose of the insurance policy in an endowment loan. The borrower pays the premiums. Part of it goes to provide insurance — the guarantee that if he dies the loan will be paid off in full. The remainder goes into the savings fund which it is hoped will grow sufficiently to ensure that when the policy matures at the end of twenty years or so, it will yield enough to pay off the loan.

There are different ways of handling those savings. With unit linked policies they are used to buy units (shares) in one or other of the funds managed by the insurance company or other financial institution. The choice is usually a managed fund where the money is invested widely in a mixture of company shares, property and government stocks. Such funds have done very well in the past but the value of units can go down as well as up. There is no guarantee that the accumulated units will be enough, when the policy matures, to pay off the loan. Of course, on the other hand, if the investments perform well, there can be more than enough to pay off the loan so that the borrower is left with a nice lump sum at the end of the day.

If you do go for an endowment mortgage pick the insurance policy with care. Make sure your adviser justifies his or her recommendation.

The other main type of policy is a "with-profits endowment policy". With this type the money is invested in the life assurance company itself. There are no units which can move up and down in value. Bonuses are declared each year and at the end of the policy a terminal bonus is added on. Once added on, bonuses cannot be taken back so there is much less chance of the policy not yielding enough to pay off the loan.

That is all very complicated but to sum up: A unit linked policy offers the possibility of a higher return but with a greater degree of risk that it will not provide enough to pay off the loan. The with-profits policy is less risky and, arguably more appropriate, to someone for whom the policy is a way of paying off a home loan.

While there are two basic types of policy there are any number of different policies on offer. Picking the right one is very important but unfortunately there is no sure fire way of predicting which policy is going to perform best over the next twenty years. Looking at how they did over the last twenty years can only provide a guide and, in any case, many of the unit linked policies have only been around a few years. Unfortunately some lenders do not offer the borrower a wide choice of policy. Indeed some lenders only offer one type of policy usually from their own insurance company. They may perform very well - only the future will tell. In the past the with-profit policies of British mutual insurance societies have generally performed well. These are insurance companies which are effectively owned by the policyholders — there are no shareholders.

The costs — an example

The following example assumes the purchase of a £60,000 second hand house with a mortgage of £50,000. On a new house there would be no stamp duties on the house although there would be on the mortgage. This is only an illustration of the possible costs.

Legal fees (based on 2% of price including VAT)	£1,200
Survey fees	£100
Land registry fees etc.	£250
Search fees	£60
Stamp duties on house	£3,000
Stamp duties on mortgage	£50
Total	£4,660

Unit linked policies have, in general, performed reasonably well over the longer term although they can move sharply down at times — as the sharp losses suffered by many funds in recent years proves all too well. And the variation between best and worst is great.

There is no sure way of picking the winners although you can reduce the risk by picking a with-profits policy from one of the mutual societies mentioned above or a unit linked policy with a good long-term track record. There are, no doubt, other policies which have performed well in the past and which may perform even better in the future. If one is being recommended to you simply ask the seller, be he an insurance broker or a lender, to justify the choice. Why is he recommending that policy rather than another? That is a very simple question which is relevant to a lot more than buying an insurance policy.

In all of the financial services area the buyer should ask the seller "why this and not another". You do not have to know what the others are. Be assured that there are alternatives so why is the adviser recommending this one. And be sure that you understand the answer. Do not be put off by jargon. Do not be afraid of appearing ignorant. If the adviser cannot explain adequately it is his ignorance and not yours. The good adviser will have looked at the alternatives and have picked the right product for you. He'll know why and be able to explain why.

A plus point for endowment mortgages is that there is no need for an additional mortgage protection policy. If the borrower dies, the loan is automatically paid off. But a mortgage protection policy is not all that costly.

Costs of getting a mortgage

Obviously, first of all, you need the cash for the deposit. As outlined above, although 90% loans are available you may find it hard to get more than an 80% loan on any house — maybe even less on an old house. If it is an old house which you are going to renovate, it may be possible to increase the mortgage later as alterations and additions are made. Check this with your lender.

But there are also other costs. Auctioneers fees are paid by the seller, so there is no need to worry about those, but there will be fees to the building society or other lender, legal fees and maybe stamp duty. There will also be costs involved in satisfying yourself that the house has no structural flaws.

Let us look at these in turn.

- **Fees to the lending agency:** These are not likely to break you, but it is as well to bear them in mind since they can stretch a slim budget. They include mortgage fees, survey fees, and search fees. The rates vary from lender to lender but the following provides a rough guide:

Mortgage Law Costs: 0.5 to 0.65% of loan - some societies charge a fixed fee of up to £240, others allow you to use your own solicitor.

Application Fee: From nothing to 0.2% per £1,000 to a fixed £50 fee depending on the lender.

Survey Fees: About £1.50 per £1,000 although sometimes a fixed fee is charged. There may also be travelling expenses for the surveyor.

Search Fees: These should not amount to much more than £50 or £60.

- **Stamp duties:** Stamp duty on second-hand houses valued at more than £150,000 and on new houses valued at more than £600,000 was increased from January 23, 1997.

Stamp duty on house purchases

Less than £5,000	Nil
Between £5,000 and £10,000	1%
Between £10,000 and £15,000	2%
Between £15,000 and £25,000	3%
Between £25,000 and £50,000	4%
Between £50,000 and £60,000	5%
Between £60,000 and £150,000	6%
Between £150,000 and £160,0000	7%
Between £160,000 and £170,000	8%
Over £170,000 — secondhand houses	9%
Over £600,000 — new houses in excess of 125 sq. mtrs.	9%

There is no stamp duty payable by the first purchaser of most new houses. If, however, the house is not eligible for a State grant — if, for example, its floor area is greater than 1,346 square feet (125 square metres) — then stamp duty is payable but only on the site value which is assumed to be 25% of the total consideration paid. The rates are given above. Stamp duty is payable on the full value of most second-hand houses. There

Switching lenders could cut your costs

Most loans can be repaid at any time without penalty. So there is scope for switching lenders. Borrowing from one to repay another. Unfortunately the more expensive loans, sometimes at fixed rates, include penalty clauses. The penalty for early repayment can more than offset any potential savings on interest payments. But there should be no penalty clauses on variable rate mortgages.

So is it worthwhile switching?

Setting up a new mortgage can cost up to £1,000. It depends, of course, on the size of the mortgage, the legal costs the lender may impose, and the way it is registered. However given the current competition in the market many lenders are willing to absorb some of the costs bringing it down to perhaps below £500. So the up-front cost can be heavy. What are the potential savings?

Let's take the case of Tom and Mary who borrowed £70,000 two years ago with an annuity mortgage at a variable rate. They are currently paying 7.45 per cent - far higher than the 6.6 per cent they see one building society advertising. They are thinking of switching. Is it worthwhile?

The annual saving is simple enough to work out. It amounts to 0.85 per cent. Tom and Mary still owe almost the full £70,000 so the saving works out at about £590 a year. The real saving after tax relief would be about £440. If it costs £500 to set up the new mortgage Tom and Mary will be net winners in little more than a year.

While there is no certainty, if the current differentials remain for a little over a year they can't lose. Of course, it may be sufficient just to warn your existing lender that you intend switching unless they lower their rate. That might produce the desired result without the need to switch. That, after all, is what competition is all about

are exemptions for certain tenants of local authority houses who buy their houses from the Authority. Your solicitor will normally arrange for the payment of it and bill you. These stamp duty rates are not charged on slices of the price. On a £100,000 house, for instance, the rate is 6% on the full £100,000. There is also a stamp duty of 25p per £200 on mortgages over £10,000.

- **Legal Fees:** There are too many possible pitfalls in buying a house for you to dispense with the services of a solicitor. Ask him in advance what his fees will be - most solicitors will tell you as a matter of course. There is no fixed rate of charges, but the Incorporated Law Society recommends a rate of 2% of the purchase price including VAT. This is a recommendation — the actual fees may be higher or lower. Legal fees are subject to VAT at 21%. The VAT only applies to the fees — not to the stamp duty which the solicitor may also collect.

There are, of course, other — mainly non-financial — matters to be borne in mind. These are the fairly obvious considerations of location, house size, age, etc. In other words, is the house good value for money? Is it suitable for your particular requirements and are there any flaws which might make it bad value for money?

The importance of location and size are matters for your own judgement, but you should never buy a house without having someone give it a professional once-over, unless it is a new house and the purchase contract provides for the making good of any structural defect appearing in the first two years. How do you go about that?

The lending agency will always send out its own surveyor to examine a house before agreeing to grant a mortgage. This provides some protection, since a mortgage will not be forthcoming unless the house is reasonably sound. But remember the lending agency is only concerned that the value of the house covers 80% of the price which it is lending to you. So with a second-hand house it is a good idea to engage your own surveyor to carry out a more detailed examination.

With a new house, ask your solicitor to ensure that the purchase contract contains a guarantee that any structural defects becoming evident in the first two years will be put right at the builder's expense. For preference deal with a builder who is in the National House Building Guarantee Scheme. If not, have a survey done yourself. Having satisfied yourself that the house is sound — or at least that you know of any major defects — the next thing to check is the possibility of any new building which might affect its value in the future. It could be that the person selling knows that a large block of flats is planned on a site overlooking the, seemingly private, back garden; or that a new motorway is to be built along your side wall.

So you need to check the planning applications and approvals for the area. This can be done at the offices of your local plan-

Checking the house

Your solicitor is only concerned that the contract of sale does not put you at a disadvantage. Make sure that a check is also made for planning applications or approvals which might effect the value of the house.

ning authority. There you can examine maps of your area showing the zonings — whether agricultural, commercial or
residential — and see details of any planning approvals granted
or applications pending. Such a visit is well worth making. The
planning offices are usually located in the local urban or county
council premises.

State grants for housing   6.2

GRANTS for house purchase and improvement have been dramatically curtailed in recent years but there are some still available and a number of new schemes have been introduced. These include mortgage subsidies for tenants and tenant purchasers of local authority houses who wish to purchase private houses, and grants for improving or extending the houses of people on local authority housing lists. Local authorities can also provide subsidised sites to eligible applicants and also provide assistance to promote voluntary housing. There are grants to help the first time purchaser and grants to assist in financing some very basic home improvements — but the house needs to be in urgent need of essential repairs.

Full details can be obtained from the Department of the Environment, Housing Grants Section, Ballina, Co Mayo. The following is an outline of what is available:

First time purchasers of new houses are entitled to a grant of £3,000 provided the house is built by a registered builder. 'House' in this context can mean either a house or a flat. To qualify the buyer must never have owned a house in Ireland or abroad before, and the house must not have been occupied before. An exception is made in the case of local authority tenants who buy their existing houses and also, in certain circumstances, where an earlier house was destroyed by fire, flood or such like. Where a spouse has got a recognised divorce, a civil annulment or a legal separation, the grants may also be payable if the applicant can show that he or she needs housing.

In all cases the purchaser must occupy the dwelling on completion as his or her normal place of residence on a year round basis. This excludes holiday homes, etc. Apart from the exception mentioned above, the condition of not having purchased a dwelling before applies to both the purchaser and spouse. Neither must have owned a house either individually or jointly. In addition, the dwelling must be built to a standard not inferior to that laid down by the Department.

There are also limits to the size of the house or flat on which a grant is payable. For a house, the total floor area must be more

House purchase grants

than 38 square metres (409 square feet) and less than 125 square metres (1,346 square feet). The measurements are taken inside the external walls and exclude undeveloped attics and basements, garages and out-offices. In multi-dwelling buildings, common spaces are also excluded. The minimum floor area in the case of flats is identical as that for houses.

The 38 square metre minimum size for apartments is laid down in guidelines issued by the Department of the Environment to local authorities for use in considering planning applications. They specify that no more than half the apartments in any development should have only one bedroom and that a proportion of larger apartments of over 70 square metres should be included in larger developments. Two bedroomed apartments should have a minimum floor area of 55 square metres while those with three or more bedrooms should have a minimum floor area of 70 square metres.

If applicable, it is advisable to make the application for a grant before the house is commenced or when a deposit is paid. A provisional approval can then be given. When the house is finished and occupied, the grant is then claimed by signing the declaration on the back of the certificate of approval and forwarding it to the Department. The payment is made directly to the purchaser.

Mortgage subsidy

A tenant or tenant purchaser of a local authority house who gives up the house and buys or builds a private house with the help of a mortgage loan of at least £10,000 can qualify for a mortgage subsidy of up to £3,300 spread over five years. It is known as a mortgage allowance and at its maximum is paid as follows. The subsidy is paid directly to the lending agency and cannot exceed the actual amount of interest incurred in the year.

Year 1	£1,000	Year 4	£500
Year 2	£800	Year 5	£400
Year 3	£600		

House improvement grants

Grants can be given by local authorities towards the cost of installing special facilities for handicapped people and for essential repairs to certain houses in rural areas. Local authorities can also make interest free loans of up to £10,000 to upgrade the accommodation of people in need of local authority housing. The work must bring the accommodation up to a minimum standard to meet the housing needs of the applicant without recourse to local authority accommodation. The loan repayments are calculated on an income related basis.

Thatching grant

A grant of up to £2,000 is available for renewing or repairing thatched roofs on houses. The work must cost a total of at least £750 with the grant covering two-thirds of the approved cost up to that maximum of £2,000. The house must be more than ten years old; it must be structurally sound; and it must be occupied as a normal place of residence.

6.3 Mortgage tax relief

Mortgage interest relief still costs the Exchequer some £150 million a year. So it's a valuable tax relief. There have been significant changes in the relief over recent years — changes which have made the calculations increasingly complicated and further changes are on the way. From the 1997/98 tax year interest relief has only been allowed at the standard rate of tax — 24p in the £ from April 1998.

A cap on the total amount of interest eligible for tax relief didn't complicate the tax system too much but now there are three further limitations on the relief. All four limitations have to be taken into account in calculating exactly how much relief you've entitled to.

Let's go through the four limitations in turn:

- **Overall Ceiling:** You have to start off with a overall ceiling on the amount of interest payments you can take into account. For most people it is a notional figure which is reduced by the other limitations. Only first-time buyers can claim relief up to the full ceiling and only for five years from the first time they claimed mortgage tax relief.

  The overall ceilings are £5,000 for a married couple; £3,600 for a widowed person; and £2,500 for single taxpayers.

- **Percentage reduction:** Within the overall ceiling only 80% of the interest liability is actually allowed for tax relief. So a married couple whose interest liability for the year is, say, £6,000 must ignore the first £1,000 of that since it is above the £5,000 ceiling. The £5,000 that is taken into account is reduced to 80% or £4,000.

- **Exclusions:** In the case of a married couple the first £200 is disallowed. It's £100 in the case of other taxpayers — single or widowed. So in the example above of a married couple incurring interest payment of £6,000, the first step as outlined above, is to reduce the eligible interest to the ceiling of £5,000, then further reduce by 20% or down to £4,000, and then knock off the first £200 to bring the allowance down to £3,800. That £3,800 is the maximum relief available to a married couple who are not first-time buyers.

Will you get maximum tax relief?

If you're a first time buyer you're very likely to be borrowing enough to qualify for the maximum tax relief. The size of loan to bring you up to that threshold depends on the current rate of interest. The following are approximate levels for various rates. If your loan exceeds the relevant figure that you can safely assume that you are eligible for the maximum tax relief.

Interest:-	7%	7.5%	8%	8.5%	9%
Single	£35,700	£33,300	£31,200	£29,411	£27,700
Married	£71,400	£66,600	£62,500	£58,800	£55,500
Widowed	£51,400	£48,000	£45,000	£42,454	£40,000

How much is the maximum relief worth?

The maximum tax relief you can claim depends on your marital status, your top rate of tax and whether you're a first time buyer or not. The table shows the value of the maximum tax relief. It's reducing over the next couple of years as the maximum relief is being phased down to the standard rate of tax. This only affects people who are paying tax at the top rate.

First time buyers:-

Tax Rate:-	24p	48p		46p
		1996/97	1997/98	1998/99
Married	£1,200	£1,625	£1,300	£1,200
Widowed	£864	£1,161	£936	£864
Single	£600	£812	£650	£600

Other buyers:-

Tax Rate:-	24p	48p		46p
		1996/97	1997/98	1998/99
Married	£912	£1,225	£988	£912
Widowed	£667	£897	£723	£667
Single	£456	£613	£494	£456

- **Limit to Standard Rate:** Up to 1994 tax relief was allowed at whatever your maximum tax rate was. Now it is only allowed at the standard rate — 24p from April 1998.

  Prior to 1994 a couple paying enough tax at the then top rate of 48p in the pound could save 48p on every eligible pound of interest paid. But for the 1994/95 tax year only 75% of the eligible interest was allowed for tax relief at 48p in the pound. The remainder was allowed only at the old standard rate of 27p.

  In effect the tax relief was granted at a maximum rate of 42.75p in the £ in 1994/95; at 37.5p in 1995/96; at 32.5p in 1996/97; and at the standard rate from April 1997 onwards.

  The effect of those changes on a married couple with eligible interest of £3,800 was to reduce the tax saving from £1,624 in the 1994/95 tax year to £1,425 in 1995/96, to £1,225 in 1996/97, to £1,026 in 1997/98 and to £912 from April 1998 when the lower standard rate of 24p comes into effect.

  As mentioned above first-time buyers get special treatment during the first five years of claiming interest relief. These changes were introduced in 1996 and the benefits only applied from April 1996 although the five year limit is taken to have started whenever you first claimed mortgage interest relief.

  For example if you first claimed interest relief in 1992/93 tax year you are entitled to the relief for the 1996/97 tax year but not thereafter since your loan will be more than five years old. There is no provision to allow a rebate for years prior to April 1996.

- **Designated Areas:** There is additional tax relief available to the owner occupiers of homes in designated areas which meet certain conditions. The property must be the sole or main residence of the individual claiming the relief. If it is a converted premises there must be a certificate of reasonable cost. The total floor area must be between 30 and 90 square metres in the case of an apartment (up to 125 square metres in the case of a refurbished apartment). A house must be between 35 and 125 square metres.

  The expenditure must have been incurred after October 1985 and before July 31, 1997.

  Tax relief is allowed each year for ten years on 5% of the construction cost in the case of a new premises and 10% in the case of a refurbished premises.

For example the construction costs of a new apartment selling for £90,000 might be about £60,000. The buyer is entitled to claim tax relief on 5% of that for ten years. So relief is allowed on £3,000 a year. At 24p in the pound the actual tax saving is £720.

That relief is in addition to any mortgage tax relief calculated on the basis outlined above.

Rent Relief

Since April 1995 it has been possible to claim tax relief on the rent paid for some accommodation. For some years previously those over 55 years of age were entitled to claim tax relief of up to £2,000 (married), £1,000 (single), or £1,500 (widowed) for rent paid on private accommodation. It is not available for rent paid on local authority houses or flats.

Since the 1995/96 tax year a similar relief is available to those under 55 years of age subject to the following maximum figures: £1,000 (married); £500 (single); or £750 (widowed) The relief is only granted at the standard rate of income tax. It is, of course, possible to backdate a claim — see chapter 14.

Wills

Inheritance, wills and probate

7.

MOST people experience an understandable reluctance about drawing up a will. It brings thoughts of death and few people like to think about dying. But the failure to make a will can cause many problems for dependents. It has also resulted in many bitter family feuds. Unless there is a properly drawn up will in existence, your property will be divided up, after your death, in accordance with the dictates of the 1965 Succession Act. Such a division may not be in keeping with your wishes and could cause major problems for your spouse. A little early planning can also reduce the amount your dependents may have to pay. That is particularly so if some of the beneficiaries are distant relatives or friends. But the Probate Tax, introduced in 1993, can hit even very small estates.

But the first concern is to ensure that your wishes are known. If there is no will, the law lays down how the estate is divided up. By making a will you ensure that your property passes to the people you choose — not to the people dictated in court according to the strict rule of law. There is the added advantage that you can appoint your own executor and the administration of the estate will be much easier.

A valid will can be made by anyone over eighteen years of age — or younger if he or she is married. It must be in writing. While a simple will can be drawn up at home, it is worthwhile getting a solicitor to oversee the task. The few pounds it costs can save a lot of trouble in the long run.

If you do decide to draw up your own will, remember to word it simply and clearly. Date it, sign it, and get your signature witnessed by two people. This means that you should sign it in their presence. They do not have to read the will. Neither of the witnesses should be a beneficiary under the will. It is normal to appoint an executor or executors to carry out your wishes under the will although it is not essential. The executor can be a beneficiary under the will although he, or she, need not be. For a simple will, where the main beneficiaries are members of the immediate family, it is common to name the principal beneficiary as executor. In most cases this is the husband or wife. If either are reaching old age and might find the task difficult, it is useful to name a co-executor — perhaps an elder child or the family solicitor.

The larger banks have special departments to deal with estate matters and will normally accept being named executor for wills. Solicitors and banks, of course, make charges for this service. It can be expensive and it is usual to provide for the charges in the will. For the person leaving his estate to fairly distant relatives, it may be as well to have an outside executor who can be above any family friction which might arise. But usually a member of the family — or a friend whom you trust — is the best choice. There is nothing to stop an executor hiring a solicitor to help in administering the will if he or she thinks it necessary.

The will should, of course, be lodged in a safe place, and be sure that the executor, and some other people know where it is lodged. This is particularly important for people whose families are widely spread. There are many wills lying in solicitors' offices throughout the country forgotten and, to all intents and purposes, lost. If you are a regular user of a bank, that is possibly the best place to have the will kept.

Once made, the will remains in force until a new will is made or the person who made it gets married. On marriage an existing will becomes void and a new one should be drawn up. Remember also to review your will from time to time. You may not want to change the provisions, but perhaps you need to change the executor.

> All married people should have a will drawn up. It costs little to have the job done correctly by a solicitor. Once made, the will should be reviewed from time to time.

Wives should also make wills

A point that is often forgotten is that wives should also make wills. It is often assumed that she will always have time to do so, if necessary, after her husband's death. Yet this can lead to problems in an unfortunate situation where both die together — in a car accident, for instance. It could happen in such a case that the husband dies first leaving his entire estate to his wife but that she then dies without having time to make a will. The

Where there is no will

Surviving Relatives	Distribution of estate where there is no will.
Spouse and children	Two-thirds to spouse, one third to children in equal shares with children of a deceased child getting their parent's share
Spouse, no children	Whole estate to spouse.
Children, no spouse	Whole estate to children in equal shares with children of a deceased child getting their parent's share.
Father, mother, brothers and/or sisters	One-half to each parent.
Parent, brothers and/or sisters	Whole estate to parent
Brothers and sisters	All get equal shares with children of deceased brothers and sisters getting their parent's share.
Nephews and nieces	All get equal shares.

estate would then be equally divided among the children — if there are any. That may be in accordance with their parent's wishes. But it equally might not, if one child, for instance, was still living at home and hoped to be left the house.

There is only one important restriction on the maker of a will. A spouse cannot be cut out of the estate. Irrespective of what the will says, the spouse is legally entitled to one-third of the estate where there are surviving children, and one-half of the estate where there are no children. Apart from that restriction, however, a person may dispose of his or her property as he or she thinks fit, although the courts can overturn the provisions of a will if, for instance, a child claims that he or she has not been adequately provided for.

In many cases family homes are jointly owned by both spouses but even where one spouse has formal ownership the other spouse, very often a non-wage earning wife, has certain rights

Rights to the family home

in the family home under existing legislation. They are not rights of ownership although in the case of a judicial separation or divorce, a court may order a transfer of property from one spouse to another. There are three pieces of legislation which provide rights in this area: the Family Home Protection Act; the Married Women's Status Act; and the Judicial Separation Act.

The Family Home Protection Act provides that both spouses must agree to the sale or mortgaging of the family home. But where the house is in just one name, the other spouse has no right to any proceeds from a sale unless he or she has made some financial contribution to the purchase of the house or the mortgage repayments.

There are also provisions protecting the rights of a spouse against whom a barring order is being sought. The first step in getting a barring order is to get a protection order. Where that has been obtained neither spouse can remove or dispose any household contents until a decision has been made on the barring order.

A spouse must also be given the opportunity to take over the mortgage repayments on the family home where his or her partner has defaulted on the payments. And the courts can make orders for the protection of a home where it can be shown that a spouse is indulging in some actions which could lead to the loss of the home.

Under the Married Women's Status Act the Courts can be asked to rule on the ownership of property, including a family home. But the Courts will only grant ownership rights to a spouse who can show that he or she made financial contributions to the purchase of the house or to other household costs. Work done in the home or in rearing children is not taken into account.

The courts have much wider powers of discretion under the judicial separation and divorce legislation. Where a couple have been granted either a judicial separation or a divorce the court can make orders requiring the transfer of property from one spouse to another. In this case it does not matter whether or not a spouse has made a financial contribution. The courts may also make maintenance orders. Such orders can be reviewed from time to time, but orders made with regard to property are permanent and the courts will only review them if it can be shown that the court was deliberately misled at the time the original order was made.

Both spouses have important rights to the family home even if they are not formally joint owners.

Wills and tax planning

Tax is another thing to consider when making a will. Inheritance taxes have been hitting a growing number of people. A wide range of concessions have been introduced in recent years to lessen the impact on business assets including farms. That has greatly reduced the potential liability of those with their own businesses. Traditionally this was the section of the community who worried most about the impact of the tax. But people who wouldn't necessarily perceive themselves as wealthy are now being caught by the tax. It is still not a major worry for people inheriting from parents or spouses but the tax can be onerous for the growing number of people inheriting from more distant relatives.

Details of Capital Acquisitions Tax (CAT) and Probate Tax are given in chapter 13 but broadly speaking a person can receive any amount from a spouse without tax liability while a child can receive up to £185,500 from a parent or grandparent before coming into the tax net. But the tax thresholds for gifts or inheritances from more distant levels are much lower and because of low marriage rates in the past, particularly in some rural areas, it is not uncommon for people to receive inheritances from sisters, brothers, uncles, aunts or cousins. The tax on such inheritances can be quite steep. But it can be reduced, or eliminated, with a little advance planning.

There is a section on tax planning for inheritances in chapter 14 on page 267.

Inheritance taxes can be avoided or reduced. It is worthwhile considering the options and getting advice.

The duties of executors

The person making a will — the testator — should always seek the consent of a person named in the will to act as executor. It is, of course, quite in order to name more than one person, but there is no obligation on the persons so named to act. A person who does not wish to accept an executorship may renounce it by signing a form of renunciation before a witness. It is usual to get a solicitor to oversee this operation. When this happens it can obviously create problems so it is essential to ensure that the executor named will act, and to review the will from time to time to ensure that this is still the case. As mentioned above, it is usual to name the principal beneficiary under the will as executor so a husband will name his wife and vice versa. If there are children over 18 years of age it can be a good idea to name one of these as a co-executor as a way of reducing the burden on the spouse. It is not necessary to name a solicitor, accountant, or bank as a further co-executor. Professional advice can be obtained after the death, if required.

An executor may benefit under a will but he is not entitled to any payment for his services unless it is specifically stated in the will that such payment should be made. The executor can, however, claim for expenses actually incurred in administering the will. If the person is not a beneficiary under the will provision for the payment of a fee should be made.

You don't need to hire a solicitor to take out probate on a will. You can do it yourself.

If it is decided to accept the executorship, the first move is normally to obtain a Grant of Probate from the courts. This will formally authorise the executor to collect the deceased's assets and carry out the provisions of the will. But the will itself is sufficient authorisation and even without a grant of probate the executor can immediately take charge of the deceased's assets and start to carry out the provisions of the will.

A listing of all the deceased's assets should be made and valuations obtained where necessary. It is also necessary to obtain details of any outstanding debts. Usually these are easily ascertained but, if they are not, the executor can protect himself against further claims by putting a notice in the daily newspaper asking all creditors to supply details of their claims by a certain date.

If a creditor has not made a claim by that date, he loses the right to pursue his claim against the executor although he can still proceed against the beneficiaries under the will. If the executor does not put the statutory notice in the newspaper, he may protect himself by getting the beneficiaries to give an agreement in writing to indemnify him against any claims which emerge after the distribution has taken place.

The Probate Office in the Four Courts, Dublin 7 (phone 01 8725555 ex 179) has a special application section for those who wish to take out probate themselves. Application for probate can be made there or to one of fourteen District Probate Registries. There is, in fact, no need to get a solicitor to do the job, particularly if it is a simple will. On request the probate office will send out an application form which should be completed as fully as possible and returned. The probate office will immediately acknowledge receipt of the form and will ask the applicant to call in for a preliminary meeting. At that stage the applicant should present full details of the estate, a death certificate and the original will, if there is a will. Statements of deposit accounts held by the deceased should be produced as well as details of assurance policies and all assets owned by the deceased. A second meeting will be arranged to finalise any outstanding matters and the applicant will then be required to sign the completed documents, swear to the truth and accuracy of their contents, and pay a fee.

In some cases it may take more than two meetings to finalise the matter but once probate has been granted, the executor will find it easier to transfer funds from bank accounts into his or her own name. It is best for the executor to open a separate bank account for this purpose. The executor has further duties in making returns to the taxman and settling any tax claims outstanding or arising as a result of the will. This includes making income, probate and inheritance tax returns. Because of the tax implications it may be necessary to get tax clearance before withdrawing money from bank or other saving accounts. The following are the rules:

Where there is a joint husband/wife account, a surviving spouse is not required to present a tax clearance no matter how large the estate but the financial institution may require sight of the death certificate and/or will depending on the type of account i.e. whether two signatures were needed for withdrawals.

Where an account has more than £5,000 in it and is in the deceased's sole name, or in the joint names of the deceased and someone other than a spouse, a tax clearance is needed but such a clearance is granted quickly by the Capital Taxes Branch, Revenue Commissioners, Dublin Castle. The financial institution may also have its own rules with regard to having sight of the will, death certificate or grant of probate. For more details on joint accounts see chapter 3.

If the executor is not the spouse of the deceased, he or she has to inform the spouse of their rights under the Succession Act, 1965. As outlined above these include the right to at least a third of the estate (if there are children) or a half (if there are no children), and the right to keep the house in which they are living, together with the household chattels, in satisfaction or part-satisfaction of his or her share. Records of all transactions should, of course, be kept as should the original will.

Tax clearance is not always needed to withdraw money from a deceased person's account.

Work rights

Your rights as an employee

8.

THE source of most family finance is wages and indeed most breadwinners spend almost a third of their lives on the job. Over recent years there has been a great deal of legislation giving workers minimum rights and protection in matters like redundancy, holidays, unfair dismissal, etc. The laws apply to full time and "regular part-time" workers who are defined as having been in continuous employment with the same employer for at least thirteen weeks and be normally required to work not less than eight hours a week.

Employers cannot avoid their obligations under this legislation by simply sacking part-timers after twelve weeks and then re-employing them after a suitable interval, or by employing them for only seven hours a week. Where re-employment takes place within 26 weeks of a worker being let go, or a worker is kept on less than eight hours a week just to avoid the provisions of the Act, the Employment Appeals Tribunal can decide that the worker is in fact covered.

Regular part-time workers have pro-rata rights with full time workers. After the minimum thirteen weeks they are entitled to a written statement of terms and conditions of employment and are protected against unfair dismissal arising wholly or mainly from pregnancy or trade union membership or activities. They are also entitled to claim arrears of pay from the insolvency fund administered by the Department of Labour if their employer becomes insolvent. They are entitled to 14 weeks unpaid maternity leave and time off for postnatal care with their jobs protected for that period. Having been in a job for a year they are covered for unfair dismissal on any basis and after two years are entitled to statutory redundancy payments if made redundant. Further details of these entitlements are given below.

New legislation which was enacted during 1997 but subsequently found to be unconstitutional in just one respect would have outlawed discrimination on the basis of age, race, or religion. It will undoubtedly be enacted again in a constitutional form in the not too distant future. Legislation restricting the number of hours worked and giving rights to minimum work breaks etc. did come into force during 1997. There's a summary of its provisions later in the chapter.

Some employers try to reduce their exposure to the employment protection laws by either contracting out work to self-employed workers, or by hiring employees under contracts which effectively prevent them acquiring their full range of rights. To qualify for most of employment rights, employees have to have a minimum amount of service. Workers may be prevented from building up the required service if they are hired on a contract basis for a fixed term or for a specific job. The distinction between such workers and employees may, in some cases, be very obvious but that's not always the case. There is plenty of room for dispute where there is no written contract.

People working on fixed term contracts maybe covered by some of the employment laws

Employers who require workers for specific periods or specific jobs may limit the period of employment by contract. The contract may specify either a fixed time period or may cover the completion of a specific job. Workers taken on under such contracts are employees but they may not qualify for rights under all of the employment protection Acts.

As a rule of thumb, however, the contract must be seen to have a purpose other than simply to allow the employer avoid unfair dismissal legislation. The Employment Appeals Tribunal has for long taken the view that a worker employed under a series of fixed term employment contracts extending over the required one year is covered by the Acts.

An amendment to the legislation introduced in 1993 specifically states that employers cannot avoid the Act by using fixed term contracts and that a break of less than three months between two consecutive contracts does not constitute a break in service. This may be true even for work of a seasonal nature. It may not be possible to prevent workers building up entitlements under the Unfair Dismissals and Redundancy Acts. The

Employment Appeals Tribunal has upheld claims for continuity of service by seasonal workers who showed a pattern of such work over a number of years.

A contract worker, however, is not normally covered under the unfair dismissals legislation unless he or she did work other than that specified in the contract of employment.

While workers in large firms with union representation can be fairly certain that their entitlements are not allowed to go by default, non-union workers particularly in smaller firms may find that their employers, either by accident or design, fail to give them their full entitlements.

The following gives a brief guide to the more important legislative provisions. Explanatory leaflets may be obtained from the Department of Enterprise, Trade and Employment, Conditions of Employment Section, Dublin 4. The Department also gives further assistance and advice. In the case of disputes arising you can seek redress through a Rights Commissioner who can be contacted through the Department.

The rights of part-time workers under these labour laws should not be confused with social welfare entitlements. Part-time workers earning more than £30 a week have some cover under the PRSI system — including unemployment, sickness benefits and old-age pensions. These are detailed in chapter 12.

Redundancy entitlements

Redundancy has been the fate of an increasing number of workers in recent years and will remain a fact of life for years to come. Under the redundancy payment scheme and the Protection of Employment Act, an employer is required to give at least thirty days notice to the Minister of Labour of any intention to make collective redundancies.

Workers are entitled to minimum notice and to minimum lump sum payments based on the number of years service with the firm. There is also provision for weekly pay-related benefits during a subsequent period of unemployment — these are on the same basis as normal unemployment pay-related benefits.

Who is covered? The scheme covers employees who are in employment which is insurable for all benefits under the Social Welfare Acts or who were in such employment in the four years prior to redundancy; are between the ages of sixteen and sixty-six; and who are normally expected to work for at least eight hours a week for the same employer. Domestic servants and agricultural workers — who are not relatives and who do not reside with their employers — are also covered.

An employee becomes eligible for redundancy pay if he has been employed by the same employer for at least two years after attaining sixteen years of age and is dismissed as redundant, laid off, or kept on short-time at less than fifty per cent of normal time for four consecutive weeks or a total of six weeks in a period of thirteen weeks.

The lump sum: The lump sum is calculated as follows. It is paid by the employer who is partially reimbursed by the State:

- A half weeks pay for each year of continuous service between ages sixteen and forty-one.

- One week's pay for each year of continuous service over the age of forty-one, and

- An additional amount of one week's pay.

- Income over £15,000 a year is disregarded in making the above calculation.

The number of years' service is calculated backwards from the date of dismissal with any remaining period of over twenty-six weeks regarded as a year. A period of under twenty-six weeks is disregarded. The same rule applies in working out the period over forty-one years of age.

As an example a worker earning £20,000 a year who had ten years service, five of them under the age of 41 would be entitled to eight and a half week's pay but the pay would only be calculated at the maximum rate of £300 a week i.e. £15,000 a year. That works out at only £2,550 — not a lot after ten years service. That would be tax free but tax may be payable on any additional lump sum given by an employer.

You can reduce the tax on a lump sum by choosing the right option.

Tax and the lump sum: The taxation on redundancy lump sums can be quite heavy. As mentioned above the statutory redundancy payment is not liable for tax. On top of that at least the first £6,000 of any other redundancy payment is also tax free. Refunds of pension contributions are separately taxed at 25% but are not included in any other tax calculation.

Many workers get payments over and above the statutory amount and at least the first £6,000 of such payments is also tax free. That £6,000 is increased by £500 for each full year of service. That's the minimum entitlement. The calculation of the actual exemption starts off at £10,000, plus £500 for each full year of service. The £10,000 figure is reduced by the amount of any other tax-free payments received or credited. That does not include refunds of pension contributions but it does include tax free lump sums from pension schemes. And it also includes a valuation put on any deferred payment from a pension scheme. In no case is the £10,000 reduced below £6,000.

In some cases — particularly when there has been long service — it is possible to get more than £10,000 tax free. The taxpayer has the option of calculating the tax free lump sum on the following basis known as the Standard Capital Superannuation Benefit. For workers with long service it is likely to yield a much higher tax-free figure than the normal £10,000. The calculation is done as follows:

$$\text{I} \times \frac{\text{N}}{15} \quad \text{minus} \quad \text{P} \qquad \text{where}$$

- **I** is average salary over the past three years
- **N** is the number of years service; and
- **P** is any tax-free lump sum paid, or due, from a pension scheme.

To see how these calculations might work, let us first take the case of a man who is made redundant and leaves his pension contributions in the scheme as he is required to do. He has a right to a tax-free lump sum and a pension when he reaches retirement age.

A valuation is put on that lump sum taking account of the amount that will be paid out and the number of years to go before it is paid.

For the sake of the example we can suppose that it is valued at £3,500. The basic tax exemption on the redundancy lump sum of £10,000 is reduced by that £3,500 to £6,500. If the value of the pension lump sum was £4,500, the exemption would only be reduced by £4,000 since in no case is it reduced below £6,000.

As mentioned above some people with long service may be able to get more than stated maximum of £10,000 plus £500 per year of service tax free. The formula given above may be stated

Workers with long service can get more of a lump sum tax free by opting for the Standard Capital Superannuation Benefit calculation.

as follows: Take the average annual earnings over the last three years and multiply by the number of year's service. Dividing that figure by 15 gives the maximum tax-free lump sum including any payment from a pension scheme.

Taking an example — suppose your average earnings over the last three years works out at £18,000 and you have thirty years service. The calculation would work out as follows: £18,000 multiplied by 30 gives £540,000 and dividing that by 15 gives £36,000. So in this case the tax-free lump sum including redundancy payments and pension lump sum benefits works out well above the normal maximum of £10,000. And on top of the £36,000 the person involved also gets his statutory redundancy payments tax free. Before taxing a lump sum on this basis an employer must get approval from the Revenue Commissioners.

You can have your average tax rate over the past five years applied to any taxable lump sum.

The tax on any remaining taxable lump sum can be worked out in two possible ways — the choice is up to the tax payer. Initially, in any case, any remaining taxable lump sum, after deducting the tax free element, is treated as income in the year in which it is received and taxed as such. This might be advantageous to someone being made redundant early in the tax year who does not expect to work during the rest of that year but the other alternative is usually better.

Under the second alternative, tax is levied at the average rate you paid over the last five tax years. To work this out you take your taxable income for the five years. It is important to stress that it is your taxable income you take — that is gross income less tax allowances. You take that figure and divide by the actual tax paid. And that gives you the tax rate. A claim to have this average tax rate applied must be made to your tax office and if a refund is payable you normally have to wait until the end of the tax-year.

Tax in all these cases involves the various income levies where they are applicable.

A person who is laid off work because of a permanent disability can receive a lump sum entirely tax-free.

Repayments from pension funds are taxed at a flat rate of 25% but if the payment takes the form of a lump sum pension payment — rather than simply a refund of contributions — a tax free payment of up to $1\frac{1}{2}$ times final salary is possible. But relatively few pension schemes provide for such payments except perhaps in cases of disability. Twenty years service would be required to qualify for a tax free lump sum of $1\frac{1}{2}$ times salary from such a scheme.

Holiday entitlement

Legal entitlement to paid holidays was provided for in the Holiday (Employees) Act, 1973, which covered most wage earners. Those not covered include outworkers, seafarers, lighthouse and lightship employees, fishermen, most State officials, or employees who are relatives of the employer, maintained by him and living in his house or on his farm. The basic entitlement has been increased to three weeks and one day for 1997/98 and will be increased to three weeks and three days for 1998/99 and to four weeks in 1999/2000.

There is pro-rata entitlement for periods of employment of less than a year. The Act also provides for entitlements in respect of public holidays. For the purpose of the Act a "leave year" means a year beginning on April 1.

For the 1997/98 leave year ending in March 31, 1998 minimum holiday entitlement is calculated in one of the following three ways:

- Three working weeks and one day where the employee has worked at least 1,365 hours — this method is not used where a worker changes jobs during the leave year.

- Four fifteenths of a working week per calendar month in which the employee has worked at least 117 hours.

- Where an employee leaves a job during the holiday year he or she is entitled to 6.4 hours leave for every hundred hours worked subject to a maximum of three weeks and one day.

These are, of course, minimum entitlements. Many workers get more paid holidays by agreement.

For the 1998/99 leave year the minimum entitlements will work out as follows:

- Three working weeks and three days where the employee has worked at least 1,365 hours — this method is not used where a worker changes jobs during the leave year.

- Three-tenths of a working week per calendar month in which the employee has worked at least 117 hours.

- Where an employee leaves a job during the holiday year he or she will be entitled to 7.2 hours leave for every hundred hours worked subject to a maximum of three weeks and one day.

Regular part-time workers who work for more than eight hours a week and have been in continuous employment for at least thirteen weeks are entitled to paid leave on the basis of the relevant number of hours per hundred hours worked.

Some further points on this entitlement:

- If an employee on leave sends in a medical certificate stating that he or she is ill, the time covered by the certificate is not considered as leave.

- If board and/or lodgings is part of a workers remuneration, his holiday pay must include compensation for the loss of these during his annual leave.

- The employer determines when annual leave should be taken but he must give at least one month's notice to the employee or his trade union and the leave must be given either during the leave year or within six months after it ends.

Anyone who has worked 120 hours in the five weeks prior to a public holiday is entitled to be paid for the public holiday. Regular part-time workers are entitled to a paid public holiday if they work for the employer for at least four of the five weeks before the public holiday.

There are nine public holidays: New Year's Day; St. Patrick's Day; Easter Monday; First Monday in May; First Monday in June; First Monday in August; Last Monday in October; Christmas Day; and St. Stephen's Day.

Working hours

The Organisation of Working Time Act which was passed into law during 1997 begins to take effect from March 1, 1998. Subject to a wide range of exceptions the maximum working week is being reduced to 48 hours from the year 2000. From March 1 1998 the maximum is 60 hours reduced to 55 hours on March 1, 1999. The act doesn't apply to members of the defence forces and the garda siochana, junior hospital doctors, transport employees, those working at sea, workers who control their own working hours, or family members working on a farm or in a private house.

The maximum working week may be averaged over twelve months where workers enter into a collective agreement approved by the Labour Court. In the case of seasonal workers it can be averaged over six months. In all other cases it can be averaged over four months.

From March 1, 1998 every worker is entitled to:

- An 11 hour rest period in every 24 hours.

- One period of 24 hours rest per week preceded by a daily rest period i.e. A total of 35 hours.

- Rest breaks of 15 minutes where up to four and a half hours have been worked or 30 minutes where up to six hours have been worked.

Night workers are defined as those who normally work at least three hours between midnight and 7 am the following day and who during the year work at least half of their hours during the night period.

The 48 hour maximum working week comes into effect for night workers from March 1, 1998. The hours are normally averaged over two months but may be averaged over a longer period laid down in a collective agreement approved by the Labour Court.

For night workers whose jobs involve special hazards or heavy physical or mental strain an absolute limit of eight hours in a 24 hour period applies.

Working time is net of breaks, on call or standby time.

Sunday work

Workers who don't already get special compensation for Sunday work are entitled to a Sunday premium equivalent to that applying to similar workers elsewhere. The premium payable-should be based on the closest applicable collective agreement which applies in similar employment.

Zero hours on-call

Where a worker is requested to be available for work he or she is entitled to be paid for at least a quarter of the on-call hours even if not called upon to work subject to a payment for a maximum of fifteen hours.

So if a worker is required to be available for 48 hours a week, he or she is entitled to a minimum payment for twelve hours even if not required to work at all.

Unfair dismissal

The Unfair Dismissals Act, 1977, is aimed at protecting workers from being unfairly sacked by laying down criteria of what is unfair dismissal and providing an adjudication system for redressing such action. The Act applies to most workers who work for more than eight hours a week and who have at least a year's continuous service with the same employer. It does not cover those who have passed retiring age or those excluded from the redundancy payments scheme because of age. Neither does it cover people working for a close relative and living in the same house or farm; members of the defence forces and gardaí; FÁS trainees; apprentices; or most State and local authority employees.

Normally it is up to the employer to prove that a dismissal is fair and justified on the basis of the capability, competence, or qualification of the worker for the work he was employed to do; conduct; redundancy; or the fact that continuation of employment would contravene another statutory requirement. Dismissals are deemed to be definitely unfair if it is shown that they result from the worker's trade union membership or activities outside working hours or within working hours if normally permitted by the employer; race; religion; politics; pregnancy, or unfair selection for redundancy.

A woman who believes she was dismissed because of pregnancy may bring a claim against the employer even if she has not had a year's continuous service although a regular part-time worker must have worked for at least thirteen weeks.

To take action against unfair dismissal, the worker should seek redress within six months. This may be done by contacting a Rights Commissioner, through the Department of Labour, phone (01) 6765861, or by writing to the Employment Appeals Tribunal, Davitt House, Dublin 4. Where it is decided that the dismissal is unfair, the Commissioner or Tribunal can order any of the following: reinstatement in the old job; re-engagement in the old job, or in a suitable alternative; or financial compensation up to a maximum of two years pay.

An alternative action may be taken in cases of unfair dismissal due to sex discrimination. In this case the claim is made to an Equality Officer with the right to subsequently appeal his or her ruling to the Labour Court.

Minimum notice

Any worker who has completed at least thirteen weeks continuous employment with the one employer is entitled to receive minimum notice of dismissal. The notice depends on the length of service as outlined in the table below. An employee who has worked for over thirteen weeks is required to give at least one week's notice of leaving the job to his employer.

Minimum notice entitlement

13 weeks to two years	one week
Two to five years	two weeks
Five to ten years	four weeks
Ten to fifteen years	six weeks
Over fifteen years	eight weeks

Equality rights

The new law that was enacted in 1997, but subsequently found to be unconstitutional, would have extended the provisions of the 1977 Employment Equality Act to cover discrimination on the grounds of age, race or religion. Despite its grand sounding name that 1977 Act was in fact very limited since it only outlawed discrimination on the grounds of sex. That was later taken to include discrimination on the grounds of marital or family status but it offered no protection against discrimination on the grounds of race, age, or religion.

Dismissal on the ground of race or religion would be deemed unfair under the 1977 Unfair Dismissals Act but it wasn't until 1993 that this protection was extended to cover dismissals on the grounds of age or membership of the travelling community.

But dismissal is only one aspect of discrimination. Of greater importance to most people is the ability to get a job, and there is no doubt that there is widespread discrimination against individual job seekers on the basis of age. Just as the 1977 Act made it illegal to specify gender conditions in employment ads, the new laws would have made it illegal to specify age conditions. More importantly, of course, it would make the application of such conditions illegal.

It may not be all that easy to prove that an employer has discriminated on the basis of age. But employers might find it difficult to prove otherwise. The legislation will undoubtedly be enacted again. Hopefully the Employment Equality Agency will be gearing up for a great increase in its workload of advising potential claimants.

Insurance

Your guide to home insurance

9.

PROTECTING your assets involves more than simply picking the right investment. Fire, burglary, accident, or even storm damage can, and does, result in substantial losses every day of the week. It is up to the individual to decide whether he wants to bear the full risk of such losses himself or spread it around by taking out insurance. For this is what insurance does — spreads the risk. A large number of people pay a small premium so that the few who actually suffer loss can be reimbursed. And that someone could be you.

The cost of house insurance has risen dramatically in recent years and for a while it was even difficult to get insurance. But there is a fair element of competition in the market and it is worth shopping around. It is worth taking some time to see if you are getting the best deal — a good broker will do the comparisons for you, but there are policies not available through brokers. Some building societies, for instance, are doing special group deals with insurance companies which can be very competitive. But remember that what is cheap one year may not be so the next. So take the time to shop around each year — particularly if your premium goes up sharply.

Most people are prepared to take some risk of loss, but there are risks just not worth taking. The family house is usually the most valuable asset owned and its loss through fire could have financial repercussions extending over a lifetime. For a small insurance premium that risk can be removed.

The most important thing to remember is that you are not fully covered unless you insure for the full value of the assets. In almost all cases, an "average clause" will apply. This average clause causes many misunderstandings and problems, so it is as

Valuing your house for insurance

The Society of Chartered Surveyors, 5, Wilton Place, Dublin, 2 issues annual guidelines for valuing houses for insurance purposes. Copies are free on request but please enclose a stamped address envelope. The following is a summary of their 1997 figures. They are designed to cover rebuilding costs.

House type		Dublin	Cork	Galway
Terraced —	2 bedroom 750 sq. ft.	£66.50 sq. ft.	£60.00 sq. ft.	£60.00 sq. ft.
	3 bedroom 1,023 sq. ft.	£62.00 sq. ft.	£56.50 sq. ft.	£56.00 sq. ft.
Semi —	3 bedroom 1,023 sq. ft.	£62.75 sq. ft.	£57.25 sq. ft.	£57.00 sq. ft.
	4 bedroom 1,270 sq. ft.	£59.50 sq. ft.	£53.25 sq. ft.	£53.00 sq. ft.
Detached —	4 bedroom 1,270 sq. ft.	£60.50 sq. ft.	£55.00 sq. ft.	£55.00 sq. ft.
Bungalow —	4 bedrooms 1,572 sq. ft.	£60.25 sq. ft.	£55.50 sq. ft.	£54.75 sq. ft.
Garage: Single garage £5,000, double garage £9,000.				

well to understand what it is about. It can best be explained by a simple example. Suppose your house is worth £60,000, but you only have it insured for £30,000. If your house was completely destroyed, you would only expect to get £30,000 from the insurance company — so you are only half insured. But suppose your house is only damaged. If the damage is estimated at, say, £20,000 then the insurance company will still consider that you are only half insured and pay out £10,000 — half of the £20,000 damage.

You should reassess your insurance needs at each renewal and increase your valuation if appropriate

This quite simply is what the average clause is about. The insurance company will only pay out, on a claim, a proportion of the loss equal to the proportion the sum insured bears to the real value of the assets covered. If the sum insured is equal to only two-thirds or a half of the true value of the asset, the insurance company will only pay out two-thirds or a half of any loss incurred.

Because of the average clause it is important to reassess your insurance needs each year as you renew your policies. Remember that building costs may rise slower or faster than house prices. Market value is not necessarily a good guide to rebuilding cost. Most policies index your house value automatically to a costs index published by the Department of the Environment. If you have not got an index-linked policy, and want to be fully covered, it is absolutely necessary to increase your insurance premium each year.

There are four general areas of risk which the average householder should consider covering by insurance. These are:

- Damage or loss of the house itself.
- Damage or loss of contents — furniture, etc..
- Liability for damage to third parties arising out of defects in the building.
- All risks insurance for specific items, i.e. jewellery, etc.

Very often all four types of risk can be covered by the one general policy, although individual policies covering any one type can be taken out.

The house itself

For the sake of the relatively small premium involved it is not worth taking the risk of not insuring your house. If the house is rented, check whether or not you are liable for insuring it. With a short lease you possibly are not. With a long lease you may be. If you are buying a house with a mortgage, the building society will require you to insure the house and in some cases will have done it for you. But usually the requirement is that the house be insured only for the initial purchase price. Remember the building society is only concerned with protecting its loan to you. So even if you are paying the insurance premium through the building society — along with your mortgage repayments — it is up to you to ensure that the insurance cover is updated to reflect the rising value of the house.

The cost of insuring a house is about 15p or 16p for every £100 valuation. So the insurance on a house valued at £60,000 would be about £90 a year — a relatively small sum for the peace of mind such an insurance provides. Remember it insures you against a possible loss of £60,000. But the amount of cover you get depends on the policy. What some companies include as standard, others charge extra for.

The usual policy will cover damage to the house itself, the garage and certain outbuildings, together with walls, gates and fences. It may also cover damage to fixtures and fittings such as wash-basins, toilets, pipes and water tanks. Most policies cover loss or damage caused by:

Fire, explosion, lightning, thunderbolt, falling aircraft or other aerial devices: They exclude damage caused by supersonic bangs.

Storm damage: In many cases damage caused by flood, frost, subsidence or landslide are not covered. Neither is storm damage to fences and gates or damage to radio or television aerials. It is not unusual for some small part of any storm damage to be excluded from cover, although this can be waived on the payment of a small additional premium. Damage to radio and television aerials may also be covered.

Read the proposal form and the policy carefully to discover just what's covered and what's not.

Burglary, housebreaking or any attempt there at: The buildings policy simply covers damage to the house itself - not the contents. The cover does not apply if the house is left unfurnished, or, even if furnished, is left uninhabited for more than a set period at a time or in any one year. If you are leaving your house vacant it is best to check with the insurance company to ensure that you are covered. If you are leaving it unfurnished you will have to take out a special policy.

Bursting or overflowing of water tanks or pipes: Again it is usual to exclude some small part of any claim under this heading — the first £20 say — and the conditions on leaving the house vacant are the same as above. These small uncovered sums are aimed at saving the insurance companies a lot of administrative expense in dealing with small claims. It is usually not worthwhile paying the extra premium to have them waived. The extra premium is relatively expensive.

Impact: Damage caused by impact with the buildings, walls, gates, fences of any road vehicle, horses or cattle not belonging to or under the control of yourself or your family.

Loss of rent: If the house is left uninhabitable you are usually covered in this regard up to a set percentage of the sum insured on the building — often 10%.

Liability to Public: If you are proved liable for damages caused to another person by an accident which occurred on your property, the normal building policy will provide cover up to about £500,000.

It is possible to extend the normal policy to cover damage to underground water pipes running between your house and the boundary of your land, damage to radio and television aerials, breakage of glass, etc. It is too late finding out what is and is not covered when an accident occurs. So when you are taking out insurance you should read the proposal form carefully to see what risks are excluded and decide whether or not you want extra cover. And have a fresh look at the policy each year when the premium falls due. Circumstances change. It is a good idea, indeed, to look at all your insurance policies at least once a year, preferably long before the renewal date so that you give yourself ample time to shop around for a better deal.

House contents

The cost of house contents insurance has doubled in urban areas during the last few years and now costs anything between about 35p and 90p per £100 of value. The cost depends on where the house is, the company providing the cover and the type of cover given. There are discounts for having alarms,where the occupants are over a certain age, for agreeing to carry the first portion of any claim yourself, for being in a neighbourhood watch scheme, and even, in some cases, a no claims discount. But not all companies offer all of those discounts.

One of the main reasons for the increased cost of house insurance is the increased risk of loss. So can you afford not to be insured or to underestimate the value of your house contents. Most people do underestimate. If the contents of your house are not insured, you may be running a serious risk of loss — tot up the value of the contents of your kitchen for instance. Could you afford to replace them yourself? If it would impose an undue burden, then you would do well to be insured.

Do not assume that you are insured just because the building society looks after your insurance. It is normally only interested in having the buildings insured. Insuring the contents is generally left up to yourself. The normal contents policy covers loss arising from the same causes as the building policy considered before. Extras which may be included as standard in some policies include:

Don't assume that your building society insurance provides adequate cover.

Breakage of mirrors: only while in the house and not including hand mirrors.

Tenant's liability to landlord: Useful if you are in a rented house, this clause provides cover for damage caused to fittings, etc., for which the tenant may have to reimburse the landlord.

Employer's liability for claims by domestic staff: This covers not only full-time domestic staff but also tradesmen, etc., who may be doing repairs about the house.

Liability to third parties: This provides cover for claims arising from accidents occurring in or about the house to visitors or their property.

Death of the householder: Only if caused by someone breaking into the house or else as a result of a fire. The cover is usually for a relatively small amount.

Most policies also include provision for replacing items on a new for old basis provided it is not more than (usually) five years old. Suppose, for instance, your cooker gets burnt it will be replaced with a new cooker of the same type. Some companies, however, only provide this as an extra, so check.

There can be some important exclusions which need to be borne in mind. There may only be limited cover for loss or damage to articles temporarily removed from the house. Usually if the value of any one article — a piece of jewellery for instance — is more than 5 per cent of the total sum insured, a special policy will be required. Cash and bank notes are often only covered to a maximum of 5 per cent of the total value insured. But there may be an even more onerous money limit, as low as £25. Usually the following items are not covered at all: deeds, bonds, bills of exchange, promissory notes, cheques, securities for money, stamps, documents of any kind, manuscripts, medals, coins, motor vehicles and accessories, and livestock (other than horses).

Personal liability

Most buildings and contents insurance policies provide cover up to perhaps £500,000 against claims arising from accidents to third parties in or about the house. This is adequate to cover most eventualities, but you may consider it worthwhile to extend the cover to provide for the possibility that you, or a member of the family, will be found liable for damage outside the house. Such policies provide for claims of personal negligence for events occurring outside of business activities or motor driving — an injured golf caddie for instance. It should be possible to get cover of up to £100,000 for an annual premium as low as £1.

All risks

As mentioned above, the normal policy on house contents does not provide cover for articles whose value represents more than 5 per cent of the total sum insured. So if you have a valuable piece of jewellery, a camera or a painting, you may find that you are not covered for its loss. If you have such valuable items, an all-risks policy is worth having. Usually a valuation certificate is required for each article worth more than £100. Rates vary considerably and range upwards of £1 a year for every £100 insured - a lot more for bicycles. Some insurance companies have a minimum premium as high as £10 a year.

Pensions

Pensions - plan for retirement 10.

LESS than half of the work force — about 550,000 people — are in company or industry pension schemes in Ireland and the percentage is much smaller in some sectors. Only 19% of the 125,400 at work in the distribution sector, for instance, are in a company scheme. The majority of self-employed workers don't make any pension provision for themselves either. Only about 12% of farmers and 39% of the self-employed outside farming have pension schemes.

While many workers have some pension cover through a spouse's scheme it is clear that a very big proportion are building up no pension rights other than the basic social welfare entitlements. People seem to have a blind spot with regard to pensions preferring not to think too much about the long-term future, post-retirement. Even those in pension schemes very often pay scant attention to them, although for many years now they have been entitled to elect trustees to their schemes and have access to a wide range of detailed information.

But no law can fully protect pension scheme members. They must make use of the safeguards, keep themselves informed, and also ensure that their scheme is adequate to their needs. The law does not impose any minimum levels of benefits. So the existance of protection legislation does not provide an excuse for forgetting about your pension entitlements or lack of them. Since January 1994, pension scheme members have had the right to elect at least two of the scheme's trustees. That's an important right which should be fully utilised and members should ensure that the trustees elected take the job seriously.

On an individual basis there is a clear need to think about retirement from an early age and to ensure that provision is being

Rights under the Pensions Act

The Pensions Act which came into force in 1991 gave scheme members important rights including the right to elect trustees after January 1, 1994. The following is a brief summary of the main provisions of the Act.

Preserved pensions:

A pension fund member with over five years qualifying service, at least two of which are after January 1, 1991, is entitled to a preserved pension if he leaves the job. The value of that pension will be based on entitlements built up since January 1991 and will be revalued each year. The value will go up by the rate of inflation or 4% a year whichever is the lower figure.

The law says nothing about contributions made prior to January 1, 1991. So failing any agreement to the contrary between worker and employer they will continue to be treated as they were in the past according to the rules of the scheme. With most schemes that means that a worker who is changing jobs and who has been five years in his company's pension scheme is entitled to a refund of the contributions he made prior to January 1, 1991 plus a preserved (deferred) pension which rises in line with inflation up to at most 4% a year. The preserved pension may be transferred into a new pension scheme or into an approved pension bond.

Information entitlements:

Members of pension schemes are entitled to the following information: basic information about the scheme's benefits, contributions etc.; copies of the trust deed and rules of the scheme; an annual statement showing the individual's current entitlements; an annual report giving audited accounts, an actuarial valuation of the scheme, and an investment report. Some of that information must be given automatically to members, prospective members and their trade unions. All of it must be available at least on request. Actuarial reports are not needed for defined contribution schemes.

Adequate funding

Annual actuarial funding certificates have to be submitted each year to The Pensions Board. That certificate must show that the contributions being made are enough to cover the entitlements being built up from January 1, 1991 onwards. Any shortfall in respect of prior years has to be outlined but the funds have until the year 2001 to make it up.

Trustees:

Members in schemes covering more than fifty people are entitled to elect at least two of the scheme's trustees. At least 15% of members or a trade union must request that right.

Pension Board:

The Pensions Board can be contacted at Holbrook House, Holles Street, Dublin, 2. Phone (01) 6762622 made for those years in so far as it is possible. Social welfare will provide a floor but the benefits from a company or private pension scheme can mean the difference between hand to mouth existence and a fuller life. The average person retiring at age 65 will live another 15 years and, of course, the tendency is for people to retire earlier.

Securing an adequate pension doesn't come cheap. It has been estimated that a man would need to invest 15% of his income into a pension fund from the age of twenty in order to fund a civil service type pension at age 65. If he wanted to retire at 60 he'd need to invest 19% of his income each year and he'd need to invest 23% of income if he wanted to start drawing his pension at age 55. A woman would need to invest more since women, on average live longer than men.

Retirement is a major watershed in life and most of the financial decisions made during your working years should be made with at least half an eye on those later years. There is no need to become paranoid about it, but the post-retirement years should be kept in mind from very early on in one's working life. Individual circumstances obviously differ a great deal. For many, job-linked pension schemes will prove adequate. For others — such as the self-employed, including farmers — there may be a hope that the future will take care of itself. In this chapter we will just look at some of the questions which you should be asking yourself.

For those in pension schemes

Pension schemes are normally imposed on employees by their employers and all too often the provisions are not examined too closely. Trade unionists are, thankfully, beginning to wake up to the inadequacies of some pension schemes, and there are signs that a more questioning attitude is asserting itself. In some cases trade unions or staff associations have their own experts — or else have access to experts — who can ensure that every worker knows what his or her entitlements are, and — perhaps more importantly — what the shortcomings may be.

Most company pension schemes are of the "defined benefit" scheme. The level of benefit is laid out in the rules — for instance, one-sixtieth of final salary for every year of service. Usually the workers' contributions are fixed while the employer's contribution is open ended. The employer puts in whatever else is necessary to ensure that the promised benefits are paid. The new legislation requires employers to show each year that they are adequately funding the scheme. There are also "defined contribution" schemes where both worker and employer contributions are fixed — say as a percentage of payroll. Pensions are determined by what those invested contributions will buy when the worker retires. So the pension level is not guaranteed and the employer is not faced with an open-ended commitment as in the case of a "defined benefit" scheme. With the new legislation forcing them to adequately fund their schemes each year, employers now have a great incentive to switch to defined benefit schemes.

Few company pension schemes provide the maximum possible benefits so they are open to improvement.

In both cases the Revenue Commissioners set maximum pension levels which may be provided by schemes if they are to qualify for tax relief on contributions. With defined contribution schemes they estimate the likely level of benefit which the fixed contributions will provide given assumptions about investment returns etc. The Revenue Commissioners' maximum pension levels are more than generous. The pension may be equal to two-thirds of final salary index-linked after inflation. There may also be provision for widow's and dependant's pensions. One and a half times final salary may usually be taken as a tax-free lump sum on retirement — it is less for people with very short service. The two-thirds pension may be in addition to a social welfare pension.

So how far does your pension scheme fall short of those maximum benefit levels? With a defined contribution scheme you have to not only look at the forecast pension level but also at the assumptions on which those forecasts are based. The following are some of the more pertinent questions which should be asked:

- **Will the pension provided be adequate?** Normally schemes provide one-sixtieth of final salary for each year of service up to a maximum of two-thirds of final salary. Some schemes give one-eightieth and provide for a maximum pension of one-half of final salary. Very often there is a reduction in those levels to take account of a social welfare pension. It is up to the individual to decide what is adequate.

- **Is there provision for increases in the pension to allow for inflation after retirement?** Too few pension schemes provide for inflation. The cost of such a provision is high - contributions would have to be increased by about one-fifth to allow for an annual increase of two and a half per cent in the pension. But it's better to pay now to make some provision for inflation than to see your fixed pension dwindle in value as the years go by. There is little that can be done at that late stage.

- **Is there provision for a widow's or widower's pension should the pensioner die?** Again too often pensions die with the pensioner and no provision is made for widows or widowers. It is true that a pensioner can often provide for such an eventuality by surrendering part of his own pension on retirement. But this can be costly. Assuming both husband and wife are 65 years of age, the husband might have to accept a reduction of a pound a week in his pension in order to provide his widow with a pension of £2 a week after his death. If she were five years older than he, the reduction of £1 would buy her a pension of about £2.50 — again, of course, only payable after his death.

But it's hard to decide to give up part of your pension when you retire to provide for an eventuality that you hope will never happen. Most people turn the hope into a belief and do nothing. But the worst sometimes happens. The message is that it's better to have the provision for widows and widowers built into a scheme from the start.

- **Are the pension rights transferable from one job to another?** This is only a problem with contributions made prior to 1991 when the new pension legislation came into operation. Unfortunately the new law does not apply to past contributions. So there is still a problem. In respect of those old contributions, most pension schemes only provide two options for a worker changing jobs. He can take a return of his own contributions less 25% tax but, if he does, he loses out on the return made on that money over the years and on the contributions made by the employer. Alternatively, he can opt for a deferred pension based on present salary levels and service to be paid when he is 65 years of age. But unless he is close to 65, he loses out badly.

Getting an employer to pay more into the pension scheme can be better than a pay rise since the contributions go into the fund tax-free.

While the new laws give workers a better deal in respect of contributions made after January 1, 1991, it does nothing to change the situation in respect of earlier years. But it is possible for trustees to change the rules to provide similar flexibility in respect of those earlier contributions.

- **Is there any provision for a continuation of salary in the event of long-term disability?** This is another feature missing from many pension schemes. While it is not directly connected with retirement, it is something worth looking for in order to provide some insurance against the imposition of an early retirement because of some disability.

The next step is to decide whether or not your pension scheme is adequate for your needs. If not, you may be able to do something about it. There are, in fact, a wide range of options from getting the scheme improved to setting up your own scheme.

Pension scheme inadequate?

Having got the answers to each of those questions above you can then decide what to do about it. It is no harm to also have a check on the funding of the scheme. Under the new laws both annual reports and less frequent actuarial reports will have to be made available to members. The better fund managers and trustees have been doing this for years. Both types of report are worth looking at. Annual reports show flows of cash in and out of the fund and the value of its investments. They are strictly factual. Actuarial reports go further and try to calculate whether sufficient contributions are being made to meet the likely future liabilities of the fund. The actuary will make assumptions about the future: trends in wages, retirements, investment returns etc. His report may need expert analysis — a deficit, for instance, may not be something to be unduly concerned about if it arose because of recent improvements to the scheme or because the scheme is relatively young and, of course, provided steps are being taken to eliminate it.

Having got the relevant information it is up to you to decide whether your potential pension is going to be adequate or not. It is very much a personal decision.

If it is not, you are faced with two obvious options:

- You can campaign for an improvement in your company pension scheme, or

- You can start saving to ensure a better income for yourself when you retire.

Let us have a look at both of those in turn.

Improving company schemes

If the company pension scheme does not provide the maximum benefits allowed by the Revenue rules, it is possible to get an improvement and still have the contributions allowed for tax relief. But getting extra benefits obviously imposes an additional cost and that cost will have to be borne either by the employee or the employer. There may be circumstances where a pension fund is in surplus and additional pension rights could be given without any increase in the contributions. But usually companies use such surpluses either to reduce their own contributions to the fund or else pay *ad hoc* increases to those already out on pension. In every case, the provision of extra benefits costs someone money. It involves paying more into the fund than would otherwise be the case.

In many cases employees took a very short-sighted approach when the social welfare scheme was extended under PRSI to practically all private sector employees. Instead of continuing to contribute at the old rate into the company pension scheme, they accepted a reduction in the company scheme as an offset against the new social welfare entitlement. Instead of a possible two-thirds pension from the company scheme PLUS a social welfare pension they accepted that the company pension would be reduced by the amount of any social welfare pension. As a result they saved money — their contributions to the company pension scheme were reduced. But the company usually cut its contributions too, so the employees actually lost out. And even the savings they made in their own contributions were not all that large since they had, of course, been getting full tax relief on every penny they put into the pension scheme.

So for every 76p saved by a worker on the standard tax rate of 24p, there was a full £1 less going into the fund on his behalf and possibly another £1 less going in from the company side. For a saving of 76p, he or she was losing perhaps £2 worth of pension benefits. The situation was even worse for those paying tax at higher rates. This highlights one area where action could be taken to try and improve pension entitlements. Anyone who did accept that type of deal when PRSI came in for non-manual workers might now try to reverse the decision and go back to getting an increased pension entitlement.

There is no reason, except cost, why a scheme should not provide a full pension of two-thirds final pay available after thirty years service.

An examination of the maximum benefits allowed by the Revenue rules will highlight other areas in which improved pension benefits might be sought. At the present time, the indexation of pensions may be considered less important than it was in the past but it may also be less costly to fund — there are number of investments at present which can guarantee a return far above the rate of inflation.

But there are other areas to look out for:

- Widows' pensions — does your scheme provide such pensions automatically or is it necessary to accept a reduced pension in order to ensure that provision is made for a surviving spouse?

- Does the scheme provide for a pension of two-thirds of final salary, not including the social welfare pension?

- How many years service are necessary to qualify for a full pension? Many schemes provide for one-sixtieth of final pay for each year of service up to a maximum of forty-sixtieths (two-thirds). There is no reason, except cost, why a scheme should not provide a full pension of two-thirds final pay available after thirty years service (thirty forty-fifths).

- Are you allowed to work on beyond retirement age if that will enable you to increase your pension i.e. because of an impending pay increase?

Check list of possible pension scheme improvements.

- What is "final remuneration" under the scheme? Is it an average of the few final years or the actual final year or can the retiring person opt to take the most favourable of the last few years. The difference can be significant in terms of pension entitlement.

- Are the death-in-service benefits up to the maximum allowed?

- Is there an income continuance scheme included?

These are all areas where improvements might usefully be sought. If they can be campaigned for on a joint basis through trade union negotiations, then well and good. But if that is not possible, there is usually provision for individuals to buy extra benefits in the pension scheme by making their own voluntary contributions.

Voluntary contributions (AVCs)

Most pension schemes allow members to make additional voluntary contributions in order to increase their potential benefits. The contributions need not go into the company's own pension funds but may be accumulated on the side under the control of the individual. The funds are, however, subject to the same restrictions as to access etc. as other pension funds. The individual cannot normally benefit from them until reaching normal retirement age.

Let us look at the options open to someone wishing to make voluntary contributions. The money may be put into the existing company pension fund or, as mentioned above, it may be put into a wide range of funds set up by the various life assurance companies. The investor can pick his own fund from a long list of unit linked investments; guaranteed endowment funds; or fixed interest deposit funds. The difference between them is the degree of risk and the potential return.

Unit linked funds possibly offer the chance of the highest return but they also contain the greatest element of risk. Unit fund values can move down as well as up. Endowment funds usually offer a guaranteed minimum return plus the promises of bonuses — just like with-profit endowment assurance policies. Deposit funds retain the investment in fixed interest deposits getting whatever the going rate of return is. There is no risk of the value going down but it may fail to keep pace with inflation. The choice is up to the individual — a good managed unit-linked fund which has performed well in the past is possibly the best compromise for most. There is some risk of a downturn in values but over the long term the chances are that such an investment will at least keep pace with inflation — particularly since the returns within the fund are tax-free. That is one of the tax concessions accorded to pension funds.

Many schemes will allow the investor to switch into a safer deposit fund at any time and this can be particularly advantageous getting near to retirement age. The great trouble with unit linked funds is that they may be in the doldrums at the very time they are due to mature for you — at retirement age. If there is the facility to switch, however, one can keep an eye on things for a few years prior to retirement. If it seems that investments generally are heading for a downturn, it will then be possible to switch into the fixed-interest fund — in other words get out as close to the top as possible. Whoever sells you the plan, and benefits from the commission, ought to be on hand at that stage to advise on what best to do.

Care must be taken in choosing the best fund for your extra pension contributions.

There can be no rule of thumb on what extra payments into a pension fund will buy in terms of extra benefits. It depends on the performance of the investment and on annuity rates at the time of retiring. What happens is that the sum built up may be used to buy a pension at pension age. How much pension it buys will depend on interest rates at that time. The Revenue Commissioners' rules require that additional voluntary contributions should be made on a regular basis — once started the intention should be to continue them. But it is flexible in this regard if a problem arises as a result of illness or reduced earnings. It is also possible to make sizeable voluntary contributions in the years prior to retirement.

Making additional voluntary contributions may enable you to get a higher tax-free lump sum on retirement but not always. There is a maximum lump sum entitlement of one-and-a-half times final remuneration — lower if you have less than twenty years service. Making extra voluntary contributions will not increase that maximum. So if your existing contributions will enable you to get that maximum, no amount of additional contributions will increase your lump sum entitlement — they will have to be used to buy extra pension benefits.

Part-time workers

Part-time workers don't have any automatic right to join company pension schemes. The European Court of Justice ruled late in 1994 that workers could not be precluded from schemes on the grounds of sex. But it is still perfectly legal to deny pension rights to part-time workers where there is no question of sexual discrimination.

But even without any legal requirement there is likely to be growing pressure to include part-time workers in company schemes if for no other reason than the sharp increase in the number of part-time workers employed. But there is no easy way of extending pensions schemes to include part-time workers on an equal basis with full-time staff.

Most schemes currently limit entry to full-time permanent employees. There is no difficulty in changing the full-time requirement but there is a need to define "permanent". Having got over that hurdle, the larger question is how to calculate actual pension benefits in a defined benefit scheme.

In such schemes full-time workers normally get one-sixtieth of their final pay for each year of service. And there is no great problem extending that to part-timers either on the basis of their actual pay or by calculating service on the basis of equivalent full years. So a part-time worker who was with the firm 40 years and is on £6,000 a year would get a pension of £4,000 i.e. forty/sixtieths (two-thirds) of £6,000. A full time employee on £12,000 would get a pension of £8,000 assuming the same service.

That seems fair enough but problems can arise where social welfare benefits are taken into account, as they are in most schemes. Normally the company pensions is effectively reduced to take account of the State social welfare pensions. Should an equivalent reduction be taken from a part-timers pension or should the reduction be on some pro-rata basis. There is no easy formula to ensure equality in all cases.

The same sort of problem arises with regard to disability benefits (income continuance schemes). These are normally underwritten by insurance and the insurance companies insist on limiting benefits. A common maximum benefit is two- thirds of salary less twice the State disability benefit for a single person. Applying this formula to low-paid part-time workers could result in no benefit being payable or, at most, a very small one.

Pensions and marital breakdown

The rights of spouses to benefits from a pension scheme are not defined in any law. But the laws covering judicial separation and divorce allow the courts to make orders allocating such benefits between spouses in the event of separation or divorce. So part or all of the pension rights of one spouse may be allocated to the other even though he or she had not made any financial contribution to it. The actual application of these powers depend on the courts and individual circumstances. All pension rights are covered from both defined contribution and defined benefit company schemes, personal pension plans and State schemes.

Pensions for the self-employed

The self-employed are just as eligible for tax relief on pension contributions as the employed individual. It is simply a matter of organising their own personal pension scheme and there is no shortage of schemes tailor-made by the various assurance companies for this purpose. No self-employed person should really be without one. In general, tax relief may be claimed on up to 15% of income for those under 55 years of age and 20% for those over that age. That new 20% limit was introduced in 1996. For someone paying tax at 46p in the pound that means that a net payment of 54p will buy a full £1 worth of benefit — less commission and charges, of course. There is the additional tax advantage in that the money in the pension fund accumulates entirely tax free and up to a quarter of the fund available on retirement can be taken in the form of a tax free lump sum.

All-in-all, there is no better way for a self-employed person to save for the future. There is only one drawback — the fact that the money in the fund cannot normally be drawn out before age 60 at least. That can be a good thing in that it may protect your savings against your temptations but it may not seem that way if you badly need the money to save your business from impending doom.

In what follows, we are considering a self-employed person acting as a sole trader. A person working for their own company is in a more advantageous position on the pension front. While such a person may consider himself to be self-employed, he is actually an employee — the company is a legal entity of itself. As an employee, he can be a member of a company pension scheme. And it can be a special top hat scheme for managers and/or directors, or even a special scheme specifically for the managing director.

So while the self-employed person may not normally be granted tax relief on contributions of more than 15% of income paid into a pension scheme, there is no absolute limit on the amount a company may claim in tax relief on contributions it pays into a pension scheme for employees. The only limit is that the pension benefits from such a scheme must not exceed the very generous upper limits detailed earlier in the chapter.

It can be better for a self-employed person to make pension contributions through his or her own company rather than as a sole trader.

As previously outlined, these include a pension of up to two-thirds final salary indexed to inflation or salary levels, together with a tax-free lump sum of one and a half times final salary, dependants' pensions, and sizeable death-in-service benefits.

So there can be advantages in working for your own company rather than operating as a sole trader i.e. chargeable to income tax under schedule "D". The pluses and minuses involved go beyond the scope of this book, however, since they include many factors apart altogether from the benefits in the form of extra tax relief on pension contributions. The advantages on this front are likely to be particularly attractive to someone coming close to retirement with no provision for pension benefits but all the pluses and minuses need to be considered and professional advice sought.

But let us have a look at the rules as they apply to the self-employed. As always, it is first necessary to get a couple of definitions straight. The most important is that of "net relevant earnings". This is basically earned self-employed income cal-

Employees in small businesses

Only about one-in-ten small firms have pension schemes for their staff and even a smaller number of sole traders make pension provisions for their workers. Sole traders are people who operate a business on their own account without having established a company. They are self-employed but very often they also employ others. If they want to make some pension provision for those workers they can either pay them extra and let them take out their own private pension plans, or else they can set up their own executive plan. That second option can be the most tax efficient even where the employee actually pays the lion's share of the contribution.

Tax relief is only given on contributions to an executive scheme where the employer pays at least one-sixth of the overall cost. That may simply be the cost of the life assurance attaching to the pension scheme.

The employer gets the tax relief on his or her own contributions but in addition doesn't have to pay PRSI on the employees contribution. The worker also saves PRSI on his or her own contributions. Contributions to a private scheme have to be made out of income after PRSI is deducted.

Let's take an example. Joe's a publican with one full-time worker, his son Sean who is paid £15,000 a year. Joe is already making some pension provision for himself and wants to start making early provision for his son. He wants £2,000 to go into the fund at the lowest possible net cost.

He could give Sean a pay rise and let him put the £2,000 into the pension fund. He'd get tax relief on it so the after tax cost would be £1,040. If Sean put the full £2,000 into a pension fund the tax relief would offset the tax which would otherwise be due. So there would be no tax implications for him. But there are PRSI implications.

Between them they'd have to pay 18.75% of the £2,000 in PRSI — the 6.75% employee rate and the 12% employer rate. So the PRSI cost would be £365.

That can be saved if instead of giving the money to Sean, Joe paid the money directly into an executive pension scheme.

culated on much the same basis as it is for the taxman. It is net of losses and capital allowances and of any payments such as interest on which tax relief is given but before deducting other tax allowances. The other definition of importance is that for normal retirement age. In general it must be between ages 60 and 70 but it may be as early as 50 or as late as 80 for occupations where such early or late retirement "is customary". So a professional footballer or a disc-jockey might get away with a scheme which provided a pension at age 50. It is hard to think of any job other than farming where retirement at age 80 might be considered customary but maybe there are others. In order to get tax relief the pension scheme must be approved by the Revenue Commissioners. And to be approved it has to meet certain conditions. The most important of these are as follows. The scheme must be designed to provide a retirement pension although it may also provide benefits for dependants in the event of death before or after retirement.

- Those benefits can normally only come in three ways: a non-assignable pension for the individual normally starting at some age between 60 and 70, part of which may be taken as a lump sum on retiring; a non-assignable pension for the surviving spouse of the individual commencing on his or her death; and a refund of premiums plus reasonable interest if on the death of the individual no pension is provided for a surviving spouse. But there may also be provision for early or later retirement in special circumstances, as mentioned above, and there may also be provision for the payment of pensions to surviving dependants other than a spouse.

- No more than a quarter of the value of the pension fund on retirement may be taken as a lump sum. Such a lump sum is taken tax free. The scheme may either be an annuity contract or a trust scheme. If it is a trust scheme it must be established and administered within the State.

Tax relief is only given on a maximum of 15% (20% if over 55 years of age) of net relevant earnings in any year of which no more than 5 percentage points can be in respect of securing benefits for dependants.

If more than the relevant 15% or 20% is paid in during any year, then the excess may be carried forward and claimed in future years if the contribution falls below the threshold. It is also possible to back date the relief to prior years for which tax assessments have not become final.

It can be advantageous to pay more than the amount allowable for tax relief into a pension scheme because of the other tax concessions mentioned above — the fact that the fund accumulates free of tax.

Self-employed — picking the right pension plan

Someone shopping for a pension plan has at least decided what they need. That's a start. The next step is to decide how to satisfy that need. The need is to provide income during retirement. The way to satisfy that need is to invest money in a pension fund. It is, of course, possible to save for retirement in various other ways but the pension fund route offers the advantages of significant tax relief. The downside is that the money becomes inaccessible. A portion will become available as a tax-free lump sum on retirement but the rest has to be drawn down as a pension.

Once the decision has been made to invest in a pension plan it's a matter of picking the best plan. That varies with the individual. The following are the basic choices which have to be made. There is no single right answer. A lot depends on the individual and there is an element of luck involved as well.

Personal Pension or Company Pension?

Where the self-employed person works for his or her own company there are advantages in having the company set up the scheme. The net cost is likely to be lower and the restriction on the size of contributions which qualify for tax relief is less onerous. It can be worthwhile setting up a company simply for this purpose but that has other implications. The choice may be particularly important for someone trying to fund a pension fairly late in life. Professional advice is advisable.

Regular premium or lump sum?

Many personal pension plans now allow the flexibility to alter contribution levels from year to year and they also spread the setup costs over the life of the plan. That flexibility can be very important to someone whose income may fluctuate. An alternative is to make annual lump sum contributions into a pension fund. Each investment is a separate transaction. The lump sums may go into different funds or even different companies. On retirement they are simply brought together to buy a pension. The advantage is flexibility. The disadvantage is that it is all too easy to forget the initial good intentions and fail to make the investment each year. With a regular contribution plan there is some degree of compulsion.

Company and type of fund?

The final decision is where to actually invest your money. There are many companies and a wide range of funds to consider. Professional advice is well worthwhile. The investment performance of the fund can make a very significant difference to the size of pension you eventually enjoy. Past trends may, or may not, be a good guide to likely future performance. With-profits funds offer a more secure return than unit-linked options in bad times but in the good times the return on unit funds can be significantly higher. Work out your own approach to risk. Take advice, and make your choice.

So savings in the pension fund are not taxed while interest, or capital gains, earned on savings outside such a fund would be liable for tax.

PRSI and the self employed

With very few exceptions all self-employed people aged between 16 and 66 with income of over £30 a week are liable to pay PRSI although the first £10,764 is exempt. People who have been told in writing by the Revenue Commissioners that they do not need to make a return of income for tax purposes are liable for a flat rate payment of £104 a year — £2 a week . Other self-employed people pay at a rate of 5%. PRSI is paid with income tax. Those not liable for tax get special books and can make payments — through installments — at any post office. It is important to make the payments in full since the rules state that if the annual payment is even a pound short, no contributions are credited while if they are correct or over, a full 52 weekly contributions are credited for the relevant year.

The self employed get very good pension value from their PRSI contributions.

It is important to register with the Department of Social Welfare. There is a form to fill out. Even if you have not filled out a form you are still liable to pay PRSI. The registration only ensures that it gets credited in the right way. Benefits from the scheme are significant.

In the past the self-employed — mainly farmers — did not normally become eligible for contributory old age pensions. Mind you, many of them did get means tested non-contributory pensions since they could reduce their means by either passing on the farm or simply ceasing to work it. Now they are able to become eligible for full contributory old age pensions which, of course, are not subject to any means test. And the current rate is over £120 a week for a married couple.

Self-employed, Class "S", contributions do not, of course, provide unemployment benefits. What is provided for is old age, widows and orphans pensions. Three years contributions are sufficient to provide widow's and orphan's cover while eligibility for an old age pension requires ten years contributions.

Some self-employed people were already paying PRSI as voluntary contributors. They include people who became ineligible for normal full rate PRSI and opted to continue paying on a voluntary basis in order to maintain certain benefits. They now pay slightly less than they did but retain eligibility for the extra benefits conferred by voluntary contributions. These include retirement pensions — which starts at 65 whereas the old age pension starts at age 66 — and a death grant.

Queries with regard to PRSI for the self-employed should be addressed to the Self-Employed Section of the Department of Social Welfare at Aras Mhic Dhiarmada, Dublin 1, phone (01) 8740100.

Those over 56 years of age who have no previous PRSI or social welfare contributions will be unable to build up sufficient contributions to qualify for an old age pension. Ten years of contributions are required and they have to stop paying at age 66 when they reach retirement age. In the meanwhile they are eligible for widow's and orphan's pensions for their dependants should they die. Those who did pay full rate PRSI or social welfare in the past — since 1953 — are able to claim credit for those contributions in satisfying the ten year requirement.

Consumers

Enforcing your consumer rights 11.

THERE have been significant advances in consumer rights in recent years. The Small Claims Courts have been available throughout the country since 1993. The maximum amount which can be claimed is £600 but that is to be increased on a phased basis up to £1,000. There is an ombudsman to adjudicate on insurance complaints and the Central Bank has been given responsibility for overseeing the activities of financial advisers who were not already covered by the various consumer protection measures dealing with insurance. The regulation of investment advisers, as opposed to insurance intermediaries, is in a state of flux at present but should be hardened up considerably during 1998. There's a financial ombudsman to deal with complaints against banks and building societies; the insurance industry has introduced a system of self-policing. All of these add to the growing body of protective measures introduced partly as a result of EC membership. Some have the backing of law while in other cases professional bodies have been encouraged to adopt their own voluntary codes of conduct by the threat of legislation.

The Ombudsman for Credit Institutions can make awards of up to £30,000 to individuals who are found to have a legitimate complaint against a bank or a building society. He is appointed and financed by the financial institutions but they have a vested interest in allowing him his independence and making the system work. The Government has the power to appoint its own ombudsman but it prefers the self-policing method as long as it works — it's cheaper for one thing.

Before going to the ombudsman you must first make a complaint to the company itself. All the banks and building societies have designated managers to deal with complaints. Obviously you should try to sort out any problem at local level first, then take it to the head office of the bank or building society, if there is one. If you are still not satisfied, you can then take the matter to the ombudsman. He is unlikely to look at a complaint unless it has been though the complaints procedures of the institutions involved.

He is open to complaints from individuals, organisations and sole traders. He will also consider complaints from companies so long as their annual turnover is under £250,000. He can't consider matters of bank policy. For instance he will not adjudicate on a complaint about the general level of bank charges. But he can, of course, deal with a complaint about the application of those charges in an individual case.

All licenced banks and all building societies are party to the ombudsman system together with the State owned ACCBank and ICCBank.

Insurance

There is also an Insurance Ombudsman who deals with disputes between private policyholders and insurance companies. She can deal with cases involving amounts of up to £100,000 and the insurance companies have agreed in advance to be bound by her decisions. Individuals, however, are not so bound. They can reject her decision and seek redress elsewhere, through the courts, for instance. As with the Financial Ombudsman the dispute has to be initially processed through the insurance company itself and it is only when the company admits that the matter has reached an impasse, that the ombudsman will get involved. All companies providing life assurance in Ireland and about 90% of the general insurance companies participate in the scheme.

Before reaching the Ombudsman, disputes may go through a number of channels. The industry has adopted codes of conduct and implemented some self-policing machinery. The Department of Industry and Commerce retains a large degree of discretion and is the ultimate overseeing authority but it has encouraged the establishment of self-policing bodies for insurance brokers; other insurance intermediaries; and the insurance companies themselves.

•   In most cases the consumer's first point of contact with the insurance industry is through an intermediary — a bro-

Where to complain

INSURANCE	Brokers	Paul Carty National Director Irish Brokers Association 87, Merrion Square, Dublin, 2.
	Companies	Irish Insurance Federation Russell Court, St. Stephen's Green Dublin, 2.
	Overall	Department of Enterprise and Employment Kildare Street, Dublin, 2. Insurance Ombudsman 77, Merrion Square, Dublin, 2.
FINANCIAL INTERMEDIARIES		Central Bank of Ireland Dame Street, Dublin, 2. Department of Enterprise and Employment Kildare Street, Dublin, 2.
BANKS/BUILDING SOCIETIES		Ombudsman for Credit Institutions 8, Adelaide Court, Adelaide Road, Dublin, 2.
DATA PROTECTION		Data Protection Commissioner Block 4, Irish Life Centre Talbot Street, Dublin, 1.
SOLICITORS		The Law Society, Blackhall Place, Dublin, 7 Independent Adjudicator of the Law Society 26/27 Upper Pembroke Street, Dublin, 2
EUROPEAN UNION		The European Ombudsman 1, avenue du President Robert Schuman B.P. 403 F - 67001 Strasbourg Cedex

ker or agent. If there is cause for complaint and it cannot be sorted out between the customer and the intermediary, then there are a number of further steps which can be taken. Where you go depends on the sort of complaint and on the type of intermediary.

Let us first look at a complaint about the service of the actual intermediary — for instance a belief that misleading claims were made when a policy was sold, or that a broker did not give really independent advice. It is important to distinguish the type of intermediary involved.

The word "broker" now has a definite meaning. To ensure that he or she can give independent advice, a "broker" must be able to sell the products of at least five insurance companies and that cannot be made up of a mixture of life and general insurance companies. In addition there are "agents" who represent four or less companies and "tied agents" who only sell the products of one company.

If the intermediary is a broker and he is a member of the Irish Brokers Association (IBA) you can complain to it. The IBA was formed out of a merger between the two organisations, NIIBA and the CIB. It has agreed complaints procedures with the Department of Industry and Commerce. The first complaint should be to the broker, then to the IBA. But if you think that the complaint is not being adequately dealt with, you can appeal to the Department itself. (All the addresses are given on the previous page.)

- **Agents:** Those brokers who are not members of either organisation, and all agents are subject to no overseeing body other than the Department. So that must be the first port of call when a complaint is not dealt with at local level.

- **Companies:** In many cases, of course, the complaint will arise over the actual product sold — the policy itself rather than in the choice of policy. In such cases the insurance company must have a role to play and complaints can, of course, be taken directly to insurance companies. Where satisfaction cannot be reached with the company itself, complaints can be brought to their self-policing organisation, the Irish Insurance Federation.

Like the brokers' organisation it is funded and controlled by the companies themselves so it cannot be said to be completely independent, but the industry, both companies and brokers, has a vested interest in seeing that complaints are properly dealt with, and that abuses are kept to the minimum. In all cases a final appeal can be made to the Department of Industry and Commerce.

Financial advisers

There are many savings and investment products which are not linked to insurance. Financial advisers or brokers are not regulated under the insurance schemes outlined above when they are selling these. Regulation in this area covers those who take deposits, sell shares, or act as intermediaries for various types of non-insurance linked investments such as unit trusts and BES schemes. The system of regulation is in a state of flux but control is vested in the Central Bank and the Department of Enterprise and Employment who are likely to continue to share the overseeing role.

Solicitors

Solicitors are members of the Law Society of Ireland and it is to that body that complaints should first be directed after, of course, they have first been made to the individual concerned. The Law Society has its own complaints procedures. Complaints may be referred to the Disciplinary Tribunal of the High Court or, in the case of excessive fees, to the Taxing Master, at the Four Courts, Dublin, 7.

Where a complainant is dissatisfied with the manner in which the Law Society has dealt with a complaint he or she may refer it to the Independent Adjudicator of the Law Society whose role is to ensure that complaints about the conduct of a solicitor are dealt with fairly and impartially by the Law Society.

In all cases the first complaint is made to the Law Society. The Adjudicator only considers the Society's handling of a complaint against the solicitor, not the actual complaint itself. The Adjudicator cannot award compensation and cannot consider any matters which have been dealt with by the Society's Compensation Fund Committee, the Disciplinary Tribunal of the High Court or the Taxing Master.

Complaints have to be made in writing and should include a copy of the Society's decision and confirmation that the subject matter of the complaint has not already been considered by the Disciplinary Tribunal of the High Court. For the address see the table on page 189.

Going to Court for a fiver

Have you ever bought faulty goods or paid for less than adequate service? Who hasn't? Complaints often go unheeded. So what else can you do? Did you know that you can go to court for only £5. That's the cost of taking an action in the Small Claims Courts which have been operating throughout the country since 1994. Demand for the service has been growing but at a slow enough pace. Just over 2,700 claims were processed last year. In the majority of those the claimant got some redress.

Unfortunately winning the case is only half the problem. Collecting the actual awards has sometimes been a problem. A survey by the Consumers Association a couple of years ago found that only about two-thirds of consumers got their awards while the other third reported difficulties. However, the Small Claims procedure is always worth a try. The most you can lose is £5 and some of your time.

There is a limit to the size and type of claim covered by the scheme. The maximum amount that can be claimed is £600 and the dispute must relate to the purchase of goods or services for private use from someone selling them in the course of business. Also covered are claims for minor damage to privately owned property and the non-return of rent deposits. Precluded are claims for accidents, damages or for the recovery of payments under a loan or hire purchase agreement. Up to 1995 the monetary limit was set at £500 and there was a promise to raise that by annual instalments of £100 to £1,000 by the end of the decade. That process seems to have got stalled at £600.

So how do you go about making a claim?

The scheme is administered by the Small Claims Registrar at local District Court Offices throughout the country. You can look up the address and telephone number in the telephone directory. The first approach is to the Registrar. He or she will provide help in drawing up a statement of claim. There's a special form to make the job relatively easy. The non-refundable fee of £5 is payable at this stage.

A copy of the claim is sent to the person against whom it is made — the respondent — and he or she has fifteen days to reply. If no answer is received the claim is automatically treated as undisputed and the District Court will make an order for the amount claimed to be paid within a stipulated time.

Access to personal files

Individuals have a right of access to most personal files relating to themselves which companies and other organisations are holding on their computers. Most public sector organisations, financial institutions, providers of credit ratings, holders of direct mail lists, and those who keep sensitive information

If the claim is disputed the Registrar will try to reach an agreed settlement between the parties at an informal meeting. It is held in private. Both parties may be asked to outline the facts of the case and they may be asked questions by the Registrar.

His aim is not to make a judgement but rather to reach an agreed settlement. Either side can bring forward witnesses or present expert reports. But the parties have to pay for these themselves.

If the Registrar fails to get a settlement agreed, the matter is referred to the District Court and is heard before a judge. The hearing may not be in private and will, of course, be more formal. The parties may be asked to answer questions on oath. The Registrar attends the Court hearing to outline the facts as he has ascertained them.

There is provision for witnesses to be summoned to appear before either the Registrar or the Court. The Registrar will help in issuing the summons but it is up to the individual requesting the witness to pay any expenses involved. There is nothing to stop either party hiring a solicitor to represent them but the whole idea is to keep the cost down and there is no need for a solicitor. Having won an award the next problem is to get the payment and that unfortunately can sometimes prove difficult. Enforcement is far from adequate. A company may have closed. The person may have no assets or they may just refuse to pay.

Many people have won cases to no avail. The Consumer Association surveyed 470 people. One third of those who won awards had still to receive them a year later. However the scheme had worked well for the other two-thirds. Of the 2,749 applications made last year, some 1,430 were settled by the Registrar. A further 234 cases went by default to the claimants because the claims went unanswered. Of 647 cases actually heard by a judge, degrees in favour of the claimants were made in 380.

People who don't get their awards can go back to the Small Claims Registrar and have the matter passed to a sheriff or county registrar for collection. But even that is not a sure fire way of getting the money. Last year a total of 356 degrees were passed to sheriffs for collection. Of those only 195 were enforced.

Still, on the basis of those figures most claimants win something. For a fiver its worth a try.

with regard to such things as racial origin, political or other beliefs etc. are required to register with the Data Protection Commissioner.

That register is open to the public and will contain details of the type of information held. Only files held on computer are covered by the law but the right of access covers not only the files of those companies and organisations required to register but anybody with personal information on computer files. The individual has a right, first of all, to be told what sort of information is kept on file — in response to a written enquiry, and then to see the files relating to him or herself.

The holder of the files has duties with regard to maintaining the accuracy of the data, not keeping more data than is necessary for the specified purpose, nor keeping it for longer than necessary. He also has to take adequate measures to keep the files secure. There are certain files exempt from the requirement. These include police and prison files.

Your first approach should be to the person or organisation you think is holding files on you. You should write to them on the following lines —

"Please send me a copy of any information you keep on computer about me. I am making this request under the Data Protection Act."

You should give any information which might help the individual or organisation to identify you. You should get the information within forty days and you may be asked to pay up to £5. If you experience any difficulty or if you want to see the register of data holders you can contact the Data Protection Commissioner at Block 4, Irish Life Centre, Talbot Street, Dublin, 1, phone (01) 6748544.

Credit ratings

The Irish Credit Bureau, of which most of the leading finance houses are members, provides members of the public with details of their personal credit rating as shown on the Bureau's books. It has been doing this since before the enactment of the Data Protection legislation. The information provided included the name of the company which registered the information, the relevant account number and what is called the "conduct grading" of the account — likely to be only one word "satisfactory" or "unsatisfactory".

The members of the Finance Houses Association who use the Bureau are: ACCBank; Allied Irish Finance; Anglo Irish Bankcorp; Bank of Ireland Finance; Bowmaker; Credit Finance; Equity Bank; First Southern Bank; Lombard & Ulster Bank; Merchantile Credit; National Credit Company; Northern Bank Finance; and Smurfit Finance.

The Bureau can be contacted at Newstead House, Newstead, Clonskeagh, Dublin, 14. If you are finding difficulty in getting loan finance and you have no idea why, then you should contact the Bureau as well as your bank and ask for details of the information they have on you. Mistakes have been made. In 1995 the Ombudsman for the Financial Institutions granted an award for damages to a man who had been refused business loans as a result of a mistake in the information held on a bank's files. The fact that he had paid off a loan early was mistakenly entered as something else on his file and he was effectively blacklisted. So it can happen.

Consumer Credit

The Consumer Credit Act which was passed into law in 1995 is designed to provide a range of protection for borrowers. Its provisions have been coming into force under various Ministerial Orders.

Consumers have been slow enough to view loans as a service which the lender is only too anxious to sell. Banks, building societies, finance houses, moneylenders, and pawnbrokers all make their money by lending money. For many years lenders were so pleased at even being considered for a loan that they seldom looked too closely at the cost and even less seldom shopped around for the best possible deal.

That has been changing. Credit is more easily available. Consumers are better informed. There is growing competition among lenders. But there are still difficulties.

- Competition can only work if the consumer has the information needed to compare products. That information on costs and conditions has not always been easily accessible in clear terms.

- The fine print in some contracts has clearly favoured the lender and the borrower may not have the knowledge or the bargaining power to reject the onerous terms. Very often he or she doesn't know the conditions are there until they run foul of them.

- Concerns have been expressed in the past at some of the methods used to enforce loan agreements — calling at the borrower's workplace, for instance.

The Consumer Credit Act tackles those difficulties curtailing the rights of lenders and enhancing the rights of borrowers. It is a wide ranging piece of legislation and its full implications will take time to emerge. The Director of Consumer Affairs has responsibility for overseeing its operation and he also takes on a price-control task over bank and building society charges.

Let's have a look at some of the provisions:

- **Information:** All loan agreements will have to be written in plain language and contain a minimum amount of information on interest rates, charges, repayments, what happens in the event of a default etc. If there are two possible meanings to any clause the Courts will have to favour the one most beneficial to the borrower. That provision applies to all consumer agreements under a different Act which ensures that the Courts will not uphold "unfair conditions". A condition will be considered to be "unfair" if contrary to the requirement of good faith, it causes a significant imbalance in the parties rights and obligations under the contract to the detriment of the consumer".

The borrower must also be given time to read and understand the agreement.

- **Refused a loan:** A person who is refused a loan will have the right to request and get information including the name and address of "any single person" from whom the lender sought information on the financial standing of the would-be borrower. The request has to be made within 28 days of the refusal and the lender has 14 days to comply.

One lawyer has suggested that the wording of the Act would allow the lender to only supply one name even when more than one person was contacted. That advice may be taken on board by some financial institutions, so it is worth remembering and checking should you have a need to use these new rights of disclosure.

- **Interest Rates:** The only interest rates which can be quoted in advertisements and agreements will be annual percentage rates worked out under a fixed formula so that the consumer can compare rates on a like with-like-basis. A provision, which doesn't apply to bank or building society loans allows the borrower to apply to the Circuit Court claiming that the terms of an agreement are "excessive". The Court will take all the circumstances into account including "the age, business competence and level of literacy and numeracy of the consumer".The Court can effectively rewrite the agreement reducing or eliminating further repayments.

- **Cooling-off Period:** All loan agreements with the exception of housing loans, credit cards and overdrafts must allow for a ten day cooling-off period during which the consumer can withdraw from it. But the borrower can waive the right.

- **Early Repayment:** The borrower must be compensated for making an early repayment of the loan. The formula on which such compensation is based will have to be agreed by the Central Bank or the Director of Consumer Affairs. The same compensation will have to apply where the borrower is forced to pay off the loan early because of some condition of the loan.

- **Enforcement:** The lender is barred from contacting a consumer at his or her place of work except in some cases where the borrower has a live-in job. Any contact at home, by phone or personally, has to be between 9 in the morning and 9 in the evening although the wording of the Act would seem to allow calls to be made before 9 am on a Monday morning. The Act reads "between 9 o'clock in the evening on any week day and 9 o'clock on the following day".

The lender has to give ten days notice in writing of any action he wants to take under the agreement. It has to detail the action and the date on or after it is intended to take that action.

Where the action has been prompted by a breach of the agreement on the part of the borrower no action can be taken for 21 days. If the borrower gets back on track within that time period the lender must not include any reference to it in the customer's credit record.

- **Lender's Liability:** In future a lender may be liable to make good any defect of goods or services bought with a loan. In certain circumstances where the loan is arranged through the supplier, the lender can become liable.

The customer will first have to pursue his or her rights against the supplier of the goods or services but where that fails maybe because the shop has gone out of business the claim can be then pursued against the lender.

Switching house insurance

Building societies no longer have the right which they once imposed to require borrowers to take out house insurance with a particular company or even from one of a group of companies. On new loans, however, they must arrange mortgage protection insurance. Taking out house insurance through a society, of course, need not be a bad thing. Since the new requirement became law some societies have organised very attractive house insurance packages which are cheaper in many cases than can be obtained elsewhere. These are usually not available through insurance brokers but it is worth checking them out to see how your society's policy compares with whatever you have.

Redemption fees

Building societies cannot charge redemption fees when a borrower pays off his or her loan early. But there is nothing to stop other financial institutions from doing this. Many finance houses still do. Building societies may not impose higher interest rates on larger loans either but they may charge more for different categories of loan — for instance loans for purposes other than house purchase or loans to people who have not met certain savings criteria before applying for the loan.

Insurance — right to cancel

Under a voluntary agreement entered into by the life assurance companies, people buying regular premium savings and investment type policies are sent a letter outlining details of the policy; warning them that it is a long-term contract and that they stand to lose if they cancel it in the early years; and telling them that they have fifteen days to withdraw from the policy without loss. The insurance cover under the policy remains intact during this cooling-off period.

Additional disclosure including, perhaps, information on surrender values during the first five years of a policy, investment returns required to meet specific funding targets, and the impact of lower than expected investment returns, is likely to be required under new laws to be enacted in order to comply with EC directives.

Broker charges

Some insurance brokers charge clients a fee in addition to the commission they get on general insurance. Those charges must be itemised on the bill. It may also become compulsory to give details of the commission, as well. This is provided for in the Insurance Act but has not yet come into force and, indeed, may never come into force. The level of commissions on general insurance is controlled by the Department of Enterprise and Employment while commissions on life assurance policies are fixed by voluntary agreement between the companies involved.

Deposit insurance

Bank and building society deposits have always been relatively safe but there is now some guarantee against loss.

Both groupings now have guarantee schemes which provide some measure of protection against loss in the event of a bank or building society failure. In such an event depositors are guaranteed to get back 80% of the first £5,000 on deposit; 70% of the next £5,000 and 50% of the next £5,000. So someone with £15,000 on deposit would get back at least £10,000.

European Union

The European Ombudsman investigates complaints about mal-administration by Institutions and bodies of the European Community. These include the Commission, the European Parliament, the Committee of Regions, the European Investment Bank, and the European Investment Fund. You don't have to have been individually affected by the mal-administration, but you must first contact the institution or body concerned to inform it of your complaint. A letter of complaint is sufficient.

Complaints should be made in writing. There is a standard form which may be used if you like. You can get a copy from the Ombudsman's office — see page 189 for the address. The Ombudsman tries to find a mutually acceptable solution to the complaint. He can recommend how it might be solved. If the recommendation is not accepted, the Ombudsman can make a special report about the case to the European Parliament.

Goods and services

Consumer protection in the supply of good and services is provided by an 1980 Act which updated a lot of earlier legislation. The one main drawback is that the consumer's final redress must be through the courts. If the retailer, shopkeeper, or what have you, refuses to rectify a claim, the final judgment on who is right has to be made in court. The Small Claims Court offers a low cost route where the amount involved is less than £600.

The Act provided for the establishment of the office of Director of Consumer Affairs. He can investigate various practices and take direct action against traders who do not comply with the general provisions of the Act. But he has not really got a role in dealing with specific individual complaints.

The provisions of the Act are mainly related to dealings between a trader and an end-consumer of a product or service. Some of the protections do not apply to deals between two traders — a retailer and wholesaler, for instance so a consumer may not be covered by the full Act if he does a deal at a "trade price".

Your contract is almost always with the seller not the manufacturer.

When something goes wrong it is almost always the retailer who is, in law, responsible for putting things right. It is he who sold the goods and it is between him and the consumer that the contract was made — a contract for sale, remember, need not be in writing. Even if the manufacturer provides a guarantee against defect in the product it is still the retailer who is responsible to see that things are put right. There are five general areas of protection given to the consumer under the Act.

- **The goods sold must be made of "merchantable quality".** The goods must be capable of being used for the purpose for which they are normally sold. It does not matter if the retailer did not know about the fault. He has a responsibility to the consumer but if there are defects he may cover himself by pointing them out. Goods marked "seconds" or "slightly defective", for instance, would not be expected to be of top quality. The buyer also has responsibilities — he or she is expected to have examined the goods and have no complaint if the defects could reasonably have been noticed before purchase.

- **The goods must be fit for their intended purpose.** In some cases the purpose is obvious but in other cases the consumer may be relying on the retailer for advice and he is expected to have some skill in this matter. If he says the product or service will do the job, or serve the purpose, then you have a claim against him if it turns out otherwise.

- **The goods must be as described.** Goods can be described in advertisements, pictures, or orally by the salesman and if these descriptions are not in keeping with the truth, then the purchaser has a claim for redress. The trader may also be liable for criminal prosecution under the 1978 Consumer Information Act.

- **The goods must conform with the sample.** This provision applies when the consumer buys on the basis of seeing a sample of the goods.

- **The trader can be assumed to be able to pass ownership.** This is a difficult area of law but, in general, the trader is assumed to be able to pass ownership of the goods to the purchaser. If, for instance, there is an unpaid hire purchase debt on the goods and the hire purchase company comes looking for them, the buyer may have a claim against the seller.

These rights are enshrined in the Act and in general, the trader cannot limit them. If a consumer has a valid complaint, then in general, he has a right to get his money back. He may, in some cases, be entitled to compensation and, indeed, may have a claim against the manufacturer if the goods are so defective that they cause damage. But that is another area of law. Retailers cannot rely on such notices as "no exchange", "no money refunded", "returned goods only exchanged for credit notes", or "no liability accepted for faulty goods". Indeed such notices are illegal under the Act. But remember that the consumer is not exonerated from all responsibility.

I t is one thing having new consumer rights, it may be another thing altogether using them. The consumer may have a claim against the trader but how does he get redress, and what form will this redress take. The Office of Consumer Affairs has suggested the following guidelines:

- If the goods are incapable of doing what they are supposed to do from the very beginning, it is likely that the consumer is entitled to a full refund, and may refuse all offers of repair, replacement, or adjustment.

- If goods are not as described, the consumer is not bound to accept them. This is an important provision since it can be difficult for a retailer to claim that even a minor instance of false description was not important.

- The consumer's right to reject goods could be lost if he does not act promptly on discovering the cause of complaint. It could also be affected if he altered the goods or if he does anything which implies that he has accepted them.

- If the goods have been used for some time before the fault is detected, a repair may be all that the consumer can expect but the repair should be a permanent one which restores the goods to the quality that they should have had when sold allowing, of course, for wear and tear.

- If the consumer is entitled to his money back, a credit note is never good enough, although credit notes can be offered by retailers as a token of goodwill claiming that the consumer has no case for redress.

If you have a complaint, your claim is against the retailer. It is his responsibility to see that matters are corrected. If you fail to get redress you could try the Small Claims courts.

Using your rights

Social Welfare

Social welfare entitlements

12.

A FULL explanation of the workings of the social welfare system would require a book in itself, and, even then, it would not be complete since there are a lot of grey areas which are left to the discretion of the officials in the Department. A booklet giving a fuller summary of the system "Guide to Social Welfare Services" is available from Information Service, Department of Social Welfare, Aras Mhic Dhiarmada, Dublin 1, while information and advice can be obtained from local social welfare offices and local Community Information Centres throughout the country. A full list of these information centres is available free of charge and post-free from the National Social Services Board, 71 Lower Leeson Street, Dublin 1, (Tel: (01) 6682422). In this short chapter only a small number of topics are covered. But first a brief overview of the system.

Basically there are two types of social welfare payments — benefits and social assistance or allowances. Entitlement to benefits is based on meeting certain PRSI contribution requirements and also meeting some other conditions such as being unemployed, over 65 or widowed etc.. The self-employed have been covered by PRSI since 1988 and most workers earning more than £30 a week are also covered. This £30 rule replaced the old rule which laid down that it was necessary to work more than 18 hours a week to come into the PRSI net.

From April 1998 a private sector employee is not liable for PRSI on the first £100 of weekly earnings. Also from April 1998 those earning less than £207 in any week are exempt from health and income levies — totalling $2\frac{1}{4}$%. That was increased from the £197 which applied during the 1997/98 tax year. Most public servants pay a lower rate of contribution and are entitled to fewer benefits but since April 1994 new entrants to the public service are paying full rate PRSI and gain entitlement to the full range of benefits. Public servants paying PRSI at the lower rate are exempt from paying on the first £20 a week.

Entitlement to any social welfare *benefit* is not normally affected by the claimant's. Widows'/widowers' contributory pensions are an exception. Entitlement to social *assistance*, on the other hand, is not based on any contribution requirement but on the basis of a means test. An example of the difference between the two is that the contributory old age pension is a benefit — there is no means test — while the non-contributory old age pension is a form of social assistance subject to a means test.

Part-time workers

Part-time workers who earn more than £30 a week are covered for a range of social welfare benefits including unemployment benefit, disability benefit and invalidity pensions. As with full-time workers, there is no PRSI on the first £100 earned each week. Those earning less than £207 in any week are not liable for the normal health and employment levies totaling $2\frac{1}{4}$%. Those earning over £100 a week are in the normal PRSI net. The £30 threshold for social welfare cover replaced the often abused 18 hour rule under which those who worked under eighteen hours a week were not in the PRSI net at all.

Part-time workers who earn more than £30 are eligible for a wide range of PRSI benefits.

To be eligible for benefits part-time workers need to have worked for 39 weeks in insurable employment and also have 39 contributions paid or credited in the previous contribution year. The same 39 contributions may satisfy both conditions. Having satisfied these contribution conditions part-time workers are entitled to the same PRSI benefits as full time workers but unemployment, disability and invalidity benefits are paid at reduced rates. Those benefits are paid on a pro-rata basis depending on the part-timer's weekly earnings during a specified tax-year. For those claiming in 1998 the relevant tax-year is 1996/97.

Contributory old age pension

In order to qualify for a contributory old age pension, it is necessary to have a minimum annual average of contributions either paid or credited over a specified number of years. The number of years can, however, differ with the individual — a fact which can result in some anomalies. A man who paid contributions for only three years could get a full old age pension while someone who paid for over ten years can find himself ineligible for any pension. But let us look at the conditions in detail. To be eligible the claimant must:

- Have an average of at least 10 contributions either paid or credited for each year between the date he or she first entered insurable employment — or 1953 if later — and the end of the contribution year prior to reaching age 66. An average of 48 contributions a year is required to qualify for a full pension while an average of 20 will be enough for a 'reduced' pension which is not much lower. Since November 1997 those with an average of between ten and twenty qualify for a pro-rata pension provided they have a minimum of 260 paid contributions. Those with an average of 15 to 19 contributions a year qualify for a pension of 75% of the maximum rate while those with between 10 and 14 contributions qualify for a pension of 50% of the maximum rate.

- Those not seeking a pro-rata pension only need to have worked for three years in insurable employment for which contributions have been paid at any time — a total of 156 paid contributions. This requirement can be met by contributions prior to 1953. It is intended to increase the requirement to 260 by the year 2002 for all claimants and to 520 by the year 2012.

- Have entered insured employment before reaching 56 years of age if born after October 1, 1922, or 57 if born between April 1, 1919 and September 1, 1922.

In assessing a claim the Department first looks at the insurance record back to 1979 and if the claimant qualifies for a full pension on that basis they do not look back any further. If the claimant does not qualify for a full pension on the basis of his or her contributions from 1979, then the rules above are applied.

The pro-rata pensions available from November 1997 represent an extension of schemes which have been available on a limited basis since 1988. For those eligible, an average of 5 to 9 contributions provides a pension of a quarter of the reduced rate; 10 to 14 provides a half pension; and 15 to 19 a three-quarters pension. The people eligible under this concession are those who did not stamp cards prior to 1974 because they were in white-collar jobs and went above the income levels at which social welfare contributions were compulsory. People who stopped paying full rate PRSI because they went into public service jobs were brought into this scheme in November 1991.

Means tests

Broadly your entitlement to social assistance as opposed to benefits is determined by whatever means you have. There are other conditions as well but once you meet those your entitlement and maybe the size of the payment is determined by your means. If you have some cash income, savings, or, in some cases, if you are living with people who have an income, you may be considered ineligible for social welfare payments, or entitled only to a reduced payment. Your means are taken as including the following:

- Any cash income.

- The value of property personally used, such as a farm but not including the applicant's own home.

- The notional income from savings and investments.

In the case of unemployment assistance, the value of any benefit or privilege enjoyed — such as board and lodgings in a parent's house — is also taken into account.

None of these are as clear cut as they seem. And the same criteria are not used for all entitlements. Claimants for unemployment assistance have their means calculated as follows:

Cash income may seem clear cut, but the Social Welfare Act requires the means test officer to assess the income which the applicant for unemployment assistance "may reasonably expect to receive" in the coming year — not his means in the past year, you will note. Income which an applicant may earn from self employment is also included.

If the officer finds it impossible to make an estimate of likely income in the coming year, he may take the income in the year just past as the means. The Department says that in estimating earnings "particular attention is paid to the availability of opportunities for self-employment in the particular case."

Income from any of the following is not taken into account: supplementary welfare allowance; rent allowance; pensions and allowances in respect of the War of Independence; the first £80 a year of other army pensions or allowances.

A married applicant whose spouse is working can still claim an allowance for an adult dependent in respect of the spouse provided his or her earnings do not exceed £90 a week gross. A full dependant's allowance is paid if the income is below £60.

Pensions, savings and means tests

Capital is taken into account in calculating the means of claimants for social welfare assistance. Capital in this context includes savings, investments and the cash value of property owned by the claimant but not used personally i.e. a second house which is, or could be, let to provide an income.

New rules for calculating means attributable to such capital were introduced in October 1997 in respect of claimants for the Old Age Non-contributory Pension, Blind Pension, Widow(er)'s Non-contributory Pension, and Carers Allowance.

The assessment is done as follows:

The first £2,000 is ignored.

The yearly value of the next £20,000 is assessed at 7.5%.

The yearly value of the capital in excess of £22,000 is assessed at 15%.

So the annual means of someone with £25,000 in savings is assessed as follows

The first £2,000 is ignored leaving £23,000. £20,000 of that is assessed at 7.5% and £3,000 at 15%. The sums work out as follows: 7.5% of £20,000 is £1,500 while 15% of £3,000 is £450. That gives a total of £1,950 a year or £37.50 a week. The old age pension must be reduced accordingly.

An individual can have capital of up to £6,160 and still qualify for a full non-contributory old age pension or a blind pension. A couple can have £12,320. Above those levels and the pension starts being reduced. With capital above £36,266 an individual ceases to qualify for a pension. It's £72,532 in the case of a couple.

Above that and the benefit is progressively reduced. It is totally withdrawn when income goes over £90. The income of the spouse may be taken into account in deciding eligibility. The spouse is allowed a set sum for personal and travelling expenses, and the balance is then treated as the income of the applicant in assessing his or her means.

Farm income is assessed on the basis of actual gross income less the actual expense incurred in running the farm. Income includes any grants, etc. — with the whole calculation done on the basis of the year preceding the assessment.

Savings and investments are also treated as means. The income is worked out on a notional basis as follows: it is assumed that 5% is earned on the first £400 and 10% on any savings over that amount. So, that if you have £500 in the bank, you are assessed as having an annual income of £30 i.e. 5% of £400 plus 10% of £100. That is divided by 52 to give a notional weekly income. The same method is used in calculating a notional income from other assets, such as a second house. A similar notional income is calculated to arise from land or buildings owned by a farmer and not used in his own farm business. Such assets are assumed to be yielding some form of rent.

Board and lodgings is taken into account where a son or daughter is still living at home. The assessment of its value is a complicated process which involves taking into account the income of the entire household in which the applicant for unemployment assistance is living. The Department of Social Welfare operates on the basis of guidelines looking at each case "on its merits". The following is how the calculations might be made in the case of an unemployed son or daughter.

The minimum unemployment assistance payable to people living at home is £25 a week.

Where the family's main income does not come from farming a sum of £105 is deducted from the parents' net income (£95 in a single parent family). There is a further deduction to allow for rent or mortgage repayments and what is left is divided by the number of non-earning members in the household to arrive at the notional value of board and lodgings to the applicant for unemployment assistance. That figure is included in the calculation of his or her means. The maximum taken into account is 17% of net family income. Where the family's main income is from farming, £91.50 is deducted from the parents' income (£74 for a single parent family). The minimum assessment for the value of board and lodgings in this case is £3.10 a week and, as in the case of an urban family, the maximum taken as means is 17% of net family income.

Family income supplement

This scheme provides supplementary benefits for families on low incomes. To be eligible it is necessary for one member of the family to be working for at least 19 hours a week and for the family income to fall below set levels depending on family size. It is also necessary for some member of the family to be entitled to the normal childrens' allowances i.e. Child Benefit. The aim of the scheme is to help families on low wages who might otherwise be better off on social welfare. Claiming the benefit does not affect eligibility for a medical card.

Family Income Supplement

To be eligible your income must be less than the figure shown below. The payment is equal to 60% of the difference between your income and the income in the table.

Family size	Family income must be below	Family size	Family income must be below
One child	£212	Five children	£297
Two children	£232	Six children	£317
Three children	£252	Seven children	£334
Four children	£272	Eight children	£351

The family income supplement works out as 60% of the difference between actual income and the prescribed income given in the table. Actual income is defined as net of PRSI and Levies up to October 1998. After that the income taken into account will be take-home pay net of tax, PRSI and Levies. The figures in the table are those which apply from June 1998. The thresholds were £7 lower during the previous year.

Once the actual income level is established the FIS benefit remains unchanged for some time. It doesn't fluctuate up and down on a weekly basis according to the earned income in the previous week.

To qualify it is necessary to show that the employment will last at least three months. Job-sharers can qualify. The rate of payment is adjusted immediately on the birth of a child. Applications forms are available from social welfare offices or from: Social Welfare Services Office, Ballinalee Road, Longford.

Most private sector workers making PRSI contributions are, as a result, entitled to at least some financial contribution towards the cost of dental, optical and aural services and appliances. Up to April 1997 those earning over £35,000 were ineligible. To qualify you have to meet certain contribution conditions. You must have paid Class A or Class H PRSI. Class A is the full rate paid by most private sector workers while Class H is paid by privates and NCOs in the defence forces. The number of contributions required depends on your age. If you

Treatment benefits

are under 21 you need to have paid at least 39 PRSI contributions at some time or other. Credited contributions will not do.

Who qualifies?

If you are aged between 21 and 25 you can qualify if: You have paid at least 39 contributions since first starting work; have at least 39 contributions paid or credited of which 13 must have been paid in the relevant tax-year which for applicants during 1998 is the 1996/97 tax-year or in either one of the two previous tax years, or any tax year subsequent to the relevant tax year.

If you are aged over 25 you can qualify if: you have worked and paid PRSI for at least five years — 260 paid contributions and have at least 39 contributions paid or credited in the 1996/97 tax year of which 13 must be paid contributions on the basis listed above for 21 to 25 year olds.

If you are over 66 and were entitled to benefits when the changes were first introduced in 1992 you retain entitlement for life. Otherwise you need to have worked for five years paying PRSI and have 39 PRSI contributions paid or credited in either of the two tax years before reaching age 66. At least 13 of these must be paid contributions on the basis listed above for 21 to 25 year olds. The 13 week requirement does not apply to the long-term unemployed or those in receipt of Pre-Retirement Allowance; disability benefit for more than twelve months; invalidity benefit or retirement pension.

What benefits?

If you get over all the contribution hurdles, what benefits do you get? They fall into three categories: dental; optical; and aural.

Dental: Routine preventative treatment is free — a yearly examination, x-rays, scaling, treatment of mild gum conditions. You have to pay about 30% of the cost of other procedures. That includes £5.20 for a back filling; £7.85 for a standard front filling; and £5.95 for normal extractions. A full set of dentures costs £120.60 while a half-set costs £82.20 and a partial set £60.30.

Optical: Eye tests are free but you should have prior approval. Otherwise you have to pay but can claim the cost back. Standard glasses are free while you pay £8.00 for a slightly better set or can get a benefit of £22.70 towards frames or contact lenses of your choice. If you need contact lenses for medical reasons you can get half the cost up to a maximum of £240.

Aural: You can claim up to half the cost of a hearing aid up to £240 and half the cost of any repairs. Further information is available from The Social Welfare Services Office, Treatment Benefits, Letterkenny, Co. Donegal. You can phone Dublin (01) 8748444 (which gets you through to Donegal) or direct to Donegal (074) 25566

Medical cards

Eligibility for medical cards is also normally based on the means of the applicant. If your income is below the guideline figure then you are entitled to a card. The table lists the guidelines which applied from January 1997 but the health boards have discretion to take other factors into account in special circumstances. Slightly higher levels — about £1.50 higher apply from January 1998.

The allowances are added up. For instance if you are paying £20.50 for your house each week and are married with one child under 16 you could have an income of £148.00 a week and still be eligible for a Medical Card. That's made up of £5 in respect of the rent, £15.50 in respect of the child and £127.50 in respect of a married couple.

Medical card means test

	Under 66	66 to 79	80 or over
Single — living alone	£88.00	£96.00	£100.50
Single — living with family	£78.00	£83.00	£86.00
Married couple	£127.50	£143.00	£150.00
Allowance for child under 16	£15.50		
Allowance for other dependents	£17.00		
Allowances for outgoings on house	Excess over £15.50 a week		
Reasonable expenses necessarily incurred in traveling to work	Excess over £14.00 a week		

Farmers who don't produce accounts are assessed on a notional basis. An annual income is attributed to livestock and tillage according to a table prepared by Teagasc. Recent figures are as follows:

Dairy Cow	£360
Milch Cow	£150
Calves 0-12 months	£50
Stores/Heifers/Cattle	£100
Ewes and lambs	£30
Hoggetts	£10
Sow and Bonhams	£100
Pigs (fattened)	£5
Barley per acres	£60
Wheat per acre	£60 to £100
Oats per acre	£60

These are net figures after taking account of all input costs.

The dependants of people working in other EC countries are entitled to cards irrespective of means as are those drawing state pensions from other EC countries who are neither employed or self-employed in this country.

Nursing home subvention

People are living longer thanks to improved living conditions and advances in medical science. One of the consequences is that an increasing number of elderly people find themselves in need of some nursing care — very often in a nursing home. The costs can easily exceed ability to pay so it is not surprising that the State, through the Health Boards, provides some assistance by way of subvention. But the payments are not made automatically. The person is initially assessed for "dependency" i.e. do they need nursing home care and to what degree? Secondly there is a means test which includes not only an assessment of the claimant's means but also the means of their sons and daughters.

There are some anomalies. For instance the means test treats cash differently than a house so that a person who sells their house may be excluded from a subvention to which they would otherwise have qualified.

Regulations on the payment of subventions towards the cost of nursing home care came into effect from September 1993. The rules are complicated but are better than the very confused situation which existed previously. Those already in nursing homes prior to that date continue to qualify for assistance under the old regulations but all new applicants are subject to the new assessments.

So let's have a look at how it works.

First there is the assessment of dependency. To get a subvention at all, the Health Board must be satisfied that you need nursing home care. There are three levels of dependency: medium, high and maximum. A person with medium dependency is likely to have impaired mobility requiring supervision or a walking aid. Someone with high dependency need not be bed bound but may have a combination of mental and physical disabilities. Maximum dependency would apply to someone requiring constant nursing care.

The maximum level of weekly subvention for the three categories are: medium, £70; high, £95; maximum, £120. These rates are reduced pound-for-pound where the person's means exceeds the amount of the non-contributory old age pension — £70.50 from June 1998.

So how does the means test work?

First the claimant's own income and assets are considered. The income is defined as actual income received during the twelve months prior to the application i.e. pensions, earnings, rents received, farm income etc. The income of a married or co-habiting person is taken as half the combined income of the couple.

On top of actual income a notional income is attributed to assets.

A principal residence is ignored provided it is being lived in by a dependent spouse or child, or a relative who is receiving Disability Allowance (formerly DPMA), a blind, disability or invalidity pension or a non-contributory old age pension.

Otherwise the house is assessed as providing an annual income of 5% of its market value. So a house worth £60,000 is equivalent to an income of £3,000 a year (5% of £60,000). That wouldn't be enough to exclude a person from a subvention but

Both income and assets are taken into account in the means test.

they would be excluded if they sold the house and had £60,000 in cash - see below.

Mind you if the house is worth more than £75,000 it may not happen anyway since the subvention can then be refused.

Assets other than the principal residence are taken into account in a different way. These include other property, stocks, shares, business interests, life assurance policies, valuables held as investments, and any interest in land. Assets disposed of within the previous five years can also be taken into account. So giving away assets doesn't get around this.

A value is put on the assets, the first £6,000 is disregarded and the remainder assumed to be available to pay for nursing home costs during the first year. It's not the potential income from the savings but the savings themselves which are taken into account. At the end of each year the Health Board assesses the situation again.

Let's take an example.

Suppose the person has £8,000 in savings. Taking £6,000 from that leaves £2,000 to be taken into account. It's divided by 52 to give a weekly figure of £38.46. Let's assume also that the person has a net income of £90 a week between state and private pensions. Adding that to the notional amount available from the savings gives a notional weekly figure of £128.46. An amount equal to the old-age pension is disregarded — £70.50 — so that leaves £57.96 to be taken into account. The subvention is reduced by that amount. Let's assume that the person could qualify for the £120 subvention on the grounds of maximum dependency. They'd actually only get £52.04 (£120 minus £57.96).

While the income of sons and daughters can also be taken into account in the means test this has, in fact, only been done in about 10% of cases. There are generous allowances to set off against income.

It works like this.

The test applies to all sons and daughters whether they are living at home or not. The income of sons/daughters-in-law is not taken into account. It is net income which is considered i.e. after tax and PRSI. Also deducted are mortgage repayments and/or rent, interest repayments, education fees, life insurance and medical insurance premiums. There are also deductions of £8,000 as a personal allowance, £5,000 for a dependent spouse, £2,000 for each dependent child and £2,000 for any other dependent relative. Those rates have applied since July 31, 1996.

The child, of course, cannot be forced to make a contribution towards the upkeep of a parent in a nursing home but the Health Board may, under these regulations, reduce the amount of subvention if the child's or children's means are high enough.

Under EU regulations workers throughout the community enjoy some degree of transferability of social welfare benefits. Contributions in any member country can be taken into account in determining eligibility for benefits. That, at least, is the theory. But unfortunately it does not always work out like that. It is all too easy to lose out on benefits simply by not knowing, and not conforming with, the rules.

An Irish worker leaving a job in another EU country and coming straight home does not automatically qualify for unemployment benefit here. It doesn't matter how many social welfare contributions he paid abroad or whether or not he left the job of his own accord. If he comes straight home he will not be entitled to draw unemployment benefit here.

EU regulations do allow for contributions in other member countries to be taken into account in deciding eligibility for benefits. But there are rules to be complied with. It is not just a matter of adding up all the contributions and claiming the benefit in whatever country you like. That is certainly not the case with regard to unemployment benefit. Unemployment benefit must be claimed — initially at least — in the country in which the person last worked. That is what catches people who come straight home to Ireland and hope to draw benefit. Unless they have initially registered as unemployed in the country in which they last worked and have been so registered for at least four weeks, they are only entitled to the means tested dole. That is the case right across the EU. Unemployment benefit has to be initially claimed in the country a person last worked in.

Having been registered as unemployed for four weeks, the person can then move to another EU country to look for work and continue to draw the benefit for up to three months while looking for work. At the end of the three months they either go back to the country they last worked in, or else the benefit runs out

EU entitlements

For information on benefits in other EU countries ask at your local Social Welfare office or write for leaflet SW59 from: Department of Social Welfare EIU Section, Gandon House, Dublin, 1. Telephone (01) 8748444.

So someone who leaves a job in another EC country to look for work at home should register as unemployed in that country and stay there for four weeks, if they want to be able to draw unemployment benefit here. They may be entitled to unemployment assistance (the dole) but only if they can satisfy the means test. Another alternative is to work even one week in Ireland and pay at least one PRSI contribution. That way Ireland becomes the last country worked in and unemployment benefit can be claimed here. In this case contributions both here and in other EU countries are taken into account in deciding eligibility.

The same type of rule applies to people leaving Ireland to look for work in other EU countries. If they are entitled to unemployment benefit in Ireland they can make arrangements to continue drawing that benefit abroad while they look for work. There is an upper time limit of three months but shorter if the benefit would have run out in Ireland before then. If there is three months or more of benefit to run, then three months benefit can be paid abroad. The person has to be registered as unemployed here for four weeks prior to leaving the country. They should also register as unemployed as soon as possible in the country they go to. As long as they do this within seven days they should not be at the loss of any benefit.

For booklets on the social welfare system in each country write to EC Commission Molesworth Street, Dublin, 2. Specify which country you are interested in.

It is, of course, important to let your local Social Welfare office know before you go. There are some forms to collect and bring with you. These give details of your insurance record and can save a lot of delay if you need to claim some benefit. People coming home from working in another EU country should make sure to get similar forms to bring with them. It is possible to get booklets on the social welfare systems which operate in other EU countries from the EU Office in Dublin. If you are going to work in another country of the European Union, it is no harm knowing how their systems work. It may be important to know because once you get a job there it is their social welfare system rather than the Irish one which will apply.

See the margin note for the address to write to for a booklet on whichever EU country you are going to. Your local Social Welfare office should have a leaflet on unemployment benefits and the EU. The EU booklets give a much more detailed summary of the complete social welfare position in each country.

Free travel

Free travel is available to the following: All those aged 66 years or over, residing permanently in the State; those receiving invalidity pensions from the State; those receiving a disabled person's allowance from a Health Board; blind people aged eighteen or over who are registered with the National Council for the Blind; and people who have been getting an invalidity pension or benefit continuously for at least twelve months from another EC country or a country with which Ireland has a bilateral social security agreement.

All wheelchair users and blind people who are entitled to free travel are also entitled to a free travel companion pass as are pass holders who are being cared for by someone in receipt of a carer's allowance.

From September 1998 anyone aged 75 or over who is medically certified as unfit to travel alone is eligible for a free travel pass for a companion. The pass enables the holder to have any person aged 16 or over accompanying him or her free of charge on public transport.

From April 1998 people who transfer from Invalidity Pension, Disability Allowance or Blind Person's Pension to another social welfare pension such as a widow's pension will be entitled to keep their entitlement to the free schemes.

Those receiving State pensions or allowances should receive their free travel authorisation automatically. Others can get details and an application form from any Post Office. Someone travelling with a recipient of Disabled Person's Maintenance Allowance or Blind Person's Pension is also entitled to free travel.

Free gas or electricity

The following can qualify for a free electricity allowance or free natural or bottled gas: those over 66 years of age receiving:

— **pensions from the Department of Social Welfare;**
— **social security pensions from other EC countries or from countries with which Ireland has a bilateral agreement;**
— **any other social welfare payment;**
— **an ordinary garda widow's pension from the Department of Justice;**

— pensioners who do not have social welfare pensions but whose total weekly income is not more than £30 above the Contributory Old Age Pension Rates of £83 under age 80 and £88 over 80 from June 1998.

People under 66 years of age can qualify if they are in receipt of

— Disability Pension;
— Blind Person's Pension;
— Unemployability Supplement or Worker's Compensation Supplement;
— Disability allowance;
— Disability Pension/Benefit (or equivalent) for at least twelve months from another EC country, or another country with which Ireland has a bilateral agreement.

The allowance covers the standing charge together with the cost of up to 200 units in each two-monthly billing period during the summer and 300 units during the winter. Up to 600 unused free units can be carried forward to the next billing period and unused daytime units can be offset against the cost of night-time units used for storage heaters etc..

As an alternative the claimant can have a natural gas allowance of 322 kilowatt hours during each two-monthly summer period and 498 kilowatt hours during each winter billing period. Another alternative is to opt for fourteen bottled gas refills a year.

With some exceptions the applicant must be living alone or with a dependent spouse; an invalid; dependent children under 18 or, if over, still at full time education; or, if the applicant is over 80, invalid or infirm, one other person who provides care and attention for him/her. People over 75 years of age who were previously entitled to free electricity, natural gas, or bottled gas refill allowance retain that entitlement no matter who lives with them.

Entitlement was extended to all people over 75 from June 1997. Widows and widowers aged 60 to 65 whose late spouses had entitlement to free schemes retain that entitlement. Application forms can be obtained from any Post Office, Social Welfare Office, or direct from the Department.

Anyone entitled to a free electricity allowance is also entitled to a free colour TV licence. Those entitled can obtain their licence at any Post Office by presenting a recent ESB bill, showing the free electricity allowance.

Persons aged 66 or over who receive a "living alone" allowance in addition to their pension from the Department of Social Welfare, or who would be entitled to such an allowance but for the fact that they are living with one other person who is permanently incapacitated, are entitled to an allowance to cover the full cost of a telephone rental.

The presence in the household of a child under 22 years of age or a carer who is in receipt of a carer's allowance does not affect eligibility to this concession. Since 1997 all pensioners over 75 are entitled to free telephone rental. Those in receipt of social security pensions from other EC countries or countries with which Ireland has a bilateral agreement may also qualify.

Free TV licence

Free telephone rental

Tax system

How the tax system works 13.1

All income tax payers will benefit from income tax cuts which come into effect from April 1998. The changes, that were announced in the December 1997 budget, include increased personal allowances, a reduction in both the standard and basic rates of tax, and a widening of the standard rate tax band. The incapacitated child and blind allowances were also increased as was the special allowance for widowed parents in the years after bereavement.

The overall impact of the changes will vary with the individual, but in broad terms the more you earn the more you benefit both in terms of the actual cash increase in net income and as a percentage increase.

The DIRT tax on deposit interest was reduced to 24% in line with the standard tax rate while the concessionary rate on special savings accounts was raised from 15% to 20%.

The tax exemption levels were also raised with a particularly large increase for those in the 65 to 74 year old age bracket. Those with incomes below these exemption levels pay no tax. The changes are expected to take some 15,000 people out of the income tax net.

There were also some changes in PRSI: a raising of the weekly allowance for those paying the full rate contribution and an increase of £1,000 in the income ceiling above which no PRSI is payable.

The standard Capital Gains Tax rate is being halved from 40 to 20% and the Capital Acquisitions Tax concession on houses

Budget changes 1998 — a summary

INCOME TAX
Personal allowances increased:
— by £500 to £6,300 for married couples;
— by £250 to £3,150 for single taxpayers;
— by £250 to £3,650 for widowed taxpayers.
One-parent family allowances increased:
— by £250 to £2,650 for widowed taxpayers;
— by £250 to £3,150 for other single parents.
Standard rate tax band widened:
— from £19,800 to £20,000 for married taxpayers;
— from £9,900 to £10,000 for single and widowed taxpayers.
Rate of tax: Standard rate reduced from 26p to 24p and higher rate from 48p to 46p
DIRT tax: The standard rate of DIRT reduced from 26p to 24p while the rate on
Special Savings Accounts raised from 15p to 20p.
Tax exemption limits: Raised by £100 per single or widowed taxpayer under 65; by
£400 for those between age 65 and 74; and by £300 for those aged 75 or over.
The increases are twice those levels for married couples.
Widowed Parent Bereavement Allowance: Increased to £5,000 in the year following
bereavement, £4,000 in year two, £3,000 in year three, £2,000 in year four, and £1,000 in
year five.
Incapacitated child allowance: Increased by £100 to £800
Blind person's allowance: Increased by £300 to £1,000 for an individual blind person or
from £400 to £2,000 for a blind couple
Business use of cars: The threshold used for calculating capital allowances and expenses
for the business use of cars is raised from £15,000 to £15,500 in the case of new cars --
the change took effect on budget day, December 3, 1997 .

PRSI
— Payment ceiling raised by £1,000 to £24,200; weekly allowance for classes A and H
raised from £80 to £100.
— Lower exemption limit for health and training levies (2¼%) raised from £197 to £207

CAPITAL ACQUISITIONS TAX
Concession currently available to siblings over 55 living together in a jointly owned
house is to be extended to siblings under 55 and to nephews and nieces provided they
lived in the house for ten years; the value of the concession was increased.
CAPITAL GAINS TAX
Standard rate reduced from 40% to 20%. Annual exemption reduced from £1,000 to £500
per individual and it is no longer transferable between spouses. The special rate of 26%
was abolished on budget day.

jointly owned by siblings over 55 is being extended to those under 55 and also to nephews and nieces.

A summary of these changes is given in the table on the opposite page and they are treated in more detail below.

Most people believe that they are paying too much tax — on the basis that any tax is too much. There are certainly many, many people paying more tax than they need to — simply because they don't claim all the allowances they're entitled to, or because they are not making use of every tax avoidance measure possible. Tax avoidance is no crime. It is simply using the tax system to the best advantage. It is tax evasion which is illegal.

Reducing your tax bill

The following are some ideas worth considering. Further details on each option are given later in this chapter or in chapter fourteen on page 267.

- Make sure that you are claiming all the allowances to which you are entitled. PAYE taxpayers are likely to lose rather than gain by not making an annual return. That is not always true but it generally is. Relief on insurance premiums was abolished in 1992, but have you still claims to make for past years? Have you increased your claim for medical insurance in line with the premium increases? Have you a claim for medical expenses? A careful reading of the following pages could be worthwhile.

- A married couple can make up to £2,000 in tax-free capital gains in the 1997/98 tax-year The concession is being reduced from April 1998 but it is well worth while making use of that concession before then. It could save you £400 even at the new lower rate of tax. **See page 256.**

- If you are self-employed consider employing your children on a part-time basis. As a family you can save some tax that way. **See page 222.**

- Subject to certain generous limits there is full tax relief on pension contributions so, for the self-employed, a personal pensions scheme offers a particularly favourable way of saving for the future. Workers can also benefit by putting extra money into their own schemes. **For details see chapter 10, page 169.**

- Get some of your income by way of an approved profit sharing scheme negotiated with your employer. It is possible to get up to £10,000 tax free each year. **For details see page 244.**

- You can also get certain benefits from your employer tax free. They include a subsidised canteen, crèche and some leisure facilities.

You will find other ideas throughout the book.

Pay As You Earn

The vast majority of income tax payers come under the Pay As You Earn scheme (PAYE). They have no alternative. With very few exceptions all employees come under the scheme which was initially sold on the basis that it spread income tax liability over the year. That saved taxpayers being faced with large bills once a year. That was the idea anyway. Of course, it also provides the exchequer with a nice even flow of revenue throughout the year. The tax year runs from April 6 to April 5 and it is your income during that period which dictates your liability to tax. PAYE is simply an administrative method of collecting that tax in easy stages during the year, once a week or once a month.

It is all too easy for PAYE taxpayers to be overtaxed. It is important to check that you are claiming all your allowances. You will not get them all automatically.

Employers have a legal obligation to stop tax on payments to employees and they do so on the basis of instructions given to them by the Revenue Commissioners. These instructions are summarised on your certificate of tax free allowances. A certificate should be sent to you before the start of the tax year. It will list the tax reliefs you have been allowed. Do not ignore it. The tax man can make mistakes and so can you. You may not have claimed all your allowances. Some allowances are given to you automatically but others you will not get unless you claim them. So check your allowances.

The accompanying tables will help you to work out your tax liability for the year. The check list of tax allowances on page 212 contains most of the concessions applicable to the average taxpayer. A fuller list starts on the next page. Check both. Details of the allowances for the five years up to and including 1998/99 are given in appendix 1 on page 304.

Remember that if you have failed to claim your full allowances you can claim rebates for up to ten years.

The tables are designed to help you to work out your annual tax liability, in exactly the same way the taxman would work it out. It is done on an annual basis. The PAYE system is designed to collect the tax due from your pay packages. It should ensure that your tax payments over the year add up to your full liability and no more. But in some circumstances it may result in you paying too much or too little. If it has taken too much, then you are due a rebate. If it has taken too little and the taxman finds out, you will swiftly get a demand for the difference. Your legal tax liability is worked out in the way outlined in the following table — how it is collected is simply an administrative matter. Some of the technicalities — in particular the matter of table allowances — are explained on page 208.

The tax on some income may not be collected under the PAYE system but your total taxable income is arrived at by deducting your allowances from your total gross income. Income includes all emoluments (pay) of any office or job including salaries; fees; wages; perquisites; profits; pensions; headage payments; most interest; and benefits-in-kind. Some of these like benefits-in-kind or self-employed income may not be caught in the PAYE net but the tax liability is calculated in the same way.

People who are part-time self-employed in addition to being in paid employment may be liable to pay tax on the self-employed income under what is known as schedule "D" which allows for the tax to be paid in one annual instalment — more about that later in the chapter. But the tax liability is calculated on the basis of your total income from all sources.

So what allowances can be claimed?

All the following apply to the 1998/99 tax year. Rates for previous years are given in appendix 1 on page 304. Details of tax bands and rates for past years are given on page 302.

Your liability to tax is calculated on the basis of total gross income minus allowances. You total up all your allowances, deduct that figure from your gross income, to arrive at your taxable income. In the 1998/99 tax year that taxable income will be subject to tax at the following rates: First £10,000 at 24p if you are single and twice that for a married couple and the remainder at 46p.

- **PERSONAL ALLOWANCES:**

Single person	**£3,150**
Widowed person	**£3,650**
Married couple	**£6,300**

If the taxpayer or his spouse is over, or will reach, the age of 65 during the tax year, the following higher rates of personal allowances apply.

Single person	**£3,550**
Widowed person	**£4,050**
Married couple	**£7,100**

Table Allowances

The PAYE tax scheme presents tax collectors with an administrative problem. The income tax code provides that the first portion of a person's income is free of tax. That is the portion covered by allowances. Then there is a portion subject to tax at 24p in the pound. For a single person that amounts to £10,000 in the 1998/99 tax year. Any income over that is subject to tax at 46p in the pound.

But most taxpayers would find it hard to cope with a system which taxed them lightly at the beginning of the year and progressively raised the tax take as the year went by. To get over the problem employers are instructed to stop income tax at a constant rate throughout the year. The tax allowances are also spread evenly over the year so that each month the worker gets the benefit of one-twelfth of his total tax allowances for the year. The rate of tax applied to the remaining income is the top rate to which the taxpayer is expected to be liable.

If nothing else was done it is obvious that the tax-payer would end up paying too much tax. He will have got the benefit of all his tax allowances but he would have been paying tax at say 46p on all his taxable income rather than 24p on some of it, and 46p on the balance. Taking the case of a single man the first £10,000 should be taxed at 24p. If it is taxed at 46p he will be overtaxed to the tune of 10,000 times 22p (46p minus 24p) or £2,200. The table allowances are designed to compensate for this. In the case of a single person paying tax at 46p in the pound the allowance must provide a tax saving of £2,200. Since he or she is paying tax at 46p in the pound he needs an extra allowance of £4,782. That will save him £4,782 times 46p which works out a few pence over £2,200 So what he loses one way he gains in another.

The table allowances are as follows:

	Table	1997/98		1998/99	
		Rate	Allowance	Rate	Allowance
Married	"S"	48p	£9,076	46p	£9,564
Single	"B"	48p	£4,538	46p	£4,782

CHILD ALLOWANCES:

There is an allowance of £800 in respect of an incapacitated child, although this is reduced if the amount spent in maintaining the child is actually less. The child must have become incapacitated before reaching 21 years of age, or while still receiving full-time education.

There is no tax relief in respect of other children. But tax exemption limits are increased depending on the number of children in a family. This can benefit low income families — see page 211 for details.

- **DEPENDENT RELATIVE'S ALLOWANCE: £110.**

This allowance is granted for each relative of the taxpayer, or spouse, who is incapacitated, and, even if not incapacitated, the widowed mother or mother-in-law of the taxpayer. The allowance is also granted in respect of a son or daughter of the taxpayer who is resident with him, and on whose services he or his wife depends because of old age or illness.

Although small, this allowance can be an important one to claim and it can be shared among a number of people in respect of the one person. For instance a number of children could claim it in respect of a father or mother. By doing that they can then claim tax relief on any contribution they make to the parent's medical expenses and that includes the cost of maintenance in a recognised nursing home or hospital. There is more about that under "Medical Expenses" below. The allowance is reduced by £1 for every pound by which the dependant's income exceeds the maximum pension rate — about £3,510.

> Dependent Relative's Allowance, although small, can be important in claiming allowances for a dependent's medical expenses.

- **BLIND PERSON'S ALLOWANCE: £1,000.**

This allowance can be claimed where either the taxpayer or the taxpayer's spouse is blind. If both are blind the allowance is £2,000.

- **SPECIAL HOUSEKEEPER ALLOWANCE: £8,500.**

This allowance is given to an incapacitated taxpayer who is employing a person to care for him or herself or for an incapacitated spouse.

- **PAYE ALLOWANCE: £800.**

This allowance is granted to all people liable to be taxed under the PAYE system. If a husband and wife are both wage-earning, there is a double allowance of £1,600. It is allowed to a child working full-time in a family firm but not to a spouse. The child can claim the full £800 allowance.

- **HEALTH INSURANCE:**

The allowance is granted on the amount paid in premiums during the previous year. It is granted in respect of insurance against medical expenses and for income continuance assurance in the event of ill-health. But the benefits from income continuance schemes are taxed as income. The tax relief was restricted to a maximum of 37.5p in the £ for 1995/96 and to the standard rate from April 1996. Since April 1997 the relief is only given at the standard rate which is going down from 26p to 24p from April 1998.

- **MEDICAL EXPENSES:**

Full allowance is granted for most medical expenses paid by the taxpayer in respect of himself, his wife, or any other person for whom he claims tax allowances. The first £100 is disallowed (£200 for a family). Relief can either be claimed in the tax-year during which the payment was made or in the year in which it was incurred. Medical expenses in respect of the following are not allowed: normal childbirth; normal dental treatment; eye testing; or the supply of spectacles.

Dental treatment which is not considered 'normal' in this context includes: crowns, veneers, tip replacing, gold posts, gold inlays, endodontics — root canal treatment, periodontal treatment, orthodontic treatment and the surgical extraction of impacted wisdom teeth. The tax relief is available on treatment performed outside the State provided, of course, the receipts are submitted.

A person for whom a Dependent Relative's Allowance is given is considered part of a family for this purpose. This allowance can be shared among a number of people — see above. This means that a number of children, for instance, contributing to the medical expenses of a parent can all consider the parent to be part of their families for the purposes of a claim for relief under this heading.

An alternative is for the children to covenant money to the parent who then uses the extra cash to pay for the medical or nursing home expenses. The parent then claims the tax relief. Unlike the old type covenants to student children this type of covenant can still be tax efficient. See page 288.

In certain cases — kidney patients and child oncology patients — the Revenue Commissioners accept the cost of travelling to and from treatment centres as legitimate medical expenses for the purpose of this relief. A rate of 25p a mile has been allowed since April 1997. Telephone costs and certain costs involved in

Low Income Exemption Limits

People with incomes below certain exemption limits are taken out of the income tax net altogether, although they would otherwise be liable for some tax if the calculations were done in the normal way.

The table below gives the exemption limits for the current and coming years. **It is important to remember that these are not allowances.** If your income is above the limits, then your tax liability is calculated in the normal way, except that those with incomes slightly above the limit are entitled to some marginal relief. The tax they pay will not amount to more than 40p of the difference between the exemption limit and their actual income. For example a married man aged 66 with an income of £10,100 i.e. £100 above the exemption limit, will pay £40 in tax. That would be 40% of the £100.

The exemption limits shown below are increased by £450 for each of the first two dependent children and by £650 for each subsequent child. Since the tax authorities do not automatically know how many children a taxpayer has, since the general child tax allowance was abolished, it is important that taxpayers with children make a claim if their income is below or even marginally above the relevant exemption limit.

	1997/98	1998/99
Single and widowed	£4,000	£4,100
Married Couples	£8,000	£8,200
Single and widowed 65 or over	£4,600	£5,000
Married, either spouse over 65	£9,200	£10,000
Single and widowed 75 or over	£5,200	£5,500
Married, either spouse 75 or over	£10,400	£11,000

home dialysis treatment is also allowed. Full details are available from the Revenue Commissioners' Information Office, Dublin Castle, phone (01) 8780000. The claim is made at the end of the tax year on the form MED 1 which can be obtained from the local tax office.

• **PENSION CONTRIBUTIONS:**

The contributions to an approved scheme are allowed in full subject normally to a maximum of 15% of income for those under the age of 55 and on 20% of income for those over 55. In certain cases tax relief will be allowed over those limits.

- **YEAR OF MARRIAGE:**

Married couples are taxed as single persons in the year that the marriage takes place. If they would have paid less tax as a married couple they can claim a rebate at the end of the tax year in respect of the proportion of the full tax year for which they were married.

The various options facing married couples are considered in more detail in a separate section on page 228.

- **PRSI ALLOWANCE:**

Those paying PRSI at the higher rates were entitled to this allowance. It was abolished in the 1996 budget with effect from April 1996 having been reduced from £286 to £140 the previous year.

- **INTEREST PAYMENTS:**

Apart from the few exceptions mentioned below relief is only allowed in respect of the interest on loans taken out to buy, maintain, or improve the taxpayer's principal residence, the residence of a former or separated spouse, or the residence of a dependent relative (other than a child) who is living in the house rent free. There is an upper limit on eligible interest of £2,500 for single taxpayers; £5,000 for a married couple; and £3,600 for widows and widowers.

The tax relief is allowed at the standard rate on 80% of the interest paid minus £200 in the case of a married taxpayer or £100 in the case of a single taxpayer.

For example a married taxpayer paying more than £5,000 interest a year gets the maximum relief of £3,800. That is calculated as follows: 80% of £5,000 is £4,000 and that is reduced by £200 giving the relief of £3,800.

First time house buyers get relief on the basis of 100% of the interest paid without the £200 or £100 deduction — for the first five years.

Where a taxpayer moves house and there is a delay in selling the original house, both houses can be considered to be the sole or main residence for up to one year. And during that year the interest on any loan taken out to buy the new house is allowed for tax relief in addition to the tax relief on the old loan — the limit is doubled. Interest on loans taken out to pay death duties is allowed for tax relief without any restriction. And so too is interest on money borrowed to buy newly issued shares in one's own company. More information on this latter point is given in the section on reducing your tax bill on page 267. A more detailed treatment of mortgage interest relief with detailed examples and tables is given in chapter 6-3. starting on page 136.

For the 1994/95 year the relief was restricted to a maximum of 42.5p in the pound for 48p taxpayers. That was reduced further to 37.5p for 1995/96 and to 32.5p in 1996/97. Since April 1997 the relief has been restricted to the standard rate.

Tax relief was generally allowed on 100% of mortgage interest up to April 1987. For the 1987/88 and 1988/89 tax years the relief was given on 90% of the interest paid, and in April 1989 it was reduced to 80% and remained at that level until 1993 when it was increased to 90% again for one year. That's history now but may be of interest if you are making a back claim.

- **SINGLE PARENT FAMILIES:**

  A widow or widower who has care of a dependent child or children at any time during the tax year is entitled to an additional allowance of £2,650. Other single parents are entitled to a higher allowance of £3,150. In the case of separated parents, it is possible for both to get this allowance if each has care of the child or children for any part of the year. Widows and widowers also get an extra tax allowance for the first few years after bereavement — see below.

- **WIDOWS/WIDOWERS:**

  An extra allowance of £1,500 in the year following bereavement for widows and widowers with dependent children, applied for the first time in 1990/91. It's being increased to £5,000 from April 1998, reducing to £4,000 in the second year after bereavement, £3,000 the following year, then £2,000 and finally £1,000 in the fifth year reducing to nothing in the sixth year.

- **RENT ALLOWANCE:**

  Relief at the standard rate of tax is allowed to all tenants living in private rented accommodation in respect of the rent paid. The maximum rent allowed for relief is:

Married,	£1,000
Widowed person,	£750
Single person,	£500

Alternatively a taxpayer over 55 years of age living in rented accommodation can claim an allowance of up to £1,000 in respect of the rent paid. The maximum is £2,000 for a married couple and £1,500 for a widow or widower. The allowance cannot be claimed in respect of rent paid to local authority or on tenancies of fifty years or more.

● **EXPENSES:**

Allowance is also made for expenses incurred by the taxpayer in performing his job. In the case of a PAYE worker the expenses must have been wholly, exclusively, and necessarily incurred. The 'necessarily' criterion does not apply to the self-employed taxpayer. PAYE workers may claim relief against the expense of buying tools and special work clothes, for instance. Travelling expenses to and from work are not allowed. Very often the Tax Inspector will agree a figure that can be claimed without any evidence of the expenses being incurred. But the taxpayer can claim more, provided he can justify the higher claim. The following table provides an insight into the level of agreed rates which may find favour with the Revenue. They are rates applicable to civil servants which took effect from January 1997.

Civil Service Subsistence Rates

Rank	Night Allowances			Day Allowances	
	Normal	Reduced	Detention	10 hours or more	5 to 10 hours
Assistant Principal	£71.74	£66.14	£35.87	£20.73	£8.46
Admin. Officer	£64.47	£55.15	£32.24	£20.73	£8.46
Executive Officer	£53.92	£44.61	£26.99	£20.73	£8.46
Clerical Officer	£46.65	£39.36	£23.32	£15.66	£7.73
Messenger	£38.21	£31.68	£19.08	£15.66	£7.73

The normal overnight rate applies for the first 14 nights, the reduced rate for the next fourteen and the detention rate for subsequent periods.

- **SERVICE CHARGES:**

  While water charges have been abolished the tax relief on local authority service charges remain. The relief is given at the standard rate in respect of up to £150 of local authority service charges paid in full and on time. The relief is in respect of the charges paid during the previous year.

- **COLLEGE FEES:**

  From April 1995 tax relief is allowed on fees paid for undergraduate study at approved private third level college either on behalf of the taxpayer or on behalf of a dependent. The fees must not be recouped by grants or scholarships and the relief may not exceed the tax liability of the taxpayer. The relief is given only at the standard rate.

- **ALARMS FOR THE ELDERLY:**

  An allowance of up to £800 is granted in respect of the cost of alarms installed by a taxpayer over 65 living alone.

PRSI liabilities

Pay Related Social Insurance (PRSI) is every bit as much a tax on income as income tax itself. It is normally taken to include both the health and the employment and training levies but, in fact, they are three separate items. The rate of PRSI you pay depends on your job. Most people fall into one of three main categories: private sector employees; public sector employees; and the self-employed. The following table lists the position for 1998/99:

PRSI and Levy Rates

PRSI

	Private Sector	Public Sector	Self-employed
Rate	4.5%	0.9%	5%
Ceiling	£24,200	£24,200	£23,200
Exemptions	£100 a week	£20 a week	£1,040 a year
LEVIES			
Rate	2¼%	2¼%	2¼%
Ceiling	None	None	None

Those earning less than £30 a week are not covered for PRSI while those earning less than £207 in a particular week are not liable for the levies. The threshold was £197 in 1997/98 and £188 in 1996/97. Once income goes above that threshold the levies become payable on all income.

From April 1995 the first £50 of weekly pay (£10 for public sector employees paying the lower rate PRSI) was exempt from PRSI. That was increased to £80 (£20 for lower rate PRSI payers) from April 1996 and to £100 from April 1998. It applies on a weekly basis. Once earnings in a particular year go above the ceiling of £24,200 — £23,200 for 1997/98 — PRSI is no longer stopped from the pay package and the exemption no longer applies. So someone earning say £46,400 a year will only get the benefit of the exemption for half the year.

Tax on social welfare

Many social welfare benefits have been taxable for years. But tax liability was extended to some short-term benefits — unemployment and disability benefits — from April 1994. A number of concessions were introduced subsequently. The first three days of disability benefit is not subject to tax in the 1997/98 tax year. That is to be increased to six days from April 1998. In addition the following exemptions apply:

- Child dependent additions to social welfare payments are not taxed.

- The unemployment benefit of systematic short-term workers is not taxed.

- The first £10 a week of unemployment benefit is disregarded for tax purposes.

Tax and the company car

A company car is a valuable addition to any remuneration package. On the basis of AA estimates it costs well over £6,000 a year to run an average sized car when depreciation, tax, insurance and all running costs are taken into account. That's a measure of what you save if the company provides you with a car and covers all the costs.

But a car is not one of those few benefits which an employer can provide tax-free to an employee. It is viewed as part of the recipient's salary — a Benefit in Kind (BIK) — and as such is subject to income tax. And you can forget about the AA estimates — the Revenue Commissioners have their own strict rules for putting a monetary value on your "perk".

Reducing car benefit-in-kind

The options available for reducing the tax liability on a company car fall into a number of fairly obvious categories:

Reduce the price: The lower the original market price of the car the smaller will be the benefit in kind assessment. That boils down to a choice over the type of car you want and the status you attach to it. There is, however, one way of having your cake and eating it i.e. having a high status car and at the same time reducing your tax liability. That's by buying an old but good second hand car. Such cars are also attractive to people who want to buy their own and charge the company for the business milage done.

Pay some of the costs: Paying for all the petrol you use for the non-business milage done in the car reduces the initial assessment from 30% to 26%. On a £16,000 car that reduces the BIK assessment by £640 and the tax bill by £295 (assuming tax at 46p). That would buy you about 500 litres of petrol. Only you can say whether it's worth it. Similar type calculations can be done for the other items which reduce the assessment if you pay for them yourself.

Do more milage: If you're close to one of the thousand mile cut-off points it can obviously be worth while to move into the higher bracket. For instance if you do 19,001 business miles rather than 18,999 you cut the assessment by 20% rather than 15%. That can be a significant saving just for the sake of a few miles.

Use the car pool: There is no benefit in kind assessed if the company car you use is out of a car pool. But the Revenue apply very strict rules. The car must be made available to and used by more than one employee. The car must not normally be kept overnight at or close to any of the employees' homes. Any private use must be minimal and incidental to business use.

Charge milage: If you use your own car for business use you can, of course, claim a milage allowance from your employer. To escape Revenue displeasure the payment must be based on actual milage and an acceptable milage rate. The employer has to get Revenue approval not to deduct tax from the payments and while there is no definitive milage rate the Civil Service own rates provide an indication of what may be appropriate.

Use a van: If you have a company van rather than a company car somewhat more favourable rules apply to the calculation of benefit-in-kind. It's assessed on the annual value of the van which is defined as 12.5% of its cost plus total running expenses. A portion of that is attributed to private milage in the ratio it bears to total milage.

But there are ways of reducing the tax liability or avoiding it altogether by buying your own car and charging the company a mileage rate. Or if you don't claim a mileage rate you can claim tax relief on the expense of running the car including an allowance for the capital cost of buying it. That approach is most often used by self-employed people but it can be used by employees — see page 248 See the table on the page opposite for some other options.

The maximum benefit assessed by the Revenue Commissioners is 30 per cent of the original market value of the car. It was 20 per cent up to April 1992. The full 30 per cent is applied where the company bears all of the costs involved including petrol for your private use, insurance, tax, maintenance etc. The following reductions are made if you bear some of the costs yourself.

You supply petrol for your private use	4.5%
You pay for your own insurance	3%
You pay for all repairs and servicing	3%
You pay the road tax	1%

So you could get a reduction of $11\frac{1}{2}$ points i.e. to $18\frac{1}{2}$% of the car's cost.

In addition there is a sliding scale applied depending on the amount of business mileage you do. If you do more than 15,000 business miles in the car during the year there is a further reduction in the assessment on the basis of a sliding scale starting with a 2.5 per cent reduction if you do between 15,000 and 16,000 business miles and ranging upwards to a maximum reduction of 75 per cent if you do more than 30,000 business miles. Full details of the scale are given in appendix 2 on page 312.

A special 20% relief from the tax was introduced in 1996. It's available to company representatives who spend at least 70% of their working hours away from their place of business and who do at least 5,000 business miles a year. This is an alternative to the high mileage relief.

Let's have a look at an example of those calculations:

Take the case of a salesman who does 19,500 business miles in the year. He has a middle range car with an original market value of £16,000. He pays for his own insurance and road tax and also covers all the maintenance costs on the car while his employer supplies all the petrol even for personal use.

The fact that he bears those costs himself reduces the initial assessment to 23% of the £16,000. That works out at £3,680.

That's further reduced since the business mileage is more than 15,000. On the basis of the sliding scale the reduction for 19,500 miles is 20 per cent. So the £3,680 is reduced by 20 per cent to give a final assessment of £2,944. That's the figure that's liable for tax.

At 46p in the £ that would amount to £1,354. It's painful but it may not be a high cost to pay for the benefit of a company car. Compare it with the depreciation costs on a £16,000 car you'd buy yourself. Without putting it on the road at all it must be costing at least £2,000 a year just by going down in value. In estimating motoring costs the AA assumes that cars have an economic life of eight years.

Calculating your tax liability

As outlined above, your total tax liability is calculated by initially taking your gross earnings; subtracting your total allowances to arrive at taxable income; and then applying the appropriate tax rates to the successive slices of taxable income. Let us take an example: Mr. Murphy is married with two children — both still at school. He is going to earn £30,000 during the 1998/99 tax year. In addition his company supplies him with a car which is valued as a benefit-in-kind. Mr. Murphy will pay £1,525 in interest on a house mortgage, but he will only be allowed tax relief on £1,020 of that. That is calculated at 80% of the £1,525 paid less £200. He paid £500 in VHI contributions during 1997/98. Relief on VHI is based on the previous year's premiums. He paid £1,200 into the company pension scheme. His mother-in-law is living with the family and has no means of her own so he gets an allowance of a lowly £110 in respect of a dependent relative. The calculations are shown in the accompanying table. In doing your own calculations you can use the form provided on page 224.

Mr. Murphy's total income tax liability is £6,500 for the year. The PAYE system will ensure that he pays that in weekly or monthly instalments over the period. It may be necessary to arrive at an estimate of the interest payments, but if there is any under or over payment of tax it can be sorted out in a balancing statement at the end of the year. These are not automatic so if

The Murphys — how they are taxed

GROSS PAY			£30,000
Plus Benefit-in-kind (company car)			£3,000
Less Pension contributions			£1,200
TOTAL			£31,800
Less	Married allowance	£6,300	
	Dependent allowance	£110	
	VHI premiums	£500	
	Interest	£1,020	
	PAYE allowance	£800	
	Agreed expenses	£100	
	Total allowances	**£8,830**	
Taxable Income			**£22,970**
First £20,000 at 24p			£4,800
Remainder at 46p			£1,366
Interest adjustment: 1,020 by 22p (46 minus 24)			£224
VHI adjustment: 500 by 22p (46 minus 24)			£110
TOTAL TAX			**£6,500**

you think you have been overtaxed it is important for you to claim.

Doing your own sums

The tables on the following two pages will help you to do your own sums. Even if you don't feel like getting the calculator out, at least have a look at page 241 which looks at some allowances and reliefs which are commonly missed.

The figures can be worked out by reference to the list of tax allowances given on page 225. The mortgage interest relief and VHI adjustment is based on the fact that the initial calculations allow tax relief on the £1,020 of interest and the £500 of VHI

First check your tax allowances

Personnal Allowances	1997/98	1998/99	1997/98	1998/99
Married Couple	£5,800	£6,300	....	....
Single	£2,900	£3,150	....	....
Widow/Widower	£3,400	£3,650	....	....
Single Parent				
Widowed				
- year after bereavement	£3,900	£8,150		
- 2nd year	£3,400	£7,150		
- 3rd year	£2,900	£6,150		
- 4th year	£2,400	£5,150		
- 5th year	£2,400	£4,150		
- thereafter	£2,400	£3,150	....	....
Other single parents	£2,900	£2,650	....	....
Child Allowance				
Only for disabled child	£700	£800	....	....
Age Allowance (over 65)				
Married Couple	£800	£800	....	....
Single/Widowed	£400	£400	....	....
Dependent Relative				
Maximum	£110	£110	....	....
Blind Allowance				
Individual	£700	£1,000	....	....
Couple (both blind)	£1,600	£2,000	....	....
Housekeeper Allowance				
See Text	£7,500	£8,500	....	....
PAYE Allowance	£800	£800	....	....
Interest Relief				
See text			....	....
Medical Insurance				
Previous year's VHI/BUPA contribution etc.				
(only allowed at 24p — 26p for 1997/98)			....	....
Expenses				
Usually an agreed rate for your job.			....	....
Table Allowance see page 208 — do not include it here.				
TOTAL ALLOWANCES			....	....

Then calculate your own PAYE liability

To work out your annual tax liability you must first total your tax allowances on the previous page. It lists the more usual allowances but you may have other entitlements, read the more detailed list in the chapter as well. You can then transfer the total to the table below.

	1997/98	1998/99
GROSS INCOME		
Less pension contributions		
Less tax free allowances		
Equals **Taxable income**		
That income is taxed as follows:		
MARRIED COUPLE		
1997/98		
First £19,800 at 26p in the £		
Remainder at 48p in the £		
1998/99		
First £20,000 at 24p in the £		
Remainder at 46p in the £		
SINGLE PERSON		
1997/98		
First £9,900 at 26p in the £		
Remainder at 48p in the £		
1998/99		
First £10,000 at 24p in the £		
Remainder at 46p in the £		
TOTAL TAX		

Claiming back tax for previous years

Many people pay too much tax simply because they haven't claimed all of the allowances and reliefs to which they are entitled. But, if you have missed out, it is possible to go back ten years with your claim. So although relief is no longer given on life insurance premiums, for instance, it is still possible to make a claim for premiums paid before April 1992 when they were finally abolished. The following lists some of the allowances most often missed and details of how they have changed over the years. If you have a claim all you have to do is get some tax return forms from your tax office and fill them out in respect of each year. If you can only get forms for the current year don't be afraid to simply write in the relevant dates for past years.

Rent Allowance: A taxpayer over 55 years of age living in rented accommodation can claim an allowance of up to £1,000 in respect of the rent paid. The maximum is £2,000 for a married couple and £1,500 for a widow or widower. Those limits apply since April 1991. The allowance cannot be claimed in respect of rent paid to local authority or on tenancies of fifty years or more. From the 1995/96 tax year onwards relief at the standard rate of tax is allowed to all tenants living in private rented accommodation in respect of the rent paid. The maximum rent allowed for relief is: Married, £1,000; Widowed person, £750; Single person, £500.

Medical insurance premiums: This allowance is granted on the amount paid in premiums during the previous year. It is granted in respect of insurance against medical expenses and for income continuance assurance in the event of ill-health.

Medical expenses: Full allowance is granted for most medical expenses paid by the taxpayer in respect of himself, his wife, or any other person for whom he claims tax allowances. The first £100 is disallowed (£200 for a family). These limits had remained unchanged at a lower £50 per individual (£100 per family) up to April 1994. Relief can either be claimed in the tax-year during which the payment was made or in the year in which it was incurred.

Expenses: Allowance is also made for expenses incurred by the taxpayer in performing his job. In the case of a PAYE payer the expenses must have been wholly, exclusively, and necessarily incurred. The "necessarily" criterion does not apply to the self-employed. The allowance can be given for tools and special work clothes.

Life assurance premiums: This relief was abolished for premiums paid after April 5, 1992 after being gradually reduced over some years. Previously the relief applied to maximum premiums of £1,000 per individual on policies covering the life of the taxpayer or his/her spouse. This limit did not apply to policies taken out before April 2, 1974. You can still claim back to 1988.

contributions at the full rate of 46p. But these reliefs are restricted to the standard rate of 24p — a difference of 22p in the £. So the tax liability has to be increased by 1,020 times 22p in respect of the interest and 500 times 22p in respect of the VHI. No adjustment is needed for someone who is only paying tax at a top rate of 24p since they are allowed the relief in full at that rate.

Note also that the company car is treated as a taxable benefit-in-kind which has to be included in the figures. The private use of a car is not the only benefit-in-kind which may be valued and assessed as part of the taxpayer's income. Other such items include the provision of accommodation, entertainment, services or indeed any benefits or facilities supplied by the employer and not paid for by the employee. Legitimate expenses, of course, wholly, exclusively and necessarily incurred in the performance of one's duties are not assessed for tax. Neither are subsidised canteen meals.

Self-employed income 13.2

Income from self-employment is subject to a somewhat different tax regime than wages or salaries. The earnings are, of course subject to tax in just the same way as outlined in the previous section but it is collected in a different way and there are different rules with regard to allowable expenses and costs. Both of these differences are looked at in this section.

Some self-employed people are actually employees of their own companies. The company is considered to be a separate legal entity from the tax point of view. The owner is treated as an employee and taxed as such under the PAYE system although subject to certain restrictions aimed at preventing tax evasion. Here, however, we only consider the self-employed person not working for a company. Such a taxpayer has to calculate his or her own tax liability and pay a lump sum payment before November 1 each year. Detailed tax returns must be submitted by the end of January. The November payment is an estimated amount relating to the current tax year while the January return relates to the previous tax year.

Failure to make a full and true disclosure leaves the taxpayer liable not only for interest but also for a 10% surcharge. That 10% surcharge can also be imposed when a return is not made by January 31. The original estimate of tax due, issued by the tax inspector in his "notice of preliminary tax", becomes immediately payable plus a 10% surcharge but minus, of course, any tax already paid.

The annual tax return should be made on the normal tax form to which should be added summary accounts for the business. These accounts need not be all that elaborate. A single page is sufficient for a simple business. But, of course, the back-up receipts and invoices should be available in case the tax inspector wants to see them. Under the self-assessment system a proportion of all returns are examined in detail and the taxpayers involved may be subject to a revenue audit. Most are picked according to a number of unpublished criteria but some are simply picked at random. You can reduce your chances of being picked for an audit by explaining any peculiarities in your tax return — see page 244.

Self-employed income

The business accounts for the tax office need not be over elaborate but backup receipts and invoices etc. should be available if asked for.

Avoiding an tax audit

Most revenue audits are targeted. Some taxpayers are picked at random but the vast bulk – perhaps over 90 per cent – are picked because of their past record or because their tax returns trigger some alarm bells in the Revenue computers or the tax inspector's mind.

It is not too difficult to imagine the type of return which might trigger an audit. All you have to do is put yourself in the tax inspector's shoes and consider what he or she might be looking for. An irregular trading pattern, for instance, might be considered a bit strange and worthy of investigation. It might reflect tax evasion but it might also be due to the nature of the business, lost contracts, illness of key workers – any number of possible explanations.

If there is an explanation like that it is better to add a note to the VAT or other tax return. It might just offset an audit. The same is true of the other possible factors which might put a tax inspector wondering – factors like the following:

Low drawings: Where the amount of money drawn out of a business by the proprietor seems unduly low by reference to previous periods or by reference to realistic spending needs the inspector may wonder what is sustaining the taxpayer's lifestyle. If there is a legitimate explanation, make it in an addendum to your tax return.

Fluctuating turnover: This may, of itself raise questions in a tax inspector's mind unless the business is of an obvious seasonal nature. A change in the pattern is, of course, just as likely to prompt questions.

VAT: Discrepancies between VAT and income or corporation tax returns are very easily spotted now that the Revenue has encouraged a standardisation of tax periods. In small businesses particularly there can be a legitimate explanation. If there is it is better to make it before an audit is prompted than during the audit.

Careless returns: Sloppy VAT and PAYE returns will obviously raise a suspicion that accounting procedures are not all they should be.

So self-employed people do pay their tax somewhat later than employees who are subject to the PAYE system but the advantage is no longer as great as it used to be when tax was paid on a prior year basis and it does require some planning to maximise the cash flow benefits.

In particular the choice of accounting year can be important and so too can the calculation of the preliminary tax which is paid each November. To make the right choices it is important first to understand how the system works.

Self-employed taxpayers are required to pay tax in one lump sum before November 1 each year. It is an estimated amount based on a self-assessment of the tax which will eventually be payable for the current tax year. That tax is not necessarily based on the income during the normal April to April tax year but rather the accounting year which ends during the tax year. The choice of accounting year is up to the self-employed taxpayer.

That's easier to understand from an example. Many businesses operate on a calendar accounting year e.g. from January 1 to December 31. Let's take the case of such a business operated by Ms Murphy. This coming November 1, 1998 she will have to make a preliminary tax payment based on her assessment of the tax due on her 1998 calendar accounts.

Ten months of the year will have passed so she'll be paying the tax on ten months income in arrears and on two months in advance. It's actually a bit better than that because she won't have to submit a final tax return for the year until January 31, 2000. At that stage a final assessment of her tax liability will be made and she'll have a further month to pay any additional tax.

If the preliminary tax payments she makes this November is at least 90 per cent of the tax eventually found to be due, she'll suffer no interest or penalties. Another way of avoiding interest and penalties is to opt to pay a preliminary tax of at least 100 per cent of the previous year's tax liability (after adding back some extra relief such as BES). For a growing business that's usually a far better option.

Underpaying preliminary tax can prove costly so it pays to take a bit of care in doing the calculations.

The benefit, of course, is only in terms of cash flow. The full tax eventually has to be paid but it leaves extra money in the business for at least fourteen months.

For a growing business the choice of accounting year may also be important. Let's suppose Ms Murphy's business operated on a July 1 to June 30 accounting year. The tax paid in November 1998 will be based on the income generated during the accounting year from July 1997 to June 1998. If income is growing that has to be better than paying the tax on the basis of calendar year 1998 income.

But remember some of the cash flow benefits can be offset by delays in claiming allowances. And if you change your end of year accounting date the Revenue will go back a year and calculate what your liability would have been had you used the new accounting period during the previous year. You'll get an extra tax bill if the profits in that accounting period were in excess of the actual profits assessed.

That doesn't mean that it can't be worthwhile changing your accounting year or picking a favourable starting date for the business. But there's likely to be many other factors involved in that decision and the cash flow benefits don't accrue for a few years in any case because the tax liability during the early years of the business are subject to special rules.

The profits assessed for the first tax year is the actual taxable income from the date of commencement to the following April 5. The profits assessed in the second year are those for the first twelve months of the business. It is only in the first year that the normal ongoing system starts to operate.

Let's take the example of someone who started a self-employed business during September 1997. In November 1998 they will calculate their preliminary tax on the profits made between September 1997 and April 5, 1998. In November 1999 they will pay preliminary tax on the basis of profits made during the twelve months from September 1997 to September 1998.

There are, of course, additional allowances which can be claimed by the self-employed. These are basically the costs of running the business. To be allowed as a tax deduction an employee must show that any expenses were incurred wholly, exclusively and necessarily for trade or professional purposes. The self-employed taxpayer has only to meet the "wholly and exclusively" requirements. He does not have to show that the expenses were necessarily incurred. That makes more expenses allowable.

The following are some of the more general possibilities.

- Wages paid to employees. See a later section for the benefits of formally paying wages to children who may be helping in the business.

The cost of capital items such as plant or office equipment is deducted from taxable income over seven years.

- Rent paid for business premises is allowed but it may not be worthwhile claiming a notional rent allowance for a room in your private home even if it is used as an office. Instead you can claim for the cost of heating and lighting that room. Claiming for rent could result in part of your house being considered to be a commercial premises. That can have implications for local authority rates and capital gains tax. There is no capital gains tax on a principal residence but there could be a liability on a business premises. If it is only a matter of using one room as an office it is probably best just to claim tax relief on the "running cost" of the room — perhaps, in the case of a four bedroomed house, a seventh of your total household outgoings on heat and light.

- Repairs to premises and repairs to plant and machinery are allowable costs but not the cost of improvements or additions.

- Interest paid on business loans. Restrictions of the type applicable to mortgage interest relief on a home do not, of course, apply.

- The cost of advertising.

- Other business costs include travelling, stationery, telecommunications, postage etc. Receipts should, of course, be kept. Motoring expenses are considered in more detail below.

- Bad debts are also an allowable expense. That includes doubtful debts but the expense must relate to specific debts. It cannot simply be a global provision in the expectation that a certain proportion of bills will be unpaid.

- Allowance can also be claimed in respect of capital expenditure on plant and machinery used in the business. The cost of such items is written off at the rate of 15% a year for six years with the remaining 10% written off in the seventh year. For example if you buy a computer for use in the business for £2,000, you can claim £300 as a cost against earnings in each of the first six years and £200 in the seventh year. Different allowances are made in respect of motor cars. We'll look at those in some detail in the next section.

In addition to these business expenses the self-employed taxpayer who has no other income can also deduct the same personal allowances outlined above for the PAYE payer. The only exception is the PAYE allowance which the self-employed person cannot claim. The PAYE allowance is not available either for a spouse working for a self-employed taxpayer.

The expense allowances will, of course, vary according to the type of business.

Income from rents

Income from the letting of flats, houses or other property is treated in the same way as the self-employed income mentioned above. It is added to the taxpayer's other income in arriving at his overall tax liability but it is not, of course, paid under the PAYE system. In assessing the taxable income from rents, the normal personal allowances are obtainable if they have not already been offset against other income and, in addition, the cost of the following may be deducted from the gross income before arriving at taxable income.

- Any rent payable by the taxpayer himself — i.e. ground rent on the premises.

- Any rates on the premises.

- Interest on any money borrowed to buy the premises or to improve or repair them. This interest relief is unlimited — not subject to the individual upper limit which applies to mortgage interest relief on a principal residence. In this case the interest is considered to be on business borrowings and is allowable in full against rental income.

- The cost of any goods or services which he provides to the tenants and which are not paid for separately from the rent. An example might be providing electric light in the hallways of flats.

- The cost of maintenance, repairs, insurance etc.

- Management costs i.e. cost of collecting rents, advertising for tenants etc..

- Wear and tear allowances on the cost of furniture and fittings at the rate of 15% of the cost in each of the first six years and 10% in the seventh year.

Where the costs exceed the income from the rental property, that loss is only allowed as an offset against future rental income. It cannot be used to reduce the tax due on PAYE earnings for instance.

> There is no restriction on the amount of interest relief which can be claimed against rental income.

Motor Vehicles

Any taxpayer, whether employed or self-employed, who uses his own motor car for business can claim for wear and tear on the car in addition to running expenses. It doesn t arise too often in the case of an employee since he or she is normally either supplied with a company car or has the expenses reimbursed by the employer. But self-employed taxpayers very often use their own cars.

There are restrictions on the amount which can be claimed but they have been eased over recent years. The calculations are based on the value of the car at the time of purchase subject to a maximum which was raised to £15,500 on December 3, 1997.

It was £15,000 was January 23, 1997. The two years previously it was £14,000 and for two years before that, £10,000.

The wear and tear allowed each year is calculated at 20% of the declining value of the car restricted by that initial maximum value. It is also reduced to allow for any private use of the car. A one-third private to two-thirds business is a generally accepted norm.

The following table provides an example of the calculation.

Capital allowances on a car	
Cost — as bought in 1997	£18,000
Restricted to £15,000 (increased to £15,500 from Dec. 3 1997)	£15,000
Allowance at 20% (20% of £15,000)	£3,000
Restricted for business use (2/3rds of £3,000)	£2,000
Allowance for year 1	**£2,000**
Written down value for year 2 (£15,000 minus £2,000)	£13,000
Allowance at 20% (20% of £13,000)	£2,600
Restricted for business use (2/3rds of £2,600)	£1,733
Allowance for year 2	**£1,733**

A somewhat similar restriction applies to running expenses although the calculation is a bit more complicated. In this case there are two restrictions applied. The running expenses are first of all restricted to business milage. That's obvious enough since tax relief can obviously not be claimed in relation to the private use of the car.

The second restriction is aimed at reducing the relief available on more expensive cars. So the relief is restricted on the basis of the lowest i.e. the least beneficial, of one of the following two calculations:

- A third of the amount by which the cost of the car exceeded £15,000.
- Business running costs multiplied by (cost of car minus £15,000) divided by cost of car.

The following is an example of how it works.

Allowable running costs

The following is based on a new car bought during 1997 for £17,000 which is used one-third for personal purposes and two-thirds for business. It is assumed that total running costs for the year are £3,600. After allowing for the private usage it is necessary to calculate two possible restrictions on the allowable costs and apply the lowest of the two.

Total running costs	**£3,600**
Less: one third restriction for private use	£1,200
Business costs	**£2,400**
Restriction 1:	
One third of cost of car minus £15,000 (1/3rd of £2,000)	£667
Restriction 2:	
£2,400 multiplied by (£2,000/£17,000) — see text	£282
Restriction 2 is applied:	
Business Costs — from above	**£2,400**
Less restriction 2	£282
Allowable costs	**£2,118**

To be liable for tax in Ireland you need to be resident in Ireland or, in some case, to have recently been resident in Ireland. The definition of "resident" is strictly defined in this context but it is a fairly liberal definition. For instance it is possible to be non-resident and still have a home in Ireland and there are tax concessions for people who spend as little as 90 days a year out of the country.

The tax position can be considered under three separate categories:

- Working abroad
- Non-resident
- Emigrants

Working Abroad

An individual who works part of the year outside of Ireland and Britain may qualify for a tax relief whereby part of his or her income is treated as tax free. To be eligible it is necessary to:

Have worked abroad for 90 days during a twelve month period. The ninety days must include a consecutive period of at least fourteen days. A day is included in the calculation if the individual is abroad at the end of it and if, during it, he or she devoted a substantial amount of time to actual work rather than leisure or travel. Once qualified a proportion of the individual's income is treated as tax-free. The proportion is calculated on the basis of the number of days abroad minus 15 divided by 365 i.e.

$$\frac{\text{number of days minus fifteen}}{365}$$

Non-resident status

A person is considered to be resident in Ireland for tax purposes if he or she is in the country for 183 days or more in a tax year; or is in the country for more than 30 days in that year and 280 days or more during that and the previous tax year.

You are counted as having spent a day in Ireland if you are in the country at the end of the day so you could, in fact, spend every day in Ireland provided you left the country every night.

In broad terms that means that if you spend less than 30 days in the country during a tax year you are not considered to be resident for tax purposes. If you spend less than six months here you may qualify for non-residence status provided your combined time in the country over the current and previous tax years does not exceed 280 days.

As a non-resident you are not liable for income tax on earnings you make abroad. But for the first three years after becoming non-resident, you are liable to tax on income arising in Ireland, on capital gains and on investment income from any source. So if you go abroad for three years and save up your surplus income you may not be liable for Irish income tax on your earnings but you will still remain liable for tax for three years on the interest earned on your savings.

Tax rebates for emigrants

People who leave a job in Ireland to emigrate may be entitled to a tax rebate but it has to be claimed. Such claims can be backdated for up to ten years. The size of the rebate depends on a number of factors — most notably the date of leaving the Irish job. The potential refund is highest for those who leave jobs a few months into the tax year which begins on April 6. It is lowest for those who leave towards the very end of a tax year. If you leave just prior to April 5 there is unlikely to be any rebate entitlement at all.

The entitlement arises as a result of a special concession which has existed for many years although it was only formally written into law in the 1994 Finance Act. Basically it separates for tax purposes the Irish and overseas earnings of an emigrant in the year he or she leaves the country. It also operates in the year an emigrant returns to work in Ireland.

To be considered an emigrant for the purposes of this tax concession you need to spend at least one full tax year — from April 6 to the following April 5 — out of the country. Occasional visits home, of course, don't affect the entitlement.

Let's first see how it works, how you can go about claiming the rebate, and also look at how to time a return to Ireland to make the maximum use of the concession.

Normally an Irish resident is liable for tax in Ireland on their world-wide income and while the definition of "resident" for tax purposes was eased in the 1994 Finance Act most emigrants would be considered to be resident during the year they emigrated. So technically they should be liable for Irish tax not only on their earnings in Ireland before they leave but also on their earnings abroad during the remainder of the tax year while also paying tax in their new home.

They might, of course, be able to get some relief under a double taxation agreement between Ireland and their new host country. But that's complicated to say the least. But what's known as "The Split Year Rule" allows you to ignore all of that.

If you leave Ireland to work abroad and you stay abroad for at least the following tax year, then you are only liable to pay Irish tax on income earned in Ireland before you left.

A tax rebate may be due both in the year you leave and in the year you return.

There can be no disputing your claim if you have already stayed abroad for the full tax year. But you can make the claim even before you emigrate. The Revenue Commissioners may accept that you intend staying abroad if you have sold your house, for instance, or if you have evidence of taking a long-term job abroad.

So, how does the rebate arise?

Under the PAYE system your tax allowances are spread out equally over the full year. You are allowed a proportion of them for each week or month, depending on how you're paid. So if you leave a job and emigrate after say six months you will only have got the benefit of half of your tax allowances for the year. It's the other half that entitles you to the rebate.

Suppose, for instance, that you're single earning £20,000 a year. Your basic tax free allowances for the year total almost £4,000 just counting personal and PAYE allowances. Your allowances could be more if you include medical insurance and mortgage interest or rent. Six months into the tax year — by October 5 — you'll have earned £10,000 and have got the benefit of half of those tax free allowances or about £2,000. If you leave the job and emigrate at that stage you can claim the benefit of the other £2,000 of tax allowances. At 24p in the £ that's worth £480 of a rebate.

That's only an approximation. The calculations are a bit more complicated because in this case you would have been paying tax at 46p in the pound but rest assured that there is a rebate due. Don't forget, of course, that there is the overriding condition that you are going to work outside the country for the whole of the following tax year.

The claim should be made to whatever tax office you dealt with prior to leaving Ireland. You will need to fill out a tax return for the year you left the country and possibly catch up on earlier years if you hadn't been making tax returns. Ideally you would have a copy of the P45 form you got from your Irish employer on leaving. That would show your earnings during the tax year up to the date you left and details of the tax stopped.

Even if you left Ireland up to ten years ago you may still be due a rebate and it's not too late to claim.

But the tax office should have that information if your previous employer has been making his returns.

Remember that the Revenue Commissioners will normally allow a back-claim for up to ten years.

The size of a possible tax rebate is obviously not the only thing to be considered when planning a date for either emigrating from or returning to Ireland. But its a factor to be taken into account.

The point to remember is that you can earn up to your annual tax free allowance level without any liability for income tax. Indeed you can actually earn a little more because there are low income exemption levels. For those under 65 they currently stand at £4,000 single and £8,000 for a married couple. You can earn up to those figures in any tax year without any liability for income tax. These exemption limits are going up from April 1998 to £4,100 in the case of a single taxpayer and to £8,200 for a couple

So if you have earned less than £4,000 in Ireland before you emigrate you will get a rebate of all of the tax you paid since the previous April 5. A single person returning to Ireland can earn up to £4,000 between the date they return and the following April 5 and pay no tax on it.

For example if you return at Christmas, get a job and decide to stay, you can earn up to £4,000 between then and April 5 without incurring any tax liability. Remember though, that this only applies to those who have spent at least a full tax year abroad.

Cross border workers

People who are resident south of the border and travel to work in Northern Ireland suffer a number of tax disadvantages. In his budget statement on December 3, 1998, the Minister for Finance promised to provide "suitable relief" in the 1998 Finance Act following a consideration of the complex taxation, legal and constitutional issues involved.

13.4 Capital gains tax

If you buy an asset at one price and sell it at a higher price, you have made a capital gain and since April 6, 1974, most gains of this type are liable for tax. From December 3, 1997 the tax rate on gains except those on development land was reduced from 40% to 20%. On the same day a special 26p rate on disposals of shares in certain small to medium sized companies was also abolished. There is one important concession which has remained since the tax was first introduced — with the exception of gains from the disposal of development lands gains arising simply from the effects of inflation are not liable for any tax.

An example will show how this indexation works. Suppose you bought an asset four years ago for £10,000 and have just sold it for £13,000. You have made a gain of £3,000 but the taxable gain is less because you are allowed to adjust the buying price upwards in line with the general rise in prices since you acquired the asset.

Capital gains

Let us suppose for this example that prices have risen by 20% in the four years. The Revenue Commissioners actually publish their own index numbers to be used in this adjustment process — they are given in appendix 1 on page 302. But on the assumption of a 20% rise in prices the relevant index number would be 1.2. Liability to capital gains tax is calculated like this:

Selling Price	**£13,000**
Adjusted buying price (£10,000 x 1.2)	**£12,000**
Taxable Gain	**£1,000**
Tax at 20%	**£200**

If that was the only gain made during the year, there would be no tax payable since there is an exemption limit below which no tax is payable. The first £1,000 of gains made by an individual (£2,000 for a married couple) in 1997/98 is not liable for capital gains tax. From April 1998 the allowance is £500 per individual and it not transferable between spouses.

Saving Capital Gains Tax on business assets

Business assets which have been held for ten years by an individual aged over 55 may be passed to a natural or adopted child without any liability for Capital Gains Tax. Child, in this case, is defined to include nephews or nieces who have worked full-time in the business for at least the previous five years. The child has to retain ownership of the assets for at least six years.

Shares in a family business may also qualify for this concession provided the person selling them or passing them on was a full-time director of the company for at least ten years including five years as a full-time working director.

Where the transfer is to someone other than a child the concessions are less generous. The seller has to be over 55 and no tax is payable provided the consideration is less than £250,000. Where the sale is for more than £250,000 the maximum tax payable is set at half the proceeds from the sale minus £250,000. So the maximum tax payable on assets sold for £350,000 would be £50,000. There is, of course, no Capital Gains Tax payable on transfers between spouses.

Where tax liability arises it may be possible to defer it by investing in replacement assets. This 'roll-over' relief is allowed on business assets including plant, machinery, certain land, building and goodwill. The replacement assets must normally be acquired during the period starting one year before the sale of the old assets and three years after.

A similar relief is available on the disposal of shares in a trading company in which the seller held at least a 15% voting stake and was a director employee for at least the three previous years. The money must be reinvested in new ordinary shares in an unquoted Irish company and a 15% stake built up over three years — 5% after one year. The individual must become a full time employee or director of the new company within a year.

A person who fails to meet the one year condition and pays the tax may have it refunded if he/she meets the conditions within three years.

You are also allowed to deduct from the price you get on disposing of the asset any cost involved in acquiring or selling the asset, and any expenditure wholly and exclusively incurred for the purpose of enhancing its value.

Making a gift of assets can be considered to be a disposal for tax purposes. Suppose you give a holiday home to a child. You will be considered to have disposed of the home at its current

How Capital Gains Tax is calculated

The following calculation is based on an asset acquired for £5,000 during the tax year 1979/80 and sold in 1998 for £24,000. There were selling expenses of £600. The base purchase price is multiplied by the relevant index number i.e. 3.039. If the value of the asset simply rose in line with inflation it would have risen in value by 3.039 times. It is assumed that no other capital gains were made in the year.

Selling price	**£24,000**
Less selling expenses	£600
Adjusted selling price	£23,400
Adjusted purchase price (£5,000 x 3.039)	£15,195
Capital gain	**£8,205**
Less annual exemption	£500
Taxable gain	£7,705
Tax payable (at 20%)	**£1,541**

market value and your liability for capital gains tax will arise in exactly the same way as if you had sold it. The child might also, of course, have a liability for Capital Acquisitions Tax on the gift — see page 260.

There are special concessions for business assets passing to a child on the retirement of a parent — see page 257.

The transfer of assets on the death of the owner is not a disposal for tax purposes so no Capital Gains Tax liability arises. The person inheriting the assets is deemed to have acquired them at their market value on the date of the inheritance.

Exempt gains

The following gains are totally exempt from the tax.

- Gains from the sale of your principal residence including up to one acre of land. If the price you get is based on the development value of the land then you are liable for tax on the gain attributed to that development value.

- Gains on the sale of a residence, also including up to an acre of land, which you have been providing for the sole occupation of a dependent relative as his or her sole residence. Dependent relative in this regard includes any relative who because of incapacity or infirmity is not able to maintain him or herself. Also included is the widowed mother of either spouse who need not be incapacitated.

- Bonuses on Post Office or State savings schemes.

- Gains from the disposal of Government stocks.

- Gains from life assurance policies or deferred annuities.

- Gains from the disposal of a movable tangible asset worth £2,000 or less when sold.

- Gains on assets with a predictable life of under fifty years — a car, livestock etc..

- Gains from the disposal on retirement of a farm or business to a member of one's family.

- Winnings from lotteries, betting etc..

Rates of tax

From December 3, 1997 there is only one main rate of capital gains tax — 20%. That rate applies to everything other than gains from the disposal of development land which are subject to a 40% tax.

Assets passed to a spouse on death are assumed to have been acquired by the surviving spouse at the original date of acquisition by the dead partner.

The indexation mentioned above does not apply totally to development land either. The original use value of the land may be indexed but not any development value. For example the indexation could be applied to the "agricultural use" value of the land but not to its higher value as building land.

13.5 Inheritance and gift taxes

There are two taxes which may be applied to inheritances — Capital Acquisitions Tax and Probate Tax. Both can be charged on the same estate but they are different taxes and are collected separately. Capital Acquisitions Tax may also be charged on gifts but the rate of tax is three-quarters of that charged on inheritances. If the donor dies within two years of making a gift it is treated as if it were an inheritance. There is one scale of tax rates and all gifts and inheritances taken after June 1, 1982 — irrespective of the class of donor — are added together to decide whether a threshold level has been breached and, if so, to decide the rate of tax to be applied. The threshold for gifts or inheritances to children taken during 1997 is £185,550 (the same threshold applies to gifts or inheritances passing from children to parents); £24,740 for brothers, sisters, nieces, nephews and children of deceased children; and £12,370 for non and distant relatives. Spouses get inheritances and gifts tax free. The thresholds for 1998 will be about 1.5% higher. The tax rate starts at 20% rising to 40%. Details of the earlier thresholds and rates are given in appendix 1 on page 308.

Capital Acquisitions Tax

Let us have a look at an example. Suppose a man first got a gift of £10,900 from a friend. He had received no other gifts or inheritances before that. The first £500 of that gift is tax free since that amount of any gift or inheritance from each separate donor is exempt in each tax year. And the remaining £10,400 is also tax free since the relevant threshold of £12,170 has not been breached. Suppose the man now gets an inheritance of £20,000 from an uncle. The relevant threshold in this case is £23,760. But the previous gift is also taken into account. Again the first £500 is exempt from tax leaving £19,500 to which is added the previous gift of £10,400 putting the total of taxable gifts and inheritances acquired by the man at £29,900. From that is deducted the relevant threshold level of £24,340 leaving £5,560 liable for tax. All of that is considered to be a gift since it is really part of the original £10,900 received as a gift.

Family businesses

Concessions on the transfer of agricultural and business assets by way of gift or inheritance have been greatly extended in recent years and since January 23, 1997 the value of such assets is reduced by 90 per cent for tax purposes subject to certain conditions.

It's a very valuable concession. The main condition with regard to business assets is that they are held by the recipient for at least ten years after the transfer. If this requirement is breached within six years all of the tax concession is clawed back. If it is breached between six and ten years the relief is reduced and the difference clawed back. But the claw back is limited to the additional relief granted under the past two budgets.

The business concerned must be carried on wholly or mainly within the State but the definition of business assets is quite wide ranging. It includes property consisting of a business or an interest in a business; unquoted shares or securities of an Irish company subject to some restrictions; quoted shares or securities in an Irish company which were owned by the disponer before they became quoted; building, land and machinery owned by the disponer but used by a company controlled by him or her, or else used by a partnership in which he or she was a partner.

Businesses whose sole or main business is dealing in land, shares, securities etc. are not covered by the concession.

The business assets on which the concession is claimed must have been owned by the disponer or his/her spouse for at least five years prior to the transfer in the case of a gift, or for at least two years where the transfer results from the death of the disponer. So the business assets don't have to have been in the family for very long to qualify for the relief.

Concessions on the valuation of agricultural assets have been a feature of Capital Acquisitions Tax since it was first introduced. They have been greatly extended in recent years in line with similar concessions which now apply to business assets outside of farming.

Subject, as always, to some conditions agricultural assets are valued at only 10 per cent of their true market value in calculating liability for Capital Acquisitions Tax. That 90 per cent reduction has applied since January 23, 1997.

The reduction applies to farm assets transferred to a "farmer". The definition of farmer is important as is the definition of farm assets. Another important factor may be the "valuation date" for an inheritance i.e. the date on which the transfer is deemed to take place and on which the assets are valued.

Farm assets include: farm land, buildings and woodland, machinery, livestock and bloodstock. Money may also qualify so long as the transfer is conditional on it being invested into qualifying agricultural property and that that condition is met within two years. That latter concession widens the availability of the relief considerably. The donor doesn't have to have ever been a farmer or even to have owned farm assets.

A "farmer" in this context doesn't even have to know the difference between a bull and a cow.

But in all cases the recipient has to be a "farmer". However a "farmer" in this context doesn't even have to know the difference between a bull and a cow or be able to tell the difference between wheat and barley or silage and slurry. The sole requirement is that at least 80 per cent of his or her assets are farm assets. That requirement is measured after getting the inheritance or gift, or after complying with a requirement to buy such assets.

It is not too difficult to ensure that all the necessary conditions are complied with. But it is also all too easy to fail some of the tests through a lack of adequate planning.

A recipient of a farm inheritance could fail the 80 per cent test through owning a house or apartment in Dublin for instance. Where there is a danger of such a problem arising the will may be drawn up in such a way that the recipient has time to arrange his or her affairs after the death of the donor so that the 80 per cent rule is met by the time the farm assets are transferred.

For tax purposes assets need not necessarily transfer at the time of death or on the date probate or administration is granted.

As with business assets the agricultural assets transferred must be held for at least six years to avoid a claw back of the concessions. If the assets are disposed of, and not replaced, within six and ten years there is a partial claw back. After ten years there is no claw back.

Tax can also be reduced by ensuring that the maximum possible proportion of the assets being transferred consist of farm assets at the time of the gift or on the valuation date used for inheritance tax purposes. Crops in the ground are farm assets. Crops lifted are not. In the same way livestock are farm assets. The cash from their sale is not.

Other factors to consider are outlined on page 270. There are such a wide range of factors involved that careful planning is essential and professional advice advisable.

There is a further concession in respect of business property or shares in a company left or given to the child of a brother or sister. If the nephew or niece has spent five years working in the donor's business, the tax liability is calculated as if he or she were a child of the donor. The requirement is that the nephew or niece have worked at least 24 hours a week at a place where the business is carried out, or a lower fifteen hours a week where there are no employees other than the person leaving the inheritance, or making the gift (the disponer), his or her spouse, and the recipient.

If the disponer is not domiciled in the State, or the proper law of the disposition is not Irish law, then the recipient is only liable for tax on that part of the gift or inheritance which is situated in Ireland.

Since April 1991 there has been a special relief for brothers/sisters over 55 years of age who have lived in the one house for at least five years ending on the date of death.

The relief was increased in the 1994 budget allowing for the value of the house, or portion of the house, passing to the survivor from the deceased brother or sister to be reduced by 80% for tax purposes subject to a maximum reduction of £150,000. For some years up to December 3, 1997 the reduction was 60% or £80,000.

From that date a similar concession is available to nephews, nieces, and to brothers and sisters under 55 years of age. The relative inheriting the house must have lived in it for at least ten years prior to the death and not be the beneficial owner of any other house or part of any other house. The reduction in value for tax purposes is the same as for siblings over 55 i.e. 80% or £150,000 whichever is the lesser.

The owners of heritage houses or gardens can avoid Capital Acquisitions Tax liability on their transfer by gift or inheritance

Siblings living together

There is a special relief for brothers and sisters leaving a family home to the survivor.

Other exemptions

by allowing limited public access. Up to 1997 the house had to be open for 90 days a year including not less than 60 days during the summer. That has now been reduced to a total of 60 days of which at least 40 days must be during the summer months.

While the number of days that the house or gardens have to be open has been reduced the conditions with regard to publicity have been tightened up. Full details of opening hours and admission prices must be notified to Bord Failte before January 1 each year or before July 1 this year.

A similar exemption from CAT applies to other assets of national, scientific, historic or artistic interest. This includes works of art, scientific collections, and libraries. In all cases the tax exemption may be lost if the assets are disposed of within six years of being transferred either by way of gift or inheritance.

Other assets which are exempt from CAT include: the first £500 received from any one disponer in any calendar year; charitable gifts or inheritance; pension and death in service benefits payable to an employee; certain compensation payments; reasonable payments received from a family member and used for support, maintenance or education; prizes and lottery winnings; and, of course, the proceeds of qualifying insurance policies taken out with a view to paying eventual CAT liabilities.

Probate tax

Probate Tax applies to the estates of people dying on or after June 17, 1993. While Capital Acquisitions Tax is payable by the recipients of inheritances or gifts, Probate Tax is charged on the value of the estate and is normally payable by the executor. All assets passing between spouses are exempt while the value of agricultural land is reduced by 30% in assessing the tax. The tax is charged at the rate of 2% on the value of the estate passing by will or, in the absence of a will, under an intestacy, after a death. Property passed at any time before death is not liable for the tax. So someone given warning of impending death can completely avoid the tax by passing over his or her property before death.

Where the estate is valued at £10,820 (1997) or less there is no tax payable. But once it is valued at more than £10,820 the whole estate is liable for tax at 2%. There is marginal relief for estates valued at slightly above £10,820. Where there is no surviving spouse there is no tax payable on that share of a house left to a dependent child or relative normally residing in the house. A 'dependent' must not have an income in excess of £4,472 a year. That figure is equivalent to the contributory old age pension payable to someone over 80 living alone. The dependent does not have to be drawing such a pension. The requirement is that they have an income less than that figure. There are also exemptions for property passing to charities, heritage property as defined for inheritance tax, and pension benefits.

There is no probate tax payable on property held in joint ownership if it automatically passes to the survivor without having to go through probate. That exemption does not exist in the case of Capital Acquisitions Tax. It is an important concession. But see page 21 for a note on joint bank accounts.

The tax will normally be paid by the executor of the will although the liability can pass to all the beneficiaries if the tax is not already paid by the time they get their share. Where no provision is made for the tax in the will, it is charged pro-rata on the taxable value of the individual legacies. To get a grant of probate or letters of administration it is necessary to send an inland revenue affidavit to the Revenue Commissioners. This affidavit must be accompanied by a self-assessment Probate Tax Form together with the tax due.

If the tax is paid within nine months of the death, a discount of 1.25% per month or part-month is allowed. After nine months a penalty of 1.25% per month or part-month is payable up to a maximum of doubling the tax due. The Revenue Commissioners have been granted discretion to postpone the collection of the tax where there is a lack of ready cash to pay it. Probate tax is not allowed as a tax credit against inheritance tax but it is allowed as an expense.

Joint ownership

The tax should be paid within nine months of death if heavy interest penalties are not to be incurred.

Tax saving

Cutting your tax liability

14.1

There is nothing that can be done to alter your basic tax allowances but it is possible to reduce your tax bill by making use of the many concessions and incentives available within our complicated tax system. It is not only the self-employed who can make use of these legal tax avoidance measures. At least some of them are available to the ordinary PAYE payer as well.

This chapter outlines a number of ways of reducing tax liability in addition to detailing the tax position in some specific areas — such as separated couples. Many taxpayers can save tax by simply checking their income tax position and making up-to-date returns. A lot of allowances go unclaimed. Have a look at the panel on page 241.

Most income tax allowances are applied automatically by the tax-office. But not all. If you do not make annual tax returns your certificate of tax free allowances will not take account of increased VHI or BUPA contributions, for instance.

There are other allowances which have to be claimed. Many PAYE workers are entitled to some small claim for expenses. Tax relief on medical expenses will only be given if claimed — see page 228. It is not too difficult to exceed the thresholds of £100 per individual, £200 for a family. You can claim for previous years too.

Even PAYE workers can get some of their income tax-free if they arrange things right. Other options range from subsidised canteen meals to leisure facilities. The following sections outline a few approaches which could save you some money.

Employing your child

Self-employed people may be able to cut their family tax bills by formally paying their children for work done in the business. In small family businesses it is not unusual for children to do a significant amount of work. This must be particularly true of retail businesses or farms. But the type of business does not matter.

Employing your child

The tax saving arises from the fact that any individual can earn up to £4,100 a year free of tax. That is the exemption limit which applies to single people under 65 years of age. It must be stressed that it is not a tax allowance. It has no relevance to anyone earning much more than £4,100. It is an exemption limit and any single person with an income of less than that is exempt from tax.

So a child can be paid up to £4,100 from the family business and not be liable for tax. If that payment reduces the father's taxable income by that amount, the family's overall position is improved. The child can get the money free of tax while the father would have had to pay tax at his highest marginal rate.

A child who works in a family firm is entitled to get a wage from it and can earn up to £4,100 tax free.

That is how the tax advantage arises, but remember that the child must be genuinely doing the work for which he or she is paid. And there are other factors to be considered. It is necessary for the proprietor of the business — the father or mother in this case — to register as an employer for PAYE and PRSI purposes. And it may be necessary to pay PRSI on the wages paid to the child — even though the income is too small to be liable for tax.

These requirements need not be as onerous as they might seem. In most cases there will be very little paper work after the initial registration.

There is no clear cut guideline on liability for PRSI payments. In some cases PRSI may be payable on the money paid to the child but, if it is, there could be an eventual benefit in the form of unemployment and pay related payments if you cease employing the child. The final decision rests with the Department of Social Welfare and it does not spell out in detail just who is liable for PRSI at the various rates. The following, however, is an outline of the factors it takes into account in making its decisions.

If the work is full time and there is a written or implied contract of employment, then the employee is liable for PRSI at the full rate. In deciding whether an implied contract exists the Department will take account of whether there are fixed hours involved and whether there is a fixed wage or salary.

A son living on a farm and helping his father is unlikely to be considered to have a contract of employment for instance. In this case the son would be classified as a Class K contributor and might be liable to pay $2\frac{1}{4}\%$ on all income in the form of the health contribution and youth employment levy. But they are not payable if the weekly income is less than £207 — £197 a week in 1997/98. Anyone earning less than those threshold levels of income is exempt from the levies.

Where a child is employed in a family business the work is likely to be part time and the question of whether there is a contract of employment or not may not be relevant. There are two classes of PRSI which may apply.

Class M applies to employees under 16 years of age — they pay no PRSI. Close relatives working in a family business or farm are exempt from the requirements of the Protection of Young Persons (Employment) Act 1996 provided the health and safety of the young person is not put at risk.

That exception apart the general minimum age for a regular job is 16 but a 14 year old may be employed on light work outside of school term-time subject to a maximum of 35 hours a week on holiday work or 40 hours on work experience. A 15 year old may be employed for eight hours a week during school-term. Class J may apply to children over 16 earning less than £30 a week. In this case, the employer pays $\frac{1}{2}$ % on all income.

Anyone intending to employ someone at more than £6 a week or £26 a month must register as an employer. You write to your local tax office for a form CC151. Once completed the tax man will take it from there. It is not too complicated and the savings can be worthwhile.

Reducing inheritance taxes

Inheritance taxes have been hitting an increasing number of people. Traditionally they concerned only the wealthy and their relatives but the net has been widening. The old Capital Acquisitions Tax is still not a worry for people inheriting from parents or spouses but it can be for the growing number of people inheriting from more distant relatives. And the new Probate Tax can hit all but the smallest estates.

Careful advance planning is needed to reduce inheritance taxes but such planning can be very worthwhile.

A person can receive any amount from a spouse without tax liability while a child can receive up to £185,550 from a parent or grandparent before coming into the tax net. But the tax thresholds for gifts or inheritances from more distant relatives are much lower and because of low marriage rates in the past particularly in some rural areas it is not uncommon for people to receive inheritances from sisters, brothers, uncles, aunts or cousins. The tax on such inheritances can be quite steep. But it can be reduced, or eliminated, by a little advance planning.

Reducing inheritance taxes

The calculation of Capital Acquisitions Tax liability is fairly complex with all gifts and inheritances received since June 2, 1982 taken into account in calculating the tax due on any fresh inheritance. It is detailed on page 238.

There are only three threshold levels: the £185,550 for transfers from parents or grandparents if a parent is already dead; £24,740 for transfers from brothers, sisters, aunts, and uncles; and £12,370 for transfers from anyone else. But that does not mean that you can receive £185,550 from a parent and then £12,370 from a sister all tax free.

In broad terms once you have received £12,370 from a parent, then any inheritance from a cousin is going to be fully taxable. In the same way someone who has received £12,370 from a cousin will find at least part of a subsequent inheritance from a parent liable for tax. And the rate of tax varies upwards from 20% on the first £10,000 to a high of 40%. So it can take a sizeable chunk out of any inheritance.

It can be argued that this is only right given that inheritances are unearned windfalls, but then no-one likes paying tax if there are ways of avoiding it, and there are some. Each individual case will vary. But there are a number of ways of reducing tax liability by planning the transfer. The following are some points worth considering:

- The liability for CAT is on the recipient, so the wider an estate is spread the lower the tax is likely to be. For instance an uncle wishing to leave his assets to a nephew can reduce the tax payable by leaving it to the nephew and his children. Suppose he wants to leave £30,000 to the nephew. If the nephew has not received any gift or inheritance before the first £12,370 would be tax free and the other £17,630 would be subject to tax — the first £10,000 at 20p in the £ and the other £7,620 at 30%. That would be a total tax liability of £4,289.

  It could be totally avoided if the will left the £30,000 divided equally between the nephew and his two children. They would each get £10,000 which would be below the threshold. It is true that any subsequent gifts or inheritances received would move into the tax net that much more quickly because of the fact that past inheritance are taken into account. But the tax is being delayed, perhaps for a very long time.

  The high £185,550 threshold applies not only to transfers from parents to children but also transfers in the reverse direction. This can provide a way of reducing the tax liability in those unfortunate cases where an unmarried child is facing an untimely death. He or she may wish to leave the estate to a brother or sister who would only be entitled to a £24,740 tax threshold. The tax liability can be dramatically reduced by passing the inheritance back to a parent who could then give it to a brother or sister.

- A gift or inheritance can be disclaimed — in other words refused. That right may be used to refuse tax liability in some circumstances. Suppose a parent leaves a house between a sister and brother but it has been agreed that the sister will actually get it because it was she who stayed in the family home. Ideally the will should have been changed but it wasn't. In that case the brother who inherits half the house would have to give it to the sister and a sizeable tax liability could arise since the tax threshold is only £24,740 and, of course, the sister would already have received an inheritance of half of the house from the parent. But that tax liability can be avoided by the brother disclaiming the inheritance so that the sister inherits the full house directly from the parent.

CAT liability can be reduced by leaving an estate to as many people as possible i.e. instead of just leaving it to children, dividing it among children and grandchildren.

- There are concessions for agricultural land and the recipient does not have to be a farmer provided that after the inheritance farm assets comprise at least 80% of his or her total assets. The actual assets left do not have to be farm assets either. It could comprise money with an instruction to buy farm assets with it.

- There can be an advantage in making provision in a will for the transfer of assets to be delayed for some weeks after death to allow the recipient some time to arrange his or her affairs. This could be important in meeting the 80% agricultural assets rule, for instance, allowing for the disposal of some assets. The fact that a principal resident is included in total assets can make the 80% rule hard to meet in some circumstances.

- Gifts made at least two years before death are liable for tax at only three quarters of the full CAT tax rates. But the tax has to be paid earlier so that the advantage may be eroded by the loss of the interest on which might otherwise have been earned on it. Another possible disadvantage is that a gift may be considered a disposal for Capital Gains Tax purposes so that the giver may become liable for Capital Gains Tax just as if the asset had been sold. A transfer on death doesn't give rise to Capital Gains Tax.

- Probate tax can be avoided by holding property in joint ownership with the person who you wish to have it after your death. In such a case the survivor automatically gets sole ownership of the property without it having to go through probate.

These are just some suggestions. Careful planning is obviously important since each individual case is different.

Tax and marriage

Married couples have a constitutional right to be taxed no more harshly than two single individuals would be. That was the ruling of the Supreme Court back in 1980— it still stands. Since then that right has been written into the tax code. Where a husband and wife are both income earners, they can opt to be taxed as if they were two single people. But unfortunately there is seldom, if ever, any monetary advantage in so doing. It can have relevance where the couple are separated but otherwise it is hard to envisage a situation where a married couple would be jointly better off opting for single assessment.

When it comes to deciding how they would like to be taxed there are, in fact, three options facing two income married couples. If they do nothing, they will be automatically taken to have opted for joint assessment. And neither of the other options can result in their joint tax bill being reduced. By opting for separate assessment, however, it is possible to divide the tax burden more equally between them. Opting for single assessment may achieve exactly the same end, but it could result in their overall tax bill being higher.

Let's look at each of the options in turn.

Married couples can end up paying less tax than two single people but not if they opt for single assessment.

Joint assessment

This is how most married couples are taxed. It was the only option open to them before the Supreme Court ruling in the Murphy case and the majority of couples have stuck with it.

The highest earner will automatically get the benefit of the bulk of the couple's joint tax free allowances. A spouse will only get his or her own PAYE allowance — £800 this year. That only applies, of course, if the lower earning spouse is wage earning and not working in the family company. The PRSI allowance is only given to those paying PRSI at the top rate.

The lower earner also gets the benefit of the table allowances if his or her income is high enough. These are not really allowances at all but simply an administrative device for ensuring that the tax burden is spread fairly evenly over the year as a whole. Instead of having the first portion of taxable income taxed at 24p in the £ before moving onto the higher rate of 46p, the system arranges for the highest rate to apply for the full year. The table allowance is then given to compensate for the over-taxation which would otherwise occur. The tendency to overtax by applying a 46p rate instead of a 24p rate for instance is exactly offset by providing the additional 'table' tax free allowance.

Under joint assessment, the couple is still legally taxed as one unit. And indeed either spouse can be nominated as the accountable person for tax purposes. The important point is that concessions not used by one spouse can be transferred to the other. This is the important point. The true legal liability for tax is worked out at the end of a tax year by way of a balancing statement which combines the two incomes.

Two income families should check their tax each year. The PAYE system can get things wrong.

If there is a wide difference between the two incomes it is possible that the PAYE system will result in too much tax being collected during the year. But it will be refunded at the end of the year, when the balancing statement is made out. The refunds are now allocated between the spouses in proportion to the tax paid by each.

Balancing statements are not prepared automatically so two income families, in particular should do a rough calculation each year to see that they are not being overtaxed. If they are, tax returns should be speedily prepared and a balancing statement asked for.

That is true for other taxpayers too. Many taxpayers lose out on the extra allowances they can claim — such as VHI and BUPA contributions; medical expenses etc..

Separate assessment

This is only a variation on the joint assessment option. Either spouse can opt for it provided they notify the tax office before July 6 in the year of assessment. Separate assessment then continues until the tax office is told otherwise by the spouse who first opted for it.

The total tax liability of the couple is not reduced in any way by separate assessment but most allowances are evenly split between them. Personal allowances, age allowances and blind allowances are evenly divided while other allowances may be granted to the individual bearing the cost — allowance for medical insurance, for example, would be given to the person paying them.

The important point is that any allowances unused by one person can be passed back to the other. And the same is true for unused tax bands. So if the husband has moved into the 46p tax band while the wife still has not used up all of her 24p band, there is no loss. At the very latest the overtaxing will be sorted out when a balancing statement is prepared. It should be possible to prevent that problem arising, however, by dividing the allowances up broadly in proportion to each person's income.

Separate assessment is possibly the ideal option since it allows the couple to split the tax allowances fairly between them. Under ordinary joint assessment, the wife can very often find her income very heavily taxed since her husband is getting the benefit of most of the tax allowances. Separate assessment will not reduce their joint tax bill but it does give a better incentive for the wife to work.

Single assessment

This is where the couple decide to be treated exactly as if they were two single people. Their tax liabilities are kept entirely separate. If their incomes are about equal, a couple opting for single assessment may pay no more tax between them than they would if they opted for joint or separate assessment. But if their incomes are not equal or close to it they could end up with a higher tax bill.

The reason is that one spouse cannot pass on the benefit of unused allowances or rate bands to the other. Either spouse can serve notice on the tax man for single assessment at any time during the tax year. Once served the notice is applied to that year and all subsequent years until it is withdrawn. Only the person who served the notice in the first case can withdraw it.

There may be the odd freak situation where single assessment can reduce a tax bill. Such a situation might arise where one spouse is on a very low income - just below the income tax exemption limit. But, in general, there is no financial advantage to a couple in opting for single assessment.

Separated couples

A couple who have separated can get more tax relief than a couple living together although that does not mean that they will end up paying less tax. They may pay more despite the extra reliefs. Separated couples have more options on the income tax front and they can be jointly better off by picking the right one. That is if they can agree to do so.

If a separated couple can agree on their tax affairs they can arrange matters to their advantage.

Money problems may be a contributory factor to many a marriage break-up, but they do not end with the break-up of the marriage. The Revenue Commissioners are practical enough to recognise the reality of a situation but so long as the couple are married — whether separated or not — their tax affairs remain tied together. What the Revenue Commissioners have joined together let no man pull asunder. Mind you this can work to the benefit of the couple — it certainly need not work against them. And the Revenue Commissioners would seem to have little other alternative. But to make the best of the situation the couple need to work together — which seems rather ironic in the circumstances.

What follows only deals with spouses whose marriages have not been dissolved or annulled or who haven't got a divorce — couples who are, in fact, still married although separated. They have a range of options from which to choose.

Unfortunately there can be no hard and fast rule as to which is best. It depends on their particular circumstances. It can also depend on the couple jointly opting for the best alternative — both must choose some of the options — it is not enough for one of them to do so.

But let's look at the options in turn. It is important to realise that there can be no global rule of thumb on what is best. What is best for one couple may not be for someone in different circumstances. Each person needs to do their own sums.

Option one is to remain taxed as a couple without letting the tax man know anything about the separation. Even if there are maintenance payments being made, there is no problem so long as the principal earner is willing to meet the tax bills. Normally that is the husband and he would remain responsible for the tax liabilities of his wife — but tax would be stopped under PAYE on her income.

That could work to the detriment of the wife who would normally have very minimal tax allowances and would be paying heavy tax. They could, however, agree to split the allowances more equally between them — by opting for separate assessment — more about that below.

Couples and income tax — options compared

The couple Val and Pat	Single assessment		Jointly assessed	Separated with child	
	Val	Pat	Val/Pat	Val	Pat
Gross income	£25,000	£12,000	£37,000	£25,000	£12,000
Less Allowances					
Personal	£3,150	£3,150	£6,300	£3,150	£3,150
PAYE	£800	£800	£1,600	£800	£800
Single parent				£3,150	£3,150
Taxable income	£21,050	£8,050	£29,100	£17,900	£4,900
First £10,000 @ 24p	£2,400	£1,932		£2,400	£1,176
First £20,000 @ 24p			£4,800		
Remainder at 46p	£5,083	nil	£4,186	£3,634	nil
Total tax	£7,483	£1,932	£8,986	£6,034	£1,176
Income after tax	£17,517	£10,068	£28,014	£18,966	£10,824
Combined after tax	**£27,585**		**£28,014**	**£29,790**	

The table above shows three ways in which a married couple might be taxed. Their combined tax bill is different in each case. Most married couple are jointly assessed. But they can opt to be taxed as two single individuals. The difference that can make to the combined tax bill is shown in the first three columns of figures above.

If Val and Pat opt to be taxed as two single individuals, the lower earner Pat cannot transfer the benefit of unused 24p tax band to the higher earner, Val. So they end up paying more tax than if they were jointly assessed — a combined £9,415 compared with £8,986 giving them a combined take-home pay of only £27,585 whereas if they were jointly assessed it would be £28,014.

The third example assumes that Val and Pat are separated and have a child. Provided the child is under 16 or permanently incapacitated and lives with each at some time during the year both can claim the single parent's tax allowance. Their combined tax bill, in this case, is lower than it would be if they were jointly assessed because of the benefit of the extra tax allowance for single parents.

The do-nothing approach may be alright where the wife is not going to work and the husband has agreed to support her but it can pose problems otherwise.

Maintenance payments from husband to wife (or vice-versa) can cause difficulties from a tax point of view. A spouse making such payments is entitled to deduct them from his or her income for tax purposes. In which case the payments become taxable in the hands of the recipient. But in this case both spouses are treated as if they were single individuals — each with only single person's allowances.

Of course, opting for single assessment is an option for all married couples but in the case of couples living together there can be no tax saving as a result and there may be a tax loss. That's because a low earner cannot pass unused standard rate tax band — at 24p in the pound — over to the high earner who may be paying tax at 46p in the pound.

A separated couple may, in some instances, get better tax allowances after separation than they did before because they may both be entitled to single parent's allowance.

That may also be the case with separated spouses but there is a difference. If there is a child or children for which children's allowances are being paid, the spouse looking after the child or children can claim a single parent's allowance. It is sufficient to have looked after the children at some time during the tax year so, in fact, both spouses can get this allowance which currently stands at £2,900 (£3,150 from April 1998). It is not available to a couple opting for joint assessment so it can make opting for single assessment worthwhile.

But where there is single assessment, maintenance payments may be subject to tax in the hands of the recipient. They are taxable if the recipient has sufficient income to put her or him into the tax net. This only applies to maintenance payments which are legally enforceable and only to those in respect of a spouse. Payments in respect of children are different. The person making the payment gets no tax relief on the money but it is not taxable in the hands of the recipient.

Unlike the situation of married couples living together it is possible for the joint tax bill of a separated couple to be less under single assessment than it would be under joint assessment.

But that is not always the case. Joint assessment is the option automatically applied to married couples who are living together just as the single assessment option is automatically applied to separated couples who wish to transfer tax liability for maintenance payments. But a separated couple can opt for joint assessment, if they wish.

A husband making maintenance payments may work out that he would be better off foregoing the tax relief on the maintenance payments and getting the full married allowances instead although if he does claim that allowance, it is likely that his wife would lose. But she may not. She would no longer be taxed on the maintenance payment — a gain — although she would lose a single parent allowance if she was getting it.

Whether the gains outweigh the losses depend on each individual case.

But where both spouses are resident in the State and both decide to opt for joint assessment they may do so. They are then subject to separate assessment. This means that the tax allowances are split equally between them. But if one spouse has spare allowances or spare low tax rate bands, they can be transferred to the other spouse. They can, indeed, opt to split allowances in any way they like — and agree between them.

Spouses may split their joint tax allowances between them whatever way they like.

The possibilities are practically endless. But in all cases the joint tax bill of the couple remains the same — all that differs is the split of income between them.

Share incentives

PAYE workers have few opportunities of getting tax-free income. Wages are automatically taxed and the tax definition of wages is wide. It includes practically all monies paid by an employer to an employee. Most non-cash benefits are taxable too. They are treated as benefits-in-kind and their cash value is liable to income tax. Examples are company cars and loans at preferential interest rates.

Tax-free profit sharing

It is possible to get up to £10,000 of your income tax-free each year through an approved profit sharing scheme.

But there are some benefits that can be provided tax free by an employer. They include subsidised canteen meals so long as they are available to all employees; sporting facilities available to all employees; nursery facilities; and certain bonus payments paid under an approved profits sharing scheme. Most of those need to be negotiated by the work-force as a whole - the benefit is not confined to any one individual. But that is not the case with profit-sharing schemes.

Profit sharing is often advocated as a means of improving industrial relations in a firm. Workers who are going to benefit directly from the increased profitability of a company are likely to be more productive than those who are not.

Incomes can be linked to profits by way of straight forward cash bonuses. But cash bonuses are liable for tax in the same way as wages and that reduces the incentive somewhat.

But if the bonuses are given in the form of company shares and the value does not exceed £10,000 a year no tax liability arises provided certain other conditions are met. This is a benefit-in-kind which is not taxable.

To be attractive, of course, the company should be quoted on the stock exchange so that the shares can be readily sold at some stage in the future. But they do have to be held for five years and for at least two years of that they must be held by trustees. After the two years they can be passed on to individual workers and may be sold although there is some claw back of the tax concession.

The rules of the scheme must apply equally to all workers. The level of bonuses may be related to salary or years of service or both but those are the only criteria which can be used. Blue-eyed boys or green-eyed girls cannot get special treatment.

Whatever benefit employers get from operating profit sharing schemes must be doubled when the bonus comes in the form of shares. The total amount to be given out in shares may be linked in some way to profitability or productivity in the same way as any other bonus scheme. A worker may by preference take the bonus in the form of cash. But in that case it is taxable. Those who take it is the form of shares get it tax free so long as they hold the shares for five years.

During those five years, and subsequently if they hold onto the shares, the workers have a direct interest in the performance of those shares on the stock exchange. So the employer has built in an initial incentive of a bonus scheme and an ongoing incentive in the form of share ownership.

Obviously this type of profit sharing scheme is of particular interest in companies whose shares are listed on the stock exchange although many of those schemes are, in fact, operated by firms whose shares are quoted abroad rather than in Dublin. Even before the ending of exchange controls on investment abroad, the Central Bank granted exemptions to such schemes.

There are about 180 approved participation plans currently in operation in Ireland.

More popular of course, than the profit sharing scheme, are share option schemes but they are only available to top executives. With these the executive is given the option to buy shares at today's price at some stage in the future. The more the share price goes up, the greater his gain.

There is another option known as an SAYE — a save as you earn plan. This combines a savings plan with share options generally made available to a wider range of workers in a firm.

Schemes usually grant share options to workers on the basis of the amount they are willing to save each month. The saving is out of net income — there is no tax incentive. The saving may be organised through the Post Office Instalment Savings Scheme or through a bank or building society. At the end of five years the worker can use the savings to buy shares at the original option price or just keep the money if the shares have not gone up in value in the meanwhile.

Most plans of this type in Ireland are operated by British companies because there is legislation governing their operation in Britain which provides among other things, that where a plan is operated it must be made available to all workers with more than five years service. There is no such requirement here.

Tax relief can be obtained on loan interest used to buy shares in the company you work for.

There are other ways of getting tax relief on buying shares. Tax relief can be claimed on the interest on loans raised to fund the purchase of shares in the company you work for. You need to be a full time director or employee. In the case of a private company you need only be a part-time director or employee. But the company cannot be quoted on the stock exchange so the shares cannot be very marketable and that reduces the attractions somewhat.

There are also restrictions relating to non-trading companies. But in the case of a private trading company there is no upper limit on the relief which may be obtained on loans used to buy shares in it. In the case of a non-private company, there is an upper limit of £3,000 in tax relief per individual. This limit is in addition to any tax relief on mortgage interest.

Business Expansion Scheme

（1998 99）

There is another share incentive scheme — the Business Expansion Scheme — which allows tax relief on up to £25,000 used to buy shares in certain qualified companies. In general such companies are those manufacturing, and internationally traded service companies, which are entitled to the concessionary 10% Corporation Tax. The concession is also available on money invested in certain tourism ventures aimed at bringing tourists from abroad. While investments in hotels, guesthouses, and self-catering accommodation are excluded, that still leaves a wide range of possibilities.

The concession was extended to the music industry in 1996 for projects involving the production, marketing and promotion of new artist's studio recordings and associated videos. A certification system is being developed for this and for other BES projects.

It is a generous tax concession but you do need to take care. You have three options. You can:

- Invest in a fund which will in turn invest your money in a number of BES projects thereby spreading the risk;

- Invest in a single project at arms length;

- Invest in your own project in which you will take a management interest.

The second option is obviously the most risky. The shares you buy, either directly or through an investment fund, cannot be quoted on any stock exchange. So you have no easy way of judging exactly what they are worth. There is no market price. Neither will you have any great idea of the ventures' future prospects. And, most importantly, you may have no guarantee that you will be able to dispose of the shares in the future.

You may get some basic accounts, or you may not. Either way you will not be able to do the type of detailed analysis necessary to really value the shares or to evaluate the prospects of the venture during the five years for which you have to hold the shares if the tax relief is not to be clawed back.

But the tax concession is generous. The trick is to reduce the risk as much as possible. The ideal way is to opt for one of the BES funds which allow for the investment to be spread over a number of different ventures and relying on reliable fund managers to value the initial shares that they buy. But remember that promoters usually charge a 3% fee up front and may have a conflict of interest in so far as they may also collect fees from the companies in which they invest. Also not all funds have guaranteed exit mechanisms. Be wary of any fund that doesn't.

Let's have a look at the detail.

The BES concession is aimed at encouraging risk investment in small to medium sized ventures in manufacturing, traded services, and certain tourism and music projects. Traded services are ventures which have to compete in the international market place.

The investor buys shares in the venture and gets full tax relief on that investment. So for every £1 put in, a top tax payer gets a tax rebate of 46p. But the shares have to be held for at least five years. Normally there is an exit mechanism put in place to guarantee that there is someone there to buy the shares at the end of the five years. There should also be some agreed process for valuing the shares at that stage.

Guarantees are no longer allowed. Investors have to accept a risk. But provided the shares are really worth whatever is paid for them initially, the tax relief provides a sizeable cushion against loss.

In any arms length BES investment make sure there is an exit mechanism and that you are getting initial value.

Did you ever get that urge to quit your secure job and go out on your own, be your own boss, build your own business. It's a big step, not to be lightly taken, but if you've been working in Ireland there's a little extra incentive to help tip the decision. Leave the job, set up the business and the State will give you an income tax rebate of up to £60,000 to help finance your new venture. But you do have to take up full time work with the new company. It may sound too good to be true but it's not. The incentive is known as the Seed Capital Scheme. How does it work? Let's look at an example.

Tim is in his mid-thirties, a production manager with a multinational company. He's on a very good income and his future is secure enough. Indeed one of the problems is that its a bit too secure, predictable and certain. Tim's need for achievement is not being fully satisfied. He has identified a business opportunity in manufacturing and is confident that he has the skills to make it work. He has access to some capital but could do with a bit more. So how can the Seed Capital Scheme help him.

Basically it can provide him with some capital. The more he can put up himself the easier it is to borrow the rest. He can make a back-claim for tax relief extending over the past five years on up to a maximum of £125,000 invested in the business. In essence that means that he can get back all of the tax he paid on up to £25,000 of income in each of those years. He has been paying tax at the old top rate of 48p in the pound on the top slice of his income and that top slice has been bigger than £25,000 a year. So his claim is for a rebate of £12,000 (48% of £25,000) for each year — a total of £60,000.

Had he been earning less his rebate might be less. But he's entitled to the maximum of £60,000 provided he invests £125,000 in the business. The income tax rebate doesn't exclude him from benefiting from other State incentives such as grants, the 10% tax rate on profits, and employment incentives. Tim's venture is in manufacturing but it could equally well be in a service open to international competition; tourism; a trading operation selling Irish goods abroad; certain shipping ventures; some research and development activities; and even the cultivation of crops in greenhouses.

The basic requirement is that the would-be entrepreneur is setting up a new business having been employed. The incentive isn't available to an existing businessmen moving into a new venture. To ensure that this requirement is met, the condition is that at least three-quarters of the claimant's income has to have come from paid employment and no more than £15,000 of their annual income should have come from other sources. There is nothing to stop a number of people getting together to establish a business and claim tax rebates. The only requirement is that each claimant owns at least 15% of the shares in the venture.

Someone buying shares worth £10,000 at a real cost, after tax relief, of £5,400 will be doing alright if he or she can sell those shares at the initial £10,000 at the end of the five years. A real initial investment of £5,400 will have grown to £10,000 over five years. That is a compound return of just over 12.5% a year after allowing for the initial set-up commission of 3%.

As well as the initial 3% commission there is another initial cost in that it may take up to a year to get the tax rebate. The investor in our example has to put up the £10,000 and has to wait to get the £4,600 rebate or reduction in his or her tax bill. So there is a loss of interest on that money.

Ideally the investor should spread the risk among a number of ventures by investing in a fund. The shares bought have, by the nature of the scheme, to be in relatively small enterprises. While they have the potential to grow rapidly, they also have the potential to fail miserably. A spread of risk is advisable and that is best secured by investing in a fund. Picking a good fund manager is also important.

You can reclaim the tax you paid in the last five years to invest in a new venture.

If things go well and the return is big enough there may be a liability for Capital Gains Tax but it is the full investment, before tax relief, which is taken into account as the purchase price of the shares. So in our example the purchase price is £10,000 i.e. not the actual post tax relief cost of £5,400. The first £500 of capital gains realised by an individual in any one year is tax-free so providing the net return on the investment does not exceed £10,500 on the initial real investment of £5,400 there would be no liability for Capital Gains Tax on present rules. Indeed a larger tax free gain would be possible given that the initial purchase price is adjusted upwards in line with inflation.

There is an even better use for the BES concession. That is to start your own venture. This is possibly easier in the tourism area than any other. The investment cannot just be in accommodation — that loophole which allowed people to set up tourism ventures comprising houses in Dublin 4 has been closed off. But it still leaves a lot of opportunities, particularly for people in rural areas.

Remember an investment of £100,000 in a venture will only cost £54,000 after tax relief. Spread that over say four investors and the sums involved need not be prohibitive. It is possible to start with a relatively small project. The possibilities are legion. They include the following:

- Caravan and camping site
- Holiday hostels
- Holiday camps
- Pleasure boat hire
- Horse drawn caravan hire
- Equestrian centre services
- Sailing, yachting, marina services
- Sub-aqua centre services
- Heritage houses, castles, gardens
- Game fishing services
- Chauffeur-drive for tourists
- Outdoor activity centres
- Tourism guide agencies
- Tour coach services

The best use of the BES tax incentive is to set up your own venture.

The project must be aimed at attracting tourists from abroad and must have a three year marketing plan approved by Bord Failte. There are upper limits on the amount of the total investment which goes on land and buildings. It is up to 75% in the case of hostels, holiday camps etc.; 70% in the case of caravan and camping sites and equestrian centres; 65% in the case of marina services; and 50% for most other projects.

Further information can be obtained from Bord Failte, Baggot Street Bridge, Dublin, 4. The scheme is ideally suited to individuals or groups who are already paying high amounts of income tax. They can get the project up and running while retaining their jobs but reducing their tax bills.

A variant of the BES scheme, known as the Seed Capital Scheme, allows for tax relief on up to £125,000 invested in a new project. Under this scheme the relief comes by way of a refund of tax previously paid. Someone who has left a job and takes up full-time employment with the new company can claim back the tax they paid over the previous five years. The maximum relief for each year is £ 25,000. See page 252 for details.

Investment in music and films

Tax relief similar to BES relief is available on money invested in certain film projects and music projects. They tend to be relatively high risk and are best suited to those who are actually getting involved in the management of such ventures rather than outside investors.

In the case of films the project should, at the very least, have an advance sales agreement with the distributor and, of course, have the right people involved — director and performers.

Covenants and medical expenses

With lengthening life expectancy a growing number of elderly people require nursing care in their later years. It can be costly and the means-tested state subvention is, at best, small enough. But tax relief can ease the burden.

An elderly parent paying for his or her own nursing care in a registered nursing home can claim tax relief on the expense involved. In this context nursing care is considered by the Revenue Commissioners to be a medical expense eligible for tax relief (see page 228). The concession can significantly reduce the real cost of nusing home care. In the case of an individual claim the first £100 each year is disallowed but given the overall cost involved that is small enough.

Tax efficient covenants

That's straight forward enough for an elderly person who has adequate income to pay the costs involved and against which to claim the tax relief. But tax relief is useless to someone not liable for tax and that's often the case with elderly people in this situation. Very often at least some of the cost is borne by family members, usually children. They don't automatically get tax relief but there are ways to successfully claim it.

The easiest is to have the elderly person defined as a dependent relative. That way he or she is considered to be a member of the family for tax purposes. It is then possible to include the nursing home costs and other medical expenses in a family claim for relief. This will only work, however, if the parent's income is no more than £110 above the maximum social welfare pension rate – currently about £4,312.

Provided the parent's income is below that level the child claims him or her as a dependent relative for tax purposes. A number of children can claim the same parent as a dependent. They can each then claim tax relief for any medical expenses they pay for – subject to the first £200 of each family's claim being disallowed.

The other way for children to get tax relief on contributions made to a parent's health care is by making the payments under covenant. The tax relief given on money covenanted to chil-

Sample wording for a covenant

I ....(name) of ....(address) covenant to pay my father/mother ....(name) of ....(address) an amount which after the deduction of standard rate tax amounts to £...........(sum) each year for seven years or during our joint lives or until (name of third party) says the covenant should end, the first payment to be made during March 1998.

Signed, sealed and delivered by ....(name) in the present of ....(witness's name, address and occupation)

.................(Date)

dren over eighteen years of age was finally phased out in April of last year. But there is still tax relief on covenants in favour of permanently incapacitated people or in favour of anyone over 65 years of age.

A covenant is simply a legal undertaking to make payments to someone else. In order to qualify for tax relief the payments must be capable of lasting for at least six years. It is usual to make a covenant for seven years. The giver must be a taxpayer and the recipient should ideally not be liable for income tax at all. There can be some benefit where the giver pays tax at 46p and the recipient pays tax at 24p but it is limited.

In the case we're considering the recipient is a parent who is incurring heavy medical or nursing home costs. The parent can claim tax relief on such costs – in effect they provide an additional tax allowance which can very easily push him or her out of the tax net. So the parent has unused tax allowances while the child is paying tax, let us suppose, at 46p in the pound.

Let's see how a covenant might work. The child is restricted to covenanting no more than 5 per cent of annual income. Let's take the case of a son wanting to contribute £1,000 a year towards the cost of nursing home care for his mother. Other brothers and sisters could, of course, do the same thing.

The son makes out a covenant – a sample wording is given above – and pays £760 to the parent. The parent gets the other £240 by way of a tax rebate while the son also gets an additional tax relief of £220. The cost to the son is only £540 while his mother gets the benefit of £1,000 towards the nursing home costs.

The logic behind this is relatively simple although you do not have to understand it to benefit. Because the son has entered into a legal undertaking to pass the money to his mother, the taxman considers the £1,000 to be hers rather than his. But he has already paid £460 tax on the £1,000. That tax is returned. The mechanics of the process dictate that £220 goes back to the son and £240 to the mother.

Points to watch:

Covenants may provide no saving if a parent is in receipt of some means-tested benefit since the covenanted income will be treated as means.

The covenant should include a clause allowing it to be ended on the say so of a third party e.g. a trusted friend. This is just a precaution. A covenant can always be ended by the mutual consent of the parties but circumstances could arise where it is desirable to end it for one reason or another and the mutual consent cannot be obtained. For instance the covenant could, in some circumstances, prevent the parent from claiming some means tested benefit.

How to go about it

The covenant can be drawn up using the wording in the accompanying panel. You don't need a solicitor. You can get the wording typed out or even write it out filling in the blanks as appropriate.

The person making the covenant should also get a tax form R185 from his or her local tax office. It is a single page requiring very little information such as RSI number and place of employment or source of income. That completed form together with the signed covenant and, of course, the money is given to the parent.

The parent can get a tax reclaim form from a local tax office or by phoning the special Revenue Commissioners 24 hour phone number (01) 8780100. That claim form together with copies of the covenant, form R185 and some evidence of the payment being made (a photocopy of the cheque or of the bankbook into which the money went) is returned to the tax office.

Appendices

Personal Record

Where my documents can be found:

My will is with:

The will is dated:

My birth and marriage certificates may be found:

My passport and other personal documents may be found:

I have a bank deposit box in:

FOR ALL YOUR FINANCIAL NEEDS

Irish Life is changing the way we do business with our customers.

Right now we offer a new level of service when it comes to giving you expert advice on homeloans, illness cover, investments, life assurance, savings, pensions and business finance.

We've got it in one. To find out more about any of Irish Life's products, talk to your broker, Irish Life Personal Adviser or call Irish Life on: (01) 7042000.

For an ever changing life

Irish Life

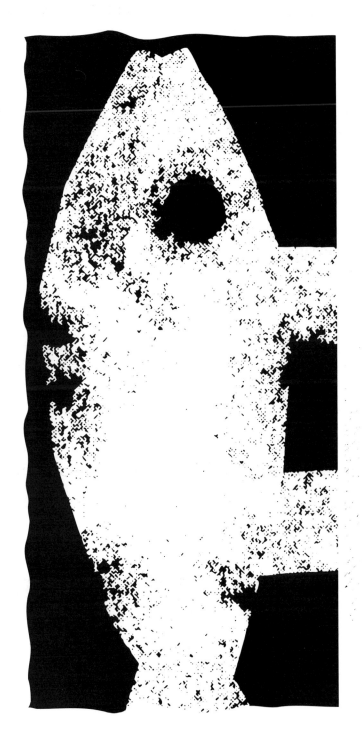

My life insurance policies may be found:

My car insurance may be found:

My house insurance policies may be found

My share and investment certificates are in:

House documentation may be found:

Other personal documents may be found:

For a rainy day...

or when they shine...

...An Post has the savings and investment plans to suit you.

All are State Guaranteed so you have the added comfort of knowing your money is totally secure. And each one, from our Education Savings Plan to our highly popular Savings Certificates, offer very attractive rates of return and tax free or tax efficient earnings. So no matter what your saving or investment requirements are, find out more about An Post's comprehensive range of options from your local Post Office.

Bank accounts etc.

I have the following bank accounts:

Bank
Address

Account number

Bank
Address

Account number

Bank
Address

Account number

Other accounts, building society etc.:

Where:

Account number

Credit Cards:

Card	Number	Expiry date and phone number to report missing

A Permanent Answer To All
Your Financial Needs....

Irish Permanent can help you with many aspects of your finances thanks to a wide range of mortgage, investment and banking products:

- **Home Loans***
- **Savings and Investments**
- **Current Accounts**
- **ATM Accounts**
- **Visa Card**[†]

- **Bureau de Change**
- **Car Finance**•
- **Personal Loans**•
- **Life and Pensions**
- **Commercial Property Loans**

*To find out how we can help you,
call to your local Irish Permanent branch.*

The People's Choice For Financial Services

Life Assurance:

Company	Policy Number	Details

Investments

Investment	Cert. number

Serving you for over a Century.
Now we offer you more products and services than ever.

MORTGAGES & LOANS
Home Loans
  Annuity/Endowment/Pension
  Fixed/Variable Rates
Home Improvement Loans
Secured Personal Loans
Refinancing
Commercial Mortgages
Residential Investment Loans

SAVINGS & INVESTMENTS
Classic Quarterly Accounts
Guaranteed Interest Bonds
Gold Saver High Interest Accounts
Special Savings Accounts
Non Resident Accounts
Regular Income Options
Foreign Currency Accounts

LIFE AND PENSIONS
Family Protection
Critical Illness Cover
Retirement Planning/Pensions
Educational Protection
Inheritance Tax Planning

INSURANCE
Home, Contents and All Risk Cover
Mortgage Payment Protection
Endowment Life Assurance
Commercial Risks
Travel Insurance

BUREAU DE CHANGE
Worldwide Money Transfers
Foreign Currency
Travellers Cheques

BANKING
Direct debits, standing orders,
cheque payment facilities,
regular statements, automated
salary credits and bill payment facilities
Cashere ATM Card with access
to 430 Cashere and Banklink
ATM outlets
Laser Card

TREASURY
Money Desk for competitive rates
Term deposits for Corporate and
large personal investors

VISA CARD

For further information on our range of services contact your local branch or phone

1850 61 62 63

Nationwide House, Grand Parade, Dublin 6.

INCOME TAX

Rates

SINGLE			MARRIED	
1994/95				
First £8,200	27%		First £16,400	27%
Balance	48%		Balance	48%
1995/96				
First £8,900	27%		First £17,800	27%
Balance	48%		Balance	48%
1996/97				
First £9,400	27%		First £18,800	27%
Balance	48%		Balance	48%
1997/98				
First £9,900	26%		First £19,800	26%
Balance	48%		Balance	48%
1998/99				
First £10,000	24%		First £20,000	24%
Balance	46%		Balance	46%

Loans for a lot more...for a lot less.

Pulling together funds for those certain extras can sometimes be a bit of a struggle. So it's nice to know you can join a movement renowned for lending a helping hand - a movement owned by its members, for the benefit of its members. We're your credit union. If you need a loan for a car... for home improvements... help with education costs... or simply a well-deserved break - we can help make it happen.

Likewise, if you want a most attractive return on your savings, it's at hand.

Savings & loans

As a member, you could be entitled to low cost loans[†] - not more than 1% per month on the reducing balance. That's just 12.6% APR. You'll also find our loans often have built in life assurance[*] for extra peace of mind.

What's more, you'll be happy to hear that individual extras - such as transaction charges - simply don't exist when you save or borrow with us. So talk to us today. And put some of your finances in much friendlier hands.

CREDIT UNION

M a n y   h a n d s   w o r k i n g   t o g e t h e r

Irish League of Credit Unions, 33-41 Lower Mount Street, Dublin, 2 Tel: (01) 6146700 Fax (01)6146701

[†]Qualification is normally subject to a credit union savings record and assessment. [*]Including Loan Protection and Life Savings. Certain conditions and limits apply.
Issued by the Irish League of Credit Unions.

Basic Allowances

	1994/95	1995/96	1996/97	1997/98	1998/99
Personal:					
— Single	£2,350	£2,500	£2,650	£2,900	£3,150
— Married	£4,700	£5,000	£5,300	£5,800	£6,300
Widowed	£2,850	£3,000	£3,150	£3,400	£3,650
PAYE	£800	£800	£800	£800	£800
Age:					
— Single	£200	£200	£200	£400	£400
— Married	£400	£400	£400	£800	£800
Incapacitated Child	£600	£600	£700	£700	£800
Dependent Relative	£110	£110	£110	£110	£110
Blind Person	£600	£600	£700	£700	£1,000
PRSI	£286	£140	nil	nil	nil
Employee caring for incapacitated person	£5,000	£5,000	£7,500	£7,500	£8,500
Single Parent					
—Widowed	£1,850	£2,000	£2,150	£2,400	£2,650
—Other	£2,350	£2,500	£2,650	£2,900	£3,150
Widow/'er in year after bereavement[1]	£1,500[1]	£1,500[1]	£1,500[1]	£1,500[1]	£5,000[2]

[1] £1,000 in second year and £500 in third year. [2] £4,000 in second year, £3,000 in third year, £2,000 in fourth year, and finally £1,000 in fifth year.

Finally, a pension that talks to you in pounds, shillings and sense: **OpenPlan.**

Unlike most other pensions, your annual **OPENPLAN** statement tells you
what your investment's worth in clear figures and plain English.
To find out more about Hibernian's revolutionary new **OPENPLAN** pension,
contact Hibernian or call your broker.

You're safe in the hands of

Head Office: Haddington Road, Dublin 4. Tel: (01) 607 8000. Fax: (01) 660 4752.

Exemption Limits

Persons with low incomes are granted complete exemption from income tax. The limits are as follows:

	1994/95	1995/96	1996/97	1997/98	1998/99
Single or widowed	£3,600	£3,700	£3,900	£4,000	£4,100
Married	£7,200	£7,400	£7,800	£8,000	£8,200
Single/w'ed over 65	£4,100	£4,300	£4,500	£4,600	£5,000
Married over 65	£8,200	£8,600	£9,000	£9,200	£10,000
Single/w'ed over 75	£4,700	£4,900	£5,100	£5,200	£5,500
Married over 75	£9,400	£9,800	£10,200	£10,400	£11,000

Since 1994/95 the limits are increased by £450 for the first and second child and by £650 for each subsequent child. So the threshold for a married couple under 65 with two dependent children is £8,900 i.e. the basis £8,000 plus twice £450. For 1993/94 the increases were £350 and £550 respectively and for the two previous years the figures were £300 and £500. Persons earning more than these exemption limits are entitled to marginal relief paying tax on the amount over the threshold at 40p in the pound.

PRSI Rates

PRSI rates (including income levies) for 1998/99 for most private sector and State employees are as follows:

	Private Sector	State Sector	Self Employed
First £22,300	$6\frac{3}{4}\%$	3.15%	$\frac{1}{4}\%$
Remainder	$2\frac{1}{4}\%$	1.9%	$2\frac{1}{4}\%$

No PRSI is payable on the first £80 weekly for the private sector; £20 weekly for the public sector; and on an annual £1,040 for the self-employed. Those earning less than £197 in any week are exempt from the $2\frac{1}{4}\%$ combined training and health levies. Also exempt are self-employed people with incomes under £10,250.

PERSONAL FINANCE

I'm thinking First

If you're looking for an outstanding performance on savings and investments, you should be thinking First. First National Building Society. For a complete range of savings and investments options, offering highly competitive rates of interest, drop into your local First National office today or simply call:

1 850 6 · 7 · 8 · 9 · 10

LINES OPEN: 8AM - 8PM MON - FRI
11AM - 4PM SAT & SUN

FIRST NATIONAL
BUILDING SOCIETY

guaranteed irish

Approved Quality System

Web-site http://www.fnbs.ie   Email: info@fnbs.ie

CAPITAL ACQUISITIONS TAX
Threshold Levels

Relationship to donor	1995	1996	1997
Child, or the minor child of a deceased child. Also from child to parent but only for inheritance tax	£178,200	£182,550	£185,550
Brother, sister, child of brother or sister or lineal descendant other than a child, or the minor child of a deceased child	£23,760	£24,340	£24,740
If none of the above	£11,880	£12,170	£12,370

No tax has been payable by spouses on inheritances received after January 1985 and gifts received after January 1, 1990. The following rates apply to inheritances, the tax on gifts is reduced by a quarter.

1993/94		Since 1994/95	
Amount	**Rate**	**Amount**	**Rate**
Up to threshold	nil	Up to threshold	nil
Next £10,000	20%	Next £10,000	20%
Next £40,000	30%	Next £30,000	30%
Next £50,000	35%	Balance	35%
Balance	40%		

There are major concessions for agriculture land passing to a farmer; for business assets, and for businesses or farms passing to a nephew or niece who has worked on the farm or in the business for at least five years. There is a special concession to reduce the tax on the transfer of a house between elderly brothers and/or sisters.

Probate Tax

A probate tax of 2% is levied on the estates of individuals who died after June 18, 1993. Where the deceased was domiciled in the State the tax applies to the net assets i.e. assets less debts, both inside and outside the State subject to certain exemptions. Where the deceased was domiciled outside the State, only the net assets situated in the State are liable for the tax. Estates worth less than £10,820 are exempt. So too are transfers between spouses. The valuation of farm land is reduced by 30% of its market value. Property held jointly at the time of death is exempt from the tax if it automatically passes to the survivor without the need for probate. Superannuation benefits are also exempt as is certain heritage property and property passing to charities. Tax not paid within nine months of the death is liable to interest at $1\frac{1}{4}$ % per month.

CITIZENS
INFORMATION
C E N T R E

A FREE & CONFIDENTIAL SERVICE

Citizen Information Centres (C.I.C.s), have been providing a free, confidential, impartial and independent information service to the public since 1974.

The Centres are operated locally by volunteer information officers, trained by the National Social Service Board.

The NSSB provides ongoing support and resource services to the Centres.

**Opening hours vary-
Check your local
Golden Pages for details**

CAPITAL GAINS TAX

Since April 1992 there has been a single flat rate of 40%, with a special low rate of 27% introduced in 1994 on certain share sales.

The first £1,000 of gains made by an individual (£2,000 for a married couple) in any one tax year are exempt from the tax. The exemption was double that prior to April 1992. Where the total proceeds of development land do not exceed £15,000 in any tax year, the tax rates are the same as on any other assets. The indexation relief (see below) does not apply to development land. Inflation is taken into account in calculating taxable gains. For tax purposes the acquisition price of the asset is multiplied by an index number which adjusts it for inflation in the intervening period. The index numbers are as follows:

Assets bought in	And sold during					
	1992/93	1993/94	1994/95	1995/96	1996/97	1997/98
1974/75	5.552	5.656	5.754	5.899	6.017	6.112
1975/76	4.484	4.568	4.647	4.764	4.860	4.936
1976/77	3.863	3.935	4.003	4.104	4.187	4.253
1977/78	3.312	3.373	3.432	3.518	3.589	3.646
1978/79	3.059	3.117	3.171	3.250	3.316	3.368
1979/80	2.760	2.812	2.861	2.933	2.992	3.039
1980/81	2.390	2.434	2.477	2.539	2.590	2.631
1981/82	1.975	2.012	2.047	2.099	2.141	2.174
1982/83	1.662	1.693	1.722	1.765	1.801	1.829
1983/84	1.478	1.505	1.531	1.570	1.601	1.627
1984/85	1.341	1.366	1.390	1.425	1.454	1.477
1985/86	1.263	1.287	1.309	1.342	1.369	1.390
1986/87	1.208	1.230	1.252	1.283	1.309	1.330
1987/88	1.168	1.190	1.210	1.241	1.266	1.285
1988/89	1.146	1.167	1.187	1.217	1.242	1.261
1989/90	1.109	1.130	1.149	1.178	1.202	1.221
1990/91	1.064	1.084	1.102	1.130	1.153	1.171
1991/92	1.037	1.056	1.075	1.102	1.124	1.142
1992/93	—	1.019	1.037	1.063	1.084	1.101
1993/94	—	—	1.018	1.043	1.064	1.081
1994/95	—	—	—	1.026	1.046	1.063
1995/96	—	—	—	—	1.021	1.037
1996/97	—	—	—	—	—	1.016

THE EASY WAY TO A HOMELOAN
PHONE
1850 654 321

EBS
BUILDING SOCIETY

Approved Quality System

Appendix 2: Motoring

Civil Service Milage

Milage allowances applicable to civil servants.

Official Milage	Under 1138cc	1139cc to 1387cc	1388cc and over
Up to 2,000	49.87p	57.70p	66.50p
2,001 to 4,000	54.98p	62.98p	72.50p
4,001 to 6,000	29.44p	33.38p	38.04p
6,001 to 8,000	27.74p	31.35p	35.69p
8,001 to 12000	24.33p	27.30p	30.98p
Over 12,001	20.92p	23.25p	26.27p

Motoring Benefit-in-kind

The value of the benefit-in-kind assessed for tax is reduced as follows as the business milage in the tax year increases. The percentage of the full charge assessed is as follows. From 1996 a 20% reduction is granted where the person supplied with the car spends at least 70% of his or her time away from the place of work and does at least 5,000 business miles in a year.

Business miles	93/94	94/95	95/96	96/99
15,001 to 16,000	97.5%	97.5%	97.5%	97.5%
16,001 to 17,000	95%	95%	95%	95%
17,001 to 18,000	90%	90%	90%	90%
18,001 to 19,000	80%	85%	85%	85%
19,001 to 20,000	70%	75%	75%	80%
20,001 to 21,000	60%	65%	70%	75%
21,001 to 22,000	55%	60%	65%	70%
22,001 to 23,000	45%	50%	55%	65%
23,001 to 24,000	40%	45%	50%	60%
24,001 to 25,000	35%	40%	45%	55%
25,001 to 26,000	30%	35%	40%	50%
26,001 to 27,000	25%	30%	35%	45%
27,001 to 28,000	20%	25%	30%	40%
28,001 to 29,000	18%	22%	28%	35%
29,001 to 30,000	15%	20%	25%	30%
over 31,000	10%	15%	20%	25%

TO UNLOCK MORE INTEREST
(WITH TOTAL SECURITY)...

You're looking for attractive rates of interest... total confidentiality...
and complete security for your investment? Better get in touch with a bank
that has it all: ICC Investment Bank. Whether you're taking the long or short
term view, ICC Investment Bank can offer you an unrivalled range of
investment opportunities, backed by over sixty years experience.
To find out more, talk to ICC Investment Bank today.

...BETTER GET IN TOUCH
WITH ICC INVESTMENT BANK

Road Tax On Private Cars

Category (engine cc)   £'s per 100 cc or part thereof

Not exceeding 1,000cc	£92 (flat rate)
1,001 to 1,500cc	£12.50
1,501 to 1,700cc	£14.50
1,701 to 2,000cc	£16.00
2,001 to 2,500cc	£19.50
Over 2,500cc	£22.00
Electrically propelled	£92 (flat rate)

Road Tax On Goods Vehicles

Vehicle Weight

Not exceeding 3000k	£150
3001 to 4000k	£190
4001 to 5000k	£245
5001 to 6000k	£340
6001 to 7000k	£460
7001 to 8000k	£580
Each extra 1000k or part thereof	£135

Road Tax On Tractors

Agriculture	£45
General haulage	£120

Road Tax On Motorcycles

All motorcycles — flat rate	£20

First Registration Charges

Motorcycles	£10
Private cars	
—not exceeding 2000cc	£20
—exceeding 2000cc	£40
Other	£40
Taxis and Hackneys — same as private cars	

"*Friendly personal service is always in fashion at TSB Bank. I like their style*".

Mary Garrigan, Boutique Owner

When Mary Garrigan went looking for a bank, she wanted one that shared her own attitudes.

She chose TSB Bank.

There she found the full range of business and personal financial services she needed. They were open when she could get to them. And above-all, they were open-minded to her plans.

Mary Garrigan knows that good customer service is part and parcel of her business success.

At TSB Bank it's also the cornerstone of ours.

TSB
B A N K

We want what's best for you.

Appendix 3:

SOCIAL INSURANCE
Maximum rates of benefit

	PRESENT RATE	NEW June '98
Retirement/Old Age Contributory Pension		
Under 80		
—Personal rate	£78.00	£83.00
—Person with qualified adult under 66	£129.00	£135.50
—Person with adult over 66	£133.40	£139.90
80 or over		
—Personal rate	£83.00	£88.00
—Person with qualified adult under 66	£134.00	£140.50
—Person with qualified adult over 66	£138.40	£144.90
Widow's/Widower's Contributory Pension		
—Under 66	£71.10	£74.10
—66 and under 80	£71.10	£76.10
—80 or over	£76.10	£81.10
Disability Pension		
Personal rate under 66	£69.20	£72.20
Personal rate 66 to 80	£78.00	£83.00
Personal rate 80 or over	£83.00	£88.00
Person under 65 with qualified adult	£114.30	£118.70
Person 65 to 80 with qualified adult	£123.10	£129.50
Person over 80 with qualified adult	£128.10	£134.50
Unemployment/Sickness Benefit		
Personal rate	£67.50	£70.50
Person with qualified adult	£107.50	£111.70
Orphan's Contributory Allowance	£45.60	£48.60
Payments for child dependants		
widow's/widower's		
—each qualified child	£17.00	£17.00
Old age and retirement pensioners		
—Each child	£15.20	£15.20
Disability pensioners		
—Each child	£15.20	£15.20
Unemployment/sickness benefit		
—Each qualified child	£13.20	£13.20

TAKE CARE
OF THE THINGS
YOU VALUE

Church & General

Church & General Insurance plc., Burlington House,
Burlington Road, Dublin 4.
Telephone: 01-702 3000. Fax: 01-660 9220.

A MEMBER OF AGF-IRISH LIFE HOLDINGS p.l.c.

SOCIAL ASSISTANCE

Maximum weekly rates of social assistance

BENEFIT	PRESENT RATE	NEW June '98
Old Age Non-Contributory Pension		
Under 80		
—Personal rate	£67.50	£72.50
—Person with qualified adult	£107.50	£113.70
80 or over		
—Personal rate	£72.50	£77.50
—Person with qualified adult	£112.50	£118.70
Widow's/Widower's non-contributory pension		
—Under 80	£67.50	£70.50
—80 or over	£72.50	£111.70
Disability allowance		
Personal rate	£67.50	£70.50
Person with qualified adult	£107.50	£111.70
Unemployment Assistance (short-term)		
Personal rate	£65.40	£68.40
Person with qualified adult	£105.40	£109.60
Unemployment Assistance (long-term)		
Personal rate	£67.50	£70.50
Person with qualified adult	£107.50	£111.70
One-parent family payment *(including one child)*	£82.70	£85.70
Carer's Allowance		
Under 66	£70.50	£73.50
66 years and over	£70.50	£75.50
Increases for child dependents		
Lone Parents	£15.20	£15.20
Others	£13.20	£13.20

Child Benefit

For first and second child	£30	£31.50[1]
For third child onwards	£39	£42.00

[1] *From September 1998*

Too busy thinking about work to think about a pension?

Self employed? Not in the company scheme? We can help you design a pension plan to take care of your needs in the years ahead. You'll get the benefit of our person-to-person service.

Our pension experts will advise on the plan that's right for your situation and help you benefit from the tax advantages available. Our advice is free, confidential and without obligation.

Call ACCBank now on

1850 234 234

or contact your local branch.

Web Sites

A selection of Irish web sites which may contain something of interest

AIB Group	http://www.aib.ie
AIB Investment Managers	http://ireland.iol.ie/aibiss
Bank of Ireland	http://www.bankofireland.ie
BCP Stockbrokers	http://www.bcp.ie
Canada Life	http://www.canadalife.ie
Church & General	http://www.churchandgeneral.ie
Coyle Hamilton	http://www.coyle.ham.ie/coyleham
Davy Stockbrokers	http://www.davy.ie
First National Building Society	http://www.fnbs.ie
Hibernian Group	http://hibernian-group.ie
ICC Bank	http://www.icc.ie
ICS Building Society	http://www.iol.ie/ics
Insurance Corporation	http://www.insurancecorporation.ie/ichome.htm
Irish Permanent	http://www.irishpermanent.ie
National Deposit Brokers	http://www.ndb.ie
NCB Stockbrokers	http://www.ncb.ie
Pensions Board	http://penionsboard.ie
TSB Bank	http://www.tsbbank.ie
Ulster Bank	http://www.ulsterbank.com
VHI	http://www.vhi.ie

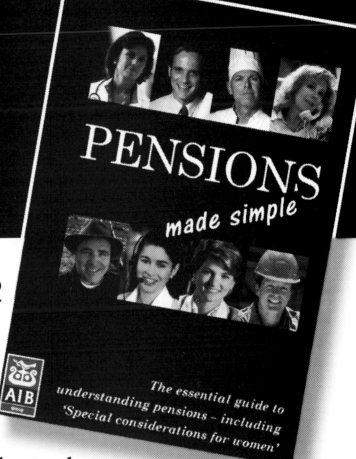

Index

Index

$$12 \overline{\smash{)}15000}$$
3

$$4 \overline{\smash{)}1250}$$
312